WOMEN'S LIFE CYCLE
AND
ECONOMIC INSECURITY

Recent Titles in
Contributions in Women's Studies

The Compassionate Memsahibs: Welfare Activities of British Women in India, 1900–1947
Mary Ann Lind

Against the Horizon: Feminism and Postwar Austrian Women Writers
Jacqueline Vansant

Sealskin and Shoddy: Working Women in American Labor Press Fiction, 1870–1920
Ann Schofield

Breaking the Angelic Image: Woman Power in Victorian Children's Fantasy
Edith Lazaros Honig

Eighteenth-Century Women and the Arts
Frederick M. Keener and Susan E. Lorsch, editors

American Women in Poverty
Paul E. Zopf, Jr.

Women Working: Comparative Perspectives in Developing Areas
Alma T. Junsay and Tim B. Heaton

Man Cannot Speak for Her. Volume I: A Critical Study of Early Feminist Rhetoric
Karlyn Kohrs Campbell

Man Cannot Speak for Her. Volume II: Key Texts of the Early Feminists
Karlyn Kohrs Campbell

Gender, Bureaucracy, and Democracy: Careers and Equal Opportunity in the Public Sector
Mary M. Hale and Rita Mae Kelly, editors

The President's Partner: The First Lady in the Twentieth Century
Myra G. Gutin

Women War Correspondents of World War II
Lilya Wagner

Feminism and Black Activism in Contemporary America:
An Ideological Assessment
Irvin D. Solomon

Scandinavian Women Writers: An Anthology from the 1880s to the 1980s
Ingrid Claréus, editor

To Bind Up The Wounds: Catholic Sister Nurses in the U.S. Civil War
Sister Mary Denis Maher

Women's Life Cycle
and
Economic Insecurity

PROBLEMS AND PROPOSALS

EDITED BY

Martha N. Ozawa

Contributions in Women's Studies, Number 108

GREENWOOD PRESS

New York · Westport, Connecticut · London

Library of Congress Cataloging-in-Publication Data

Women's life cycle and economic insecurity : problems and proposals /
  edited by Martha N. Ozawa.
     p. cm.—(Contributions in women's studies, ISSN 0147–104X ;
  no. 108)
   Bibliography: p.
   Includes index.
   ISBN 0–313–26753–7 (lib. bdg. : alk. paper)
   1. Women—United States—Social conditions. 2. Women—United
States—Economic conditions. 3. Life change events—Economic
aspects—United States. I. Ozawa, Martha N. II. Series.
HQ1421.W66   1989
305.4'0952—dc20   89–7505

British Library Cataloguing in Publication Data is available.

A paperback edition of *Women's Life Cycle and Economic Insecurity:
Problems and Proposals* is available from Praeger Publishers;
ISBN: 0–275–93348–2

Library of Congress Catalog Card Number: 89–7505
ISBN: 0–313–26753–7
ISSN: 0147–104X

First published in 1989

Greenwood Press, Inc.
88 Post Road West, Westport, Connecticut 06881

Printed in the United States of America

The paper used in this book complies with the
Permanent Paper Standard issued by the National
Information Standards Organization (Z39.48–1984).

10 9 8 7 6 5 4 3 2 1

CONTENTS

ILLUSTRATIONS

FIGURES

TABLES

PREFACE AND ACKNOWLEDGMENTS

The idea of mounting a book on the life cycle and economic insecurity of women originated in a collaborative effort between Dr. Hideo Ibe of the Japan Foundation for Research and Development of Pension Schemes and myself. He and I established an intellectual dialogue and a collaborative relationship in 1984, when we became members of the Japan-U.S. Comparative-Study Group on Social Welfare, initiated and sponsored by the foundation and the Japan Committee of the International Conference on Social Welfare. It soon became apparent to us that both the United States and Japan are facing an emerging social problem of women's economic insecurity in the midst of growing affluence. Therefore, we decided to put together a book that would focus on this problem in the two countries. That book, *Women's Life Cycle: Japan-U.S. Comparison in Income Maintenance* (*Woman's Life Cycle: Shotoku Hoshou no Nichibei Hikaku*), which contains articles by Japanese and American authors, was published in Japanese in January 1989 by Tokyo University Press.

The present book includes chapters 2 through 8 from the original Japanese book with minor modifications to place them in a more purely U.S. context. Conclusions drawn and recommendations derived from these chapters are also targeted to the U.S. situation.

This book was supported by funds from various sources. The Japan Foundation for Research and Development of Pension Schemes supported, in part, the expenses incurred in writing the chapters for this book. The chapter, "Women, Mothers, and Work," written by James P. Smith, was also supported, in part, by the National Institute of Child Health and Human Development. Partial support for the chapter "Causes and Consequences of Teenage Pregnancy and Childbearing" came from the Ford Foundation, the Robert Wood Johnson Foundation, and the Office of Adolescent Pregnancy, U.S. Department of Health and Human Services. In writing this chapter, its authors, Frank F. Furstenberg, Jr., and J. Brooks-Gunn, express their appreciation to L. H. Aiken and D. Mechanic for their permission to use part of the Furstenberg/ Brooks-Gunn chapter, "Teenage Childbearing: Causes, Consequences and Remedies," which appeared in *Applications of Social Science to Clinical Medicine and Health Policy* edited by Aiken and Mechanic.

I wish to thank Tokyo University Press and the Japan Foundation for Research and Development of Pension Schemes for permitting me to use part of the original Japanese book to mount the present book. I wish to thank Dean Shanti Khinduka of the George Warren Brown School of Social Work, Washington University, for providing me with clerical support and computer facilities. Finally, I wish to thank Wendy Almeleh of Great Neck, New York, for editorial assistance for the introduction and the concluding chapters.

Any views expressed in the chapters are those of the respective authors and do not represent the official position or policy of the foundations and agencies that supported the book or the institutions with which the authors are affiliated. I alone am responsible for the conclusions and recommendations made in the final chapter.

WOMEN'S LIFE CYCLE
AND
ECONOMIC INSECURITY

1 INTRODUCTION: AN OVERVIEW

Martha N. Ozawa

Something extraordinary is happening to American women. Although their individual economic capability has never been as great as it is today, their economic well-being in relation to that of men has been slipping. We hear increasingly about the phenomenon of the feminization of poverty. We also hear about an increasing proportion of children who are living in poverty, a fact closely related to the growing economic impoverishment of women in relation to that of men. What is happening? How are these phenomena related to each other? More specifically, why is it that women's economic position is deteriorating although their individual earning capability is growing?

This book is about women's life cycle and the growing economic insecurity that the events in their life cycle create. By illustrating what life-cycle events women go through and how these events cause women's economic insecurity, I believe I can explain why and how women's economic position is deteriorating in relation to that of men.

This book argues that the current economic condition of American women is a product of two divergent forces: women's growing economic capability, as evidenced by their greater labor force participation and their penetration—albeit slowly—into better-paying jobs, on the one hand, and women's loss of the economic benefit derived from sharing households with men, either by their choice or for reasons beyond their control, on the other hand. The net result is that women's economic lot is deteriorating in comparison to that of men. This situation is indeed paradoxical, but seems easy to understand. In years past, when women did not work outside the home but shared financial resources with the men they married, their economic condition stayed the same as that of men, as long as both men and women were alive and lived together. Thus, technically, the poverty rates of men and women were the same.

But during the past forty years, the economic condition of women has diverted from that of men. As a result, more women suffer from poverty than do men. James P. Smith, a contributing author of this book, estimates that the 1940 poverty rates for men and women were the same—34 percent—but the 1980 poverty rates were 7 percent for men and 11 percent for women. What happened? Although women's progress in the labor market has paralleled the transformation of the United States into an increasingly service-oriented economy, women have had to endure a growing number of social problems, such as teenage pregnancy and childbearing and divorce. The adverse economic effects of these social problems have more than offset the economic progress women have made in the labor market.[1] Then, too, women are also "suffering" from what appears to be social progress— that is, the growing life expectancy of the U.S. population, which results in more years of widowhood. Thus, more women than men die poor.

This dynamic socioeconomic condition is directly and adversely affecting the economic well-being of American children. Since children normally go with women when a family is struck by significant life-cycle events such as birth to a teenage girl and divorce, children's economic plight often occurs in tandem with the economic predicament of women.

What we are seeing is an emergence of a new type of economic insecurity that plagues one demographic group (women) in contrast to another (men). This economic insecurity is quite different from the traditional one, which was caused simply by economic forces. In the traditional type of economic insecurity, all persons were adversely affected by economic downturns, and all persons were relieved by economic upturns. In the new type of economic insecurity that women are facing, economic growth alone would not alleviate their plight. Indeed, women's relative economic position is declining in spite of the general economic growth and in spite of their own individual achievement in the labor market. The determining factor is social, not economic: the weakening tie between men and women as a result of the increasing incidence of childbearing out of wedlock (whether by teenagers or by adults), divorce, and the growing likelihood that women will become widows.

The growing economic plight of women is shaping the income distribution as well as the composition of poor people in a way we have never seen before. According to a series of studies by Sheldon Danziger, the growing inequality of income is largely explained by demographic factors.[2] That is, the increasing number of households headed by women is causing the distribution of income to become more unequal. Also, on the poverty front an increasing proportion of poor people are living in households headed by women.[3] In short, more and more women are staying at the bottom of the economic ladder.

Women's economic problems have profound ramifications. They are directly related to the future of American children—the future of American human capital. Currently, one in every five children lives only with his or her mother and over one-half of all children (six in every ten white children and eight in every ten black children) who were born in the 1980s are expected to live only with their mothers before they reach adulthood.[4] A series of studies by McLanahan indicated that children who grow up in female-headed households are more likely than are other children to drop out of school, to become single heads of households themselves, and to live in poverty in their adulthood, and depend on welfare.[5]

The deteriorating economic conditions and changing living arrangements of women may be related to the decline in the physical, mental, and intellectual condition of American children in general. The National Council of Organizations for Children and Youth and the U.S. Congress Select Committee on Children, Youth, and Families reported that both the physical and mental health problems of American children as a whole increased during the past two decades.[6] The National Commission on Excellence in Education stated that for the first time in American history, the educational skills of the current generation of children will not surpass, will not equal, and will not even approach those of their parents.[7] As though to validate the commission's assertion, the Congressional Budget Office reported that the average scores on scholastic achievement tests of school children started declining in the mid-1960s and hit bottom in the late 1970s.[8]

The economic plight of women has national ramifications. Thus, understanding how women's economic insecurity is created and finding its solutions are important for policymakers, academics, and concerned citizens.

To demonstrate how women's life-cycle experiences determine their economic status, the chapters in this book trace each phase of women's life cycle. The contributing authors explain how American women are educated and how ineffectively they are prepared for well-paying jobs; how they perform in the labor market later on; how teenage pregnancy and childbearing cause many women to lose the opportunity to be educated to their full potential; how badly divorce—and female headship in general—affect the economic status of women; how women fare under inheritance laws as daughters and wives and how fairly (or unfairly) these laws treat women who provide primary care to their husbands and ailing parents; how women in old age and widowhood are treated under the social security program and pension programs; and how women go through the experience of providing and later receiving long-term care and the economic impact of this experience.

These are the specific issues that the contributing authors address in their respective chapters. In so doing, they argue that the life cycle of women has a series of built-in obstacles to the achievement of an economic sufficiency that is comparable to that of men. They illustrate how obstacles in each phase of life hurt women economically. They also explain how values, expectations, and the norm regarding women's work have changed and how these changes are mitigating or aggravating barriers to women's economic independence. When appropriate, they offer their recommendations on social policies and programs to deal with the problems they identified in their chapters.

EDUCATIONAL PREPARATION OF AMERICAN WOMEN

Shirley M. Clark (chapter 2) argues that the seeds for differential economic achievement between men and women are cast in their early childhood—possibly as early as age 2½. Parents develop different expectations for boys and girls. Because they assume that girls cannot deal with the threats of the social and physical environment, they raise their daughters to believe that it is natural for girls to seek protection, supervision, and love from those close to them. But since parents do not expect that boys will need protection, they raise their sons to be protectors, supervisors, lovers, and, most important, achievers.

Parents also expect girls and boys to develop different personality characteristics. They want girls to be "feminine": neat, passive, dependent, nurturing, domestic, conforming, and obedient. They want boys to be "masculine": independent, risk taking, and responsible. Clark argues that the parents' socialization of their children is decisive in the formation of the characters of boys and girls.

At school, Clark further explains, teachers (predominantly women) take over what parents (mostly mothers) have done at home. The teachers tend to expect less from girls in academic achievement than from boys and they assume that girls will enter different academic or vocational fields from those of boys. Furthermore, teachers tend to emphasize to girls the importance of learning human-relation skills, while they tend to instill in the minds of boys the importance of achievement. Since educational preparation is directly linked to the types of jobs that boys and girls will have later on, the gender-based social stratification in the world of work originates in the school years.

A key factor that determines future occupational choices for boys and girls, Clark argues, is enrollment in courses on mathematics, which she calls a "filter" subject. Not taking mathematics for an adequate number of years forecloses, to a great extent, opportunities to pursue certain areas of academic and occupational interest. Thus, women's fate is cast in high school because few girls take enough mathematics courses at school.

The pattern of socialization and of interaction with faculty members while in college compounds the situation. In the fields in which men predominate, such as engineering and sciences—and, to a great degree, in law and medicine—few faculty members take an aggressive, supportive role in encouraging women to obtain graduate degrees.

Given the pattern of socialization at home and at school, which is not conducive to women's educational achievement, it is remarkable that nonetheless American women are making considerable progress in attaining graduate and professional degrees in male-dominated fields. (Clark reports the increasing proportion of degrees obtained by women in law, medicine, and engineering.) One may attribute the recent progress in this regard to the economic forces of the marketplace. As was mentioned earlier, the service industry is becoming a larger part of the marketplace, and manufacturing will be increasingly high-tech; both tend to create a greater demand for female labor.

WOMEN, MOTHERS, AND WORK

Economic forces appear to be the most important factor in the surge in labor force participation of women in the twentieth century, according to James P. Smith (chapter 3). The growing demand for female workers in the service sector and the availability of increasingly well educated women has further heightened women's participation, as have such socioeconomic changes as the improvement in working conditions, the decrease in farming, and the nuclearization of the family. Smith contends that economic changes have brought about attitudinal changes as well. In earlier days, work outside the home was considered acceptable for uneducated women, not for educated women. Now, it is considered not only socially acceptable but desirable.

Smith draws parallels to Japan to strengthen his argument that it was mainly economic forces that pulled women out of the home and into the labor market. He contends that in spite of cultural and other differences, the increase of women in the Japanese labor force after World War II has been similar to the increase of women in the American labor force that has taken place in this century. The only difference is that economic changes that are pulling women into the labor market have occurred faster in Japan than in the United States.

On the basis of his and his colleagues' research at the RAND Corporation, Smith indicates that marriage and childbearing have become less of a deterrent to women's work outside the home and will continue to be so in the future. Thus, women's rate of participation in the labor force will increase even more in the future.

Although the presence of children at home no longer deters American women from working, it has a negative impact on women's wages and years of employment during their lifetime. As Smith indicates, at age 30, a woman with three children earns, on average, only 77 percent of the wages earned by a woman with no children. Furthermore, women with three children typically lose 5.5 years of labor-market work. They lose these years at a crucial time in their life cycle, when other workers are developing job-related skills. All this indicates that childbearing and child rearing place women at an economic disadvantage in comparison to women without children and to men.

What about the impact of children on women's ability to save? Since information on the assets of individuals is not normally available, one cannot answer this question. However, Smith's analysis of the financial assets of families is illuminating. Smith shows that having a baby early in a marriage considerably decreases the family's net worth—an average of $1,181 in the year of birth. However, families who have a baby later in the marriage manage to save some; their net worth increases by $325 in the year of birth. Hence, Smith's analysis shows that families who have babies early forgo opportunities to save. It may be true also that families that have children later in the marriage cannot save as much as can families with no children. Moreover, one has to add to Smith's analysis college and other expenses that parents are expected to incur until the child reaches adulthood. These expenses will further erode the parents' opportunity to save. Thus, having children has a negative impact on the assets of families, which in turn probably has an adverse effect on women's economic well-being later in their life cycle, especially when they become widows.

Smith's argument that, in general, women's wages have been going up relative to those of men is contrary to the widespread belief that women's wages have stayed persistently at about 60 percent of men's wages for decades. The problem with this conventional wisdom, Smith notes, is that this wage differential is based on the wages *only* of working women. What one needs to realize is the tremendous increase in the proportion of working women. Thus, it is more meaningful to compare the average earnings of *all* women (including both working and nonworking women) with the average earnings of *all* men. On this basis, Smith concludes that women's wages grew 20 percent faster than did men's wages in the past sixty years.

In such an economic environment, Smith contends, staying at home is becoming too high a price for women to pay in the form of forgone earnings. Highly educated women will face this predicament more severely than will other women in the future. Therefore, Smith predicts, women will continue to adapt to changing labor-market conditions by further decreasing the number of children they bear unless society intervenes to reverse the trend in women's economic behavior.

ADOLESCENT PREGNANCY AND CHILDBEARING

Among all the events in the life cycle of women, teenage pregnancy and childbearing probably have one of the most adverse effects on the development of women's economic capability. These problems are discussed by Frank F. Furstenberg, Jr., and J. Brooks-Gunn (chapter 4).

Despite the devastating impact of pregnancy and childbearing on the future development of adolescent girls, these girls seem to venture into these activities rather casually. According to Furstenberg and Brooks-Gunn, American adolescents are simply behaving "naturally" in an environment flooded with media messages that it is normal for teenagers to engage in sexual intercourse. The youth environment is heavily influenced by the changing norms among adults with regard to extramarital sexual activities and the declining value attached to the institution of marriage. Many adolescents who have and keep their babies are not much different from adult women who get divorced, raise their children alone, and have sexual relationships without remarrying. Both cases involve the same life processes: engaging in extramarital sexual intercourse and raising children alone.

The public has not accepted adolescent sexual activities as an inevitable reality or expressed interest in finding a viable means to prevent the adverse effects of such activities. Thus, the public has not established a clear consensus about the importance of the use of contraceptive measures by adolescents. American adolescents' failure to use contraception consistently is the primary reason for their high rate of pregnancy in comparison to the rate of European teenagers.

The U.S. public and policymakers seem immobilized in the face of conflicting values and pressures from different constituencies. First, many conservative churchgoers believe that the institution of the family is so important that public policy should be directed toward discouraging adolescent sexual activities altogether, a view that is, of course, unrealistic in the United States. Second, some believe that encouraging the use of contraceptive measures would encourage more sexual activities, and some Catholics object to most contraceptive measures on religious grounds. Third, people who support the right-to-life movement firmly object to abortion to terminate pregnancy. Responding to pressures from conservative groups, the Reagan administration cut back heavily on expenditures for family planning and other counseling services for adolescents.

In this confused social and political environment, every year over 1 million adolescent girls become pregnant, out of wedlock in the majority of cases. Many of them do not use a contraceptive device for as long as one year after they initiate sexual intercourse. As a result, about half of them resort to abortion to terminate their pregnancy. Nine out of ten adolescents who deliver babies choose to raise them on their own, often becoming dependent on public assistance; only one out of ten such adolescents gives up her baby for adoption.

There is a considerable difference in the sexual behavior of black and white adolescents. Blacks initiate sexual activities earlier than do whites, and their rates of pregnancy and childbirth are higher than those of whites. Their rate of illegitimacy is higher as well.

The educational and later economic impact of adolescent pregnancy and childbearing is devastating, Furstenberg and Brooks-Gunn report. Teenage mothers are much more likely to drop out of high school. Having decided to raise their children, they go on welfare as a transitional measure at least. Many of these mothers attempt to return to school and catch up with their peers who did not go through the trauma of teenage pregnancy and childbearing, but they do not succeed in doing so.

In spite of heavy opposition from conservative groups, many communities have tried both preventive and ameliorative programs. However, Furstenberg and Brooks-Gunn do not have an optimistic prognosis about the effect of such programs because of the societal ambivalence about or hostility toward adolescents' use of contraception and abortion. Furstenberg and Brooks-Gunn also discuss the difficulty in serving adolescent mothers. Not only do these mothers (and *their* mothers) have educational and economic deficits, they are often not motivated to make use of programs in the community. They simply do not have the commitment, the ability, or the necessary support to go back to school and to care for their young children at the same time. In the meantime, out-of-wedlock teenage pregnancy and childbearing continue unabated, foreclosing educational and job opportunities for a considerable number of adolescent girls in the United States.

DIVORCE, FEMALE HEADSHIP, AND CHILD SUPPORT

Divorce is another important cause of economic insecurity of women. Currently, there is one divorce for each two marriages in the United States. According to Irwin Garfinkel, Sara McLanahan, and Dorothy Watson (chaper 5), 2.7 million families are headed by divorced women.

Divorce causes psychological and economic anguish to all family members. However, the problem of single-parent families in the United States does not stem from divorce alone. More and more families are headed by women who have never married or who are separated (54 percent according to Garfinkel, McLanahan, and Watson). Garfinkel, McLanahan, and Watson also report a clear difference in the causes of white and black female-headed families. For whites, divorce is the major reason; for blacks, never-married parenthood is the major reason. Thus, these authors argue, it is important to understand the problem of divorce in a broader context of female headship.

Garfinkel, McLanahan, and Watson discuss the sociological and economic reasons for the skyrocketing rate of divorce, particularly women's employment and changing values. Women's work creates an "independence effect," liberating women from their financial reliance on their husbands and allowing them to choose their own life-style. Women's work definitely causes strains in the roles traditionally played by husbands and wives. Many husbands do not adapt adequately to the changing conditions in their families that are created by women's work. As a result, tension mounts. Now that women can support themselves to some degree, they can initiate divorce to resolve their unhappy marriages. The strain may act the other way around as well. Unable to cope with strain or unwilling to make compromises, husbands may be the ones who file for divorce.

Women's determination to become economically independent is fueled not only by their belief that it is socially acceptable to pursue such a goal, given the prevailing emphasis on individualism. According to Garfinkel, McLanahan, and Watson, with half the marriages ending in divorce, American women seem to accept the likelihood that their own marriages will also end in divorce. Therefore, they attempt to mitigate the adverse effects of this probable divorce by becoming economically self-sufficient before and during marriage.

Regardless of the causes of divorce, the economic result of divorce is devastating for women with children. Although divorced mothers attempt to work more after divorce, their hourly earnings are pitifully low, and many of them face unemployment. The unemployment rate of divorced women is three times as high as that of fathers who head two-parent families.

Child support and alimony payments from noncustodial parents (fathers in almost all cases) are not high enough to offset the women's low earnings. Garfinkel, McLanahan, and Watson discuss in detail the uncertainty of private child support payments, the inefficiency and unfairness of court procedures to collect payments, and the low levels of such payments. However bad the situation is for divorced mothers, the plight of never-married mothers is far worse. Not only are they less likely to collect child support payments, but they earn less through work than do divorced women.

Because of mothers' low earnings and the inadequate child support payments from noncustodial fathers, the economic standing of divorced mothers and their children plunges overnight, forcing many of these women into poverty. Then life on welfare awaits them.

Aid to Families with Dependent Children (AFDC) is the most important vehicle through which public child support is provided. But the program is hopelessly flawed and unpopular with the public. As Garfinkel, McLanahan, and Watson discuss, AFDC is widely believed to sap a mother's will to work. It does not allow her to accumulate savings. And she and her children are treated as second-class citizens.

Plunging economic status, the inevitable reliance on welfare, the frantic search to become economically self-sufficient through work, and worry over day care all create a life of frustration and misery for many women who, for whatever reason, choose to raise their children alone. Are there any solutions to these problems?

Garfinkel, McLanahan, and Watson believe that the answer to these problems is the efficient implementation in all states of a public child-support-assurance system, like the one pioneered by the state of Wisconsin and in use in many other states. They discuss how the federal government has been instrumental in gradually shifting the burden of collecting private child support payments from the court system to the state bureaucracy. Under such a system the state government guarantees a minimum level of payment, and a state agency collects the payments on the basis of a set formula from the noncustodial parent and passes the payments on to the custodial parent. Garfinkel, McLanahan, and Watson believe that supplementing mothers' earnings with payments through a child-support-assurance system is far superior to a dependence on AFDC.

THE TREATMENT OF WOMEN UNDER THE INHERITANCE LAW

Even those women who go through the "normal" life cycle encounter obstacles to the pursuit of economic independence. In addition to the barriers of socialization and education discussed earlier is women's role in providing long-term care for their aging husbands or their frail parents. Data from the National Center for Health Statistics show that 72 percent of the primary caregivers are women—29 percent of whom are daughters; 23 percent, wives; and 20 percent, others.[9] Data from the same source indicate that for every one frail elderly person living in a nursing home, four frail elderly people are being cared for at home. Furthermore, as much as 80–90 percent of all home health care is provided by family members.[10]

In light of the heavy involvement of women in providing long-term care for the elderly, it is important to understand how women are treated under the inheritance law. Are women adequately compensated for the time and effort they exert in caring for their parents and husbands? What is the prevailing American practice with regard to inheritance? Paul L. Menchik (chapter 6) addresses these issues.

Although American settlers brought with them the European tradition of inheritance laws and practices, over time they have developed laws and practices that are uniquely American. Thus, Americans now have far greater freedom than do the French to bequeath estates as they wish. Also, unlike the British, Americans do not particularly favor sons over daughters in bequeathing estates. Another unique characteristic of American inheritance practice is the emphasis on conjugal bequests instead of lineal bequests. Thus, when a spouse is still alive, American testators generally follow the "spouse-all" bequest rule, meaning that the entire estate is transferred to the surviving spouse. Only when the deceased person has not left a will does the state inheritance law apply. Also, when the will is too harsh toward legal heirs—especially the surviving spouse—the state probate court sometimes overrules the wishes of the deceased person and distributes the wealth according to the state law.

Menchik presents empirical findings to support these generalizations. First, the majority of decedents do leave a will. Second, almost the same proportions of estates are bequeathed to sons and to daughters. Third, the overwhelming majority of testators—perhaps as many as nine out of every ten—leave the entire estate to their spouses.

There are exceptions to all these practices, of course. One important exception, Menchik notes, occurs in the so-called community-property states, in which the wealth that is accumulated during a marriage belongs equally to both spouses. In such states, the surviving spouse already has legal ownership of one-half the accumulated wealth. As a result, the testator has control only over one-half the estate for bequeathing.

What is the economic impact of inheritance on women? To understand it, one needs to investigate the scope of the estates that are usually divided among legal heirs. Menchik and Martin David conducted a study that estimated that the average estates of men are about 5 percent of their lifetime earnings, or about two years' worth of earnings.[11] What is the total in dollars? Menchik and David do not say, but the following data are instructive. The 1982 New Beneficiary Survey, conducted by the Social Security Administration, indicated that one year after retirement the median net worth of assets held by retired men and their wives was $68,300. When home equity was excluded, the net worth was only $20,000.[12] In 1982, when the survey was taken, the median annual earnings of full-time workers were $17,800.[13]

At any rate, these figures do not indicate that an enormous amount of wealth is divided among legal heirs, including widows and daughters who provided the long-term care for their husbands and fathers before these men died. To be sure, testators sometimes write wills that leave a disproportionate share of their estates to the persons who gave them physical and emotional support before their death. But these are exceptional cases. The prevailing practice is for the daughter who acted as the primary caregiver of a deceased parent to receive the same share of the estate as any of the other children. In the case of widows, the spouse-all rule usually applies, but the actual amount is relatively small. Consequently, the economic well-being of women diminishes overnight after the death of their husbands. Karen C. Holden addresses this problem in chapter 7.

WOMEN'S ECONOMIC STATUS IN OLD AGE AND WIDOWHOOD

As they get older, two types of women become financially deprived: never-married or divorced women and widows. Women who are not married at the time of retirement face an immediate financial disadvantage in relation to men because the retirement income they receive reflects the lifelong economic disadvantage they have experienced. That is, at the time of retirement, women who live alone must reckon with the effects of life-cycle events—the way they were educated, the type and duration of the jobs they held, the number of children they raised, and the divorce they experienced.

Women in their retirement years enjoy an adequate level of economic well-being as long as they live with their husbands. As a matter of fact, this group of women is economically better off in comparison not only to other groups of aged women but to the entire population, as various studies have shown.[14] But, these women face a drastic plunge in their standard of living when they become widows, as Holden illustrates.

Holden argues that a major reason why women's economic standing declines when they enter widowhood is that both the social security program and employer pension programs are not designed to provide survivors benefits that are adequate for maintaining the level of economic well-being they enjoyed while living with their husbands. Under social security, for example, the benefit declines by 33 percent when the beneficiary status changes from married couple to widow. Under most employer pension programs, the amount of the pension declines by 50 percent after the worker's death even when the worker opted for the joint-and-survivor provision. If he chose the single-life provision instead, the pension stops at the time of his death.

There are two other reasons why the widow's standard of living is so much lower than when she was living with her husband. The first is that the value of assets held in widowhood is considerably lower than that held while both spouses are still alive. The second is that as the widow advances in age, retirement incomes from all sources—except social security benefits—tend to decline in value because these incomes are fixed and thus not protected against inflation. Holden concludes that widowhood results in declining economic well-being because the loss of income caused by the husband's death cannot be fully offset by the widow's decreased need for income because she is living alone.

Do elderly couples make a conscious decision to consume more than they should while living together, thus depleting the resources that the wife will have in widowhood? There is some indication that they are doing just that. Holden shows, for example, that the overwhelming majority of retired workers choose not to take advantage of the joint-and-survivor provision even though the federal government has mandated that employers must offer this option. Instead, the majority of workers choose to receive single-life pensions.

Holden speculates that so many workers select the single-life option because (1) they need and want to use as much money as they can while both spouses are alive, (2) they are aware that inflation makes it less worthwhile to receive pensions in the distant future (to them) when widowhood begins, and (3) they fear that the wife may die first (in which case they would lose future pensions because they cannot reverse their decision once they choose the joint-and-survivor option).

Given this situation, Holden's prognosis for the future is bleak. As she points out, as the life expectancy of men and women further increases, the period of living together as well as the period of widowhood will be longer. In addition, widowhood will occur far later in the woman's life cycle, when health conditions deteriorate and the financial situation worsens.

In planning for the better economic well-being of future widows, Holden recommends that the United States maintain the scope of the social security program, since this program not only allocates resources to widows and protects benefits against inflation better than do employer pension programs but covers the entire work force and is the only source of retirement income for low-wage retirees, among whom women are overrepresented. Holden also suggests that employer pension programs be improved so that they (1) provide at least two-thirds of the deceased worker's pension to the widow and (2) are protected against inflation.

LONG-TERM CARE FOR THE ELDERLY

In many ways, the problem of long-term care is a women's problem. First, as spouses or daughters, women play the role of primary caregivers to elderly relatives in almost all cases. Second, unlike men, who are better situated financially and socially, women typically need long-term care at a stage in the life cycle that is characterized by widowhood, physical debilitation, and financial deprivation. Dorothy P. Rice analyzes the financial and health conditions of elderly people who require long-term care (chapter 8). When appropriate, she refers specifically to the plight of women.

Rice projects a large increase in the elderly population, particularly those aged 85 and over. By 2040, she estimates, the United States will have over 12 million people in this age bracket, 71 percent of whom will be women.

Women who are responsible for the primary care of frail elderly relatives are in a complex situation. On the one hand, they attempt to give as much care as they can to prevent their relatives from being institutionalized. On the other hand, they try to continue to work outside the home. The strain soon becomes unbearable, however, and something has to give. In this predicament, Rice reports, one of every ten female caregivers quits work, and one of every five women who continue to work is forced to rearrange her work schedule.

Women caregivers are indeed in an economic squeeze. If they are the wives of frail elderly husbands, they see their assets as well as their husbands' assets dissipate as the expenses for the care of their spouses mount. If they are the daughters of frail elderly fathers, they see their opportunity to earn slip away. Many of these daughters are approaching retirement themselves and are beginning to worry about their own future. At any rate, the economic condition of female caregivers is not bright. As Rice notes, 37 percent of them are poor or near poor.

A real crunch comes when women become the recipients of long-term care. By that time, most of them are living alone. For example, at age 75 and over, 45 percent of the women live alone in comparison to only 19 percent of the men. The major reason for women's living alone is widowhood; 69 percent of women in this age bracket are widowed.[15] At this stage in the life cycle of women, health and financial conditions deteriorate to the lowest level ever. Rice reports that a high percentage of women in this age bracket are suffering from chronic impairment, such as arthritis, hypertension, and heart disease, and have difficulty functioning in day-to-day activities. And, as has been mentioned, the financial status of elderly women who live alone—widows, in particular—is the lowest of any group in the United States.

Although most frail elderly women continue to be cared for in the community through the support of their daughters and other relatives, many of them eventually move into nursing homes. Life in a nursing home for women is a time of desolation and despair, when ill health and financial deprivation converge into a state of crisis. Very few women have an income that allows them to pay $22,000 a year for nursing home care, as Rice reports. Thus, according to the 1985 National Nursing Home Survey, about half the nursing home residents rely on Medicaid (a form of welfare that pays some of the medical expenses of low-income families) to pay for nursing home care from the first day of stay.[16] Even those who are initially able to pay their own way eventually have to rely on Medicaid.[17]

Foreseeing the limitations of Medicaid in providing increased funds for nursing home care and other community-based health and social services for the elderly, Price explores alternative ways to pay for long-term care. Encouraging insurance companies to offer private long-term care insurance is one idea. Extending Medicare (a social insurance program that is part of the social security program) coverage to include long-term care is another. Creating social health maintenance organizations is still another.

SETTING AGENDA

As illustrated, the United States will face an enormous challenge to sort out the causes and effects of women's growing economic insecurity. Obviously, the government needs to deal with the immediate problem of the poverty of many women—never-married mothers (teenagers and adults), divorced wives with children, and widows. However, for the long-term interest of the United States, policymakers, academics, and concerned citizens will have to go beyond addressing the symptoms of women's problems, which are manifested in childbearing out of wedlock, divorce, and widowhood.

Aside from the problem of childbearing out of wedlock, it is important to recognize that women's economic insecurity starts with divorce and widowhood, precisely because women have played the roles that are deemed desirable and necessary before they face divorce or widowhood. Divorce and widowhood bring economic insecurity to women precisely because women marry and raise children, as the society expects them to do, and spend their time and energy caring for their ailing parents and later their husbands, again as expected by society; therefore, they do not—and cannot—spend their lives in the same way as men do, developing their marketable human capital that translates into earning capability in the labor market. These nurturing and caring roles are deemed so necessary that women are socialized at home and at school to fill these roles effectively. The economic effect of all this, however, is that women are ill-prepared for supporting their children (of whom they normally have custody) and they are ill-prepared for living for a long time as widows.

How will women cope with this apparent conflict? Some women of the future may simply repeat the same economic predicament of the current generation of women. But many other women may attempt to prevent economic insecurity by not playing these traditional roles. They may find it in their individual interest to pursue education in male-dominated fields, not to marry, and not to raise children. Such a decision may solve the problem of economic insecurity facing many women and, at least in the short run, may coincide with the national interest of the United States that is confronted with a challenge of becoming competitive in the global economy. But in the long run, women's decision not to form a family may be detrimental to the United States both in terms of population policy and in terms of the preservation of the culture based on the family.

The agenda for the future seems clear. It has to do with a central question: How can society respond to the predicament of American women? Specifically, how can the society facilitate the process so that women can develop their earning capability and the society develop an environment in which women can form families through marriage and raise children?

In the final chapter, I discuss this central issue and develop a framework for developing social policies so that the United States can start addressing this perplexing problem of women's economic insecurity.

NOTES

1. V. R. Fuchs, "Sex Differences in Economic Well-Being," *Science* 232 (April 1986): 459–64.

2. S. Danziger, "Poverty and Inequality under Reaganomics," *Journal of Contemporary Studies* 5 (1982): 17–30; C. Ross, S. Danziger, and E. Smolensky, "Level and Trend of Poverty in the United States," *Demography* 25 (November 1987): 587–600; S. Danziger, "Economic Growth, Poverty, and Inequality in an Advanced Economy" (Institute for Research on Poverty Discussion Paper No. 862–88, University of Wisconsin, Madison, 1988).

3. I. V. Sawhill, "Poverty in the U.S.: Why Is It So Persistent?" *Journal of Economic Literature* 26 (September 1988): 1073–1119; S. Danziger, R. H. Haveman, and R. D. Plotnick, "Antipoverty Policy: Effects on the Poor and the Nonpoor," in *Fighting Poverty: What Works and What Doesn't*, ed. S. H. Danziger and D. H. Weinberg (Cambridge: Harvard University Press, 1986), 50–77.

4. U.S. House of Representatives, Committee on Ways and Means, *Background Material and Data on Programs within the Jurisdiction of the Committee on Ways and Means*, 1988 edition, 100th Cong., 2d sess. (Washington, D.C.: U.S. Government Printing Office, 1988), 631; L. Bumpass, "Children and Marital Disruption: A Replication and Update," *Demography* 21 (February 1984): 71–82. Also see S. Hofferth, "Updating Children's Life Course," *Journal of Marriage and the Family* 47 (1985): 93–116; and I. Garfinkel and S. McLanahan, *Single Mothers and Their Children* (Washington, D.C.: The Urban Institute Press, 1986), 46.

5. S. McLanahan, "Family Structure and the Reproduction of Poverty,"

American Journal of Sociology 90 (January 1985): 873–901; S. McLanahan, "Family Structure and Dependency: Early Transition to Female Household Headship," *Demography* 25 (February 1988): 1–16. Also see S. McLanahan and L. Bumpass, "Intergenerational Consequences of Family Disruption," *American Journal of Sociology* 94 (July 1988): 130–52.

6. National Council of Organizations for Children and Youth, *America's Children 1976: A Bicentennial Assessment* (Washington, D.C.: National Council, 1976); U.S. House of Representatives, Select Committee on Children, Youth, and Families, *Children, Youth, and Families: 1983*, 98th Cong., 2d sess. (Washington, D.C.: U.S. Government Printing Office, 1984).

7. Quoted by C. Murray, *Losing Ground: American Social Policy 1950–1980* (New York: Basic Books, 1984), 101.

8. U.S. Congressional Budget Office, *Trends in Educational Achievement* (Washington, D.C.: Congressional Budget Office, April 1986).

9. National Center for Health Statistics, *Americans Needing Help to Function at Home*, Advance Data from Vital and Health Statistics, No. 92, DHHS Publication No. (PHS) 83–1250 (Hyattsville, Md.: U.S. Public Health Services, September 1983), 1–12.

10. Ibid., 1–12.

11. P. L. Menchik and M. David, "Income Distribution, Lifetime Savings, and Bequests," *American Economic Review* 73 (1983): 672–90.

12. S. R. Sherman, "Assets of New Retired-Worker Beneficiaries: Findings from the New Beneficiary Survey," *Social Security Bulletin* 48 (July 1985): 27–43.

13. The median annual earnings of full-time male workers were $21,000 and those of full-time female workers, $17,800. See U.S. Bureau of the Census, *Statistical Abstract of the United States: 1985* (Washington, D.C.: U.S. Government Printing Office, 1984), Table 699, p. 419.

14. The poverty rate of women who live with husbands is only 7 percent, which is less than one-fourth the poverty rate of widows and less than one-half the poverty rate of the U.S. population.

15. U.S. Special Committee on Aging and the American Association of Retired Persons, *Aging America: Trends and Projections* (Washington, D.C.: U.S. Senate Committee on Aging, 1984), pp. 82, 84–85.

16. E. Hing, "Use of Nursing Homes by the Elderly: Preliminary Data from the 1985 National Nursing Home Survey," *NCHS Advance Data from Vital and Health Statistics of the National Center for Health Statistics*, No. 135 (Hyattsville, Md.: National Center for Health Statistics, May 14, 1987), p. 9.

17. M. N. Ozawa, "American Nursing Homes and Elderly Residents: An overview from the 1985 National Nursing Home Survey," *Nenkin to Koyo* 23 (1988): 4–25.

2 EDUCATIONAL PREPARATION OF AMERICAN WOMEN

Shirley M. Clark

The ideal of equal opportunity in the United States implies access to education and expectations of equality of outcomes as well. The belief that educational achievement can be translated into economic and educational success is widely held. In fact, belief in equal opportunity and the value of education, coupled with the changing social and political climate, spurred the challenges made to the educational status quo in the past twenty-five years.

During this recent period women activists have lobbied quite successfully for educational and occupational reforms. Their efforts have raised social consciousness about women's less than equal status with men and resulted in landmark legislation prohibiting sex discrimination in school and at work. From 1961 when President Kennedy formed a Commission on the Status of Women, to the passage of the Equal Pay Act of 1963, to the extension of Title VII of the Civil Rights Act of 1964 which prohibited sex discrimination in employment, to an Executive Order signed by President Johnson in 1967 to further protect women in employment, the way was opened for additional significant educational legislation and judicial rulings in the 1970s and 1980s on behalf of women's equal opportunity in both education and employment.

An even longer historical view of the education of American women over the last 200 years would lead to the conclusion that education has profoundly affected the contours of women's lives and produced revolutionary implications for the whole society. Yet it must be said that women have not yet achieved equal status with men either within or outside the institution of education. It is the purpose of this chapter to explore the differential socialization and educational preparation of American women, to consider the roles played by families and schools in this process, and to assess outcomes and consequences of this differentiation. Implications and interventions will be discussed. We begin with a focus on contemporary socialization and sex-role acquisition.

SOCIALIZATION

Why is it that girls and boys who come from the same families and attend the same schools turn out to be so respectively "feminine" or "masculine," and to have different experiences, interests, achievement levels, and expectations? Scientific research generally does not support arguments that different sex-role scripts are due to biological sex differences. Theoretical explanations of the different aspirations, preferences, interests, expectations, and behaviors of females and males focus on socialization at home and in school and the role of societal system.

Socialization is the process by which the person (biological organism) becomes a functioning member of the culture and the society, a participant in social life. It is a twofold process. From the perspective of the group, socialization is a mechanism through which members learn the values, norms, knowledge, beliefs, and the interpersonal and other skills that facilitate role performance and further group goals.[1] The girl-child learns to think of herself in certain ways and to be responsive to the approval and disapproval of others. This conditioning or internalization of the individual's motivation is responsible for the collusion between the socialized person and those whose role expectations she meets.[2] Rarely is the process one-way or coercive. Rather, the individual has a role readiness from birth to take directions from others and to fit into existing structures. Adequate enactment of the social role is the destination of socialization toward which the individual is pulled and pushed by the agents (parents, teachers, others) of socialization.

The means by which the primary socialization of infants and young children is accomplished include the use of rewards and punishments of a familiar kind: social approval or disapproval, and control over outcomes affecting the socializee. Products of socialization include learned motives (the achievement motive), learned cognitions, and personal or self-identity.[3] As the individual learns social labels or categories and applies them to the self, one of the most important of these—gender identity—emerges and crystallizes firmly at about the age 2½.[4] Sex-role socialization builds upon this basis as self expectations and social scripts interact.

In recent years recognition has grown that socialization is a process that continues over the life cycle. According to Elder, the rapidity of social change in modern society has made obsolescent a linear conception of life in which the preparatory processes of socialization are largely concentrated in the early years.[5] Attention has shifted to the adaptive and integrative requirements of role systems in late adolescence and the adult years. In fact there is considerable interest in occupational socialization and resocialization. The means employed in adult socialization are similar to those applied in primary socialization: direct teaching, modeling, information-providing, assessing, rewarding, and sanctioning. Socializing agents and agencies change at different life stages; in the early, primary phase of socialization the child is heavily dependent upon parents and adult caretakers on whom she depends and to whom she forms the attachments that will become a basic lever in subsequent learning. The primary phase is family controlled. The secondary stage, for children and youth, involves more non-family agents and agencies, e.g., teachers, schools, age-graded peers, employers, and others.

Inherent in the idea of socialization is adult role performance as the end toward which socialization efforts are directed. One of the most important roles for adults concerns attainment of appropriate femininity or masculinity. Being born female or male does not automatically result in the desired outcome. Since family and school are two of the most important groups that train us for social participation, educational attainment, and occupational consequences, it is with these two groups that attention to sex-role socialization and sex typing begins.

SEX-ROLE SOCIALIZATION AND SEX TYPING BEGINS AT HOME

By looking at the commonplace experiences of children we can identify the social processes and pressures that shape them in the direction of learned sex roles. The family group is the first and most critical agent of socialization, for it represents one's initial social contact when all of life is new and everything is yet to be learned at a time when the child's resources are minimal and alternatives are nil.[6] The family's influence is enduring, influencing behavior and dispositions far beyond the formative years.

From the moment of birth, a child's gender is probably the first trait noticed by its parents. Parents are stimulated to act according to the projected future roles of the child on the basis of sex and the traditionally appropriate attributes and skills associated with these roles. This projection into future sex-role tracks permeates gestures, thoughts, and expectations of the parents for the child and creates the climate for teaching sex roles.[7] Thus, parents begin to assign sex-role expectations to their newborn in the first hours of life (if not prenatally in the speculation about the fetus's gender and the planning of names, nursery decor, and color of clothing). In a study of babies less than a day old, researchers had hospital staff select a group of baby boys and girls who were reasonably well matched in size, weight, muscular response, and skeletal framework.[8] Parents were asked to describe their own child and comparisons were made between descriptions of babies. As expected, parents of girl babies rated their own as softer, smaller, prettier, finer featured, and so forth. In contrast, parents of boy babies rated theirs as stronger, bolder, larger featured, and better coordinated in muscle response. Other studies have found that parents select different colors, clothing, and decors to fit their expectations for sons and daughters.[9] Delicate fabrics, pastel colors, and floral motifs are chosen for girls whereas primary colors, coarser fabrics, and animal motifs are chosen for boys.

Other differences in parents' behavior toward their children in the first months after birth have been documented by researchers, as suggested in the following examples. Mothers and fathers tend to vocalize (speak, sing, and talk) much more often with daughters than with sons,[10] handle male children more roughly than female children,[11] maintain an affectionate and physically close relationship with girls more so than boys,[12] and act more protectively toward their girls relative to safety, rough-and-tumble play, and active exploration.[13] Findings such as these suggest that as early as the first year of life in many families girls are viewed as more fragile, in need of protective supervision and love. Boys, on the other hand, are viewed as stronger, ready to explore their surroundings, and less needful of parental protection. Easy generalizations are drawn concerning the head start of girls toward helplessness, passivity, and dependence, and the thrust of boys for autonomy, independence, and high activity level. The stage is set on the basis of the child's gender rather than on other personal characteristics and abilities.[14]

Since a great deal of attention in the United States has been paid of late to the goal of raising gender-aschematic children to break the bonds of these traditional, even stereotypic patterns of regarding children,[15] it is important to note that sex-role expectations are deeply ingrained and apparent even among parents who insist that they try to treat their sons and daughters alike. As reported in Maccoby and Jacklin's comprehensive analysis of research on sex differences, modern parents are often paradoxical in their responses to questions about expectations of their daughters and sons and their ideas about differences between their children on a gender-related basis.[16] Parents expect their daughters and sons to be equally neat, helpful in doing chores around the house, considerate, able to control their anger, and so forth. On the other hand, the same parents report categorically that boys are "naturally" messier, noisier, and more aggressive, whereas girls are neater, quieter, more helpful around the house, and more considerate.

What begins as sex-typed responses of parents to their children during infancy and the early years continues and becomes mutually reinforcing between parents and their children at later ages. The labeling of children as boys or girls is continuously validated and emphasized in giving children sex-typed toys, clothes, and even more important, by reinforcing behavior that is gender-appropriate. As early as age three, children are certain of their gender and that of others as well as aware of existing cultural sex-typing.[17] At this age, children are already learning of gender-appropriate behavior from other socialization agents, e.g., television, books, peers in the playgroup or nursery school, care providers, relatives, and others.

A variety of studies of preschoolers and their parents (especially their mothers who are more available to researchers than are fathers) suggests the following pattern.[18] The early warm and physically close relationships between daughters and parents continue even into early adolescence. Likewise, patterns of greater protection, support, and less punishment of daughters continue into adolescence. Alternatively, more emphasis is placed by parents on their sons' achievement, and parental love seems somewhat more conditional toward sons on the basis of their performance and success. Girls feel less the pressure to succeed but more the pressure to be "feminine" as demonstrated in qualities of sweetness, neatness, passiveness, dependence, nurturance, domesticity, conformity, and obedience. This pressure to be feminine, combined with unconditional parental love, is speculated to be associated with lower aspirations and achievement motivation. Boys, more often, are encouraged toward independence, encouraged to take chances, assume personal responsibility, and to attempt on their own more difficult tasks and problems. There is evidence of differential behavior on the part of mothers as compared to fathers, just as boys and girls are shown to react differentially to their parents' expectations and demands. Finally, fathers tend to expect more aggressiveness and competitive behavior from their sons than from their daughters, but because they seem to feel it important to curb and control their sons' aggressiveness they are firmer with them and more likely to sanction (including use of physical punishment) sons. This seems to result in decreased psychological dependency, greater distancing of boys from parents, and greater independence and autonomy.

A cautionary note should be interjected here. Determining the *actual* behavioral differences between female and male children is not an easy task, and in fact, in the most extensive search for sex differences to date, the authors concluded that there are few well-established sex differences.[19] In their quest Maccoby and Jacklin surveyed 1,600 studies suborganized by eight broad topics and several psychological dimensions such as perception, motivation, intellectual ability, social behavior, and learning. Critics of this endeavor have charged that the authors underestimated differences in some areas due to the way in which their analysis was organized.[20] The areas of least disagreement involve consistent findings that girls are more verbally precocious and more verbal; boys are more aggressive in their play. Over time, the sex difference relative to aggressiveness increases, at least with respect to observed behavior. While not so consistently found, girls show more interest in people, personalities, and social experiences in their artwork and stories. Boys show more interest in inanimate objects (machines, trucks, rockets). Some have inferred from these findings a causal explanation for female preferences for person-centered occupations and male preferences for more task-oriented work.

SEX-ROLE SOCIALIZATION AND SCHOOLING

Although the family is the primary influence in children's early sex-role development, by age five and entry into kindergarten the schools become *an* important, if not *the* most important, agent of socialization in children's and adolescents' lives. Schools are people-processing organizations. Attendance is compulsory until the middle or late teen years, as established in the laws of the fifty states, resulting in a virtual monopoly on the weekday time of the young, five days a week, approximately 180 days each year. Like other people-processing organizations, schools admit, evaluate, label, classify, teach the student role, monitor learning, and finally terminate and certify their clients. During the school day, the pervasive authority of the school extends officially over the students in a parental way. More than the family, elementary and secondary school socialization directly channels students into post-school outcomes, e.g., occupations and/or postsecondary and higher education programs. Even in a society in which the schools are not tightly coupled to the college and university level, schools are chartered to take vocational and occupational preparation and preparation for further academic work as primary responsibilities.[21]

Generally speaking, schools are highly conservative institutions engaged in cultural reproduction (of society's beliefs, values, sentiments, knowledge, and patterns of behavior) by way of the process of socialization. Of course, schools can and do contribute to social change if they are so structured and directed to teach new values, different ways of thinking, and skills needed for reform. However, schools tend to mirror society's stratification system, in spite of concerns about equality of educational opportunity. This patterning of social stratification is evident in ability grouping and curricular tracking related to students' socioeconomic background, ethnicity, and gender. Since our principal concern here is with gender stratification as that affects educational and occupational outcomes, attention will be focused on sex-segregation practices, differential treatment of the sexes, and their effects.

Public schools in the United States are coeducational and there is little evidence of official segregation by gender status. However, it is not difficult to find evidence of sex segregation practices and customs in the schools. In some elementary schools, for example, boys and girls may have separate classroom chores, lineups, and enrollment lists.[22] Playgrounds may be invisibly demarcated into male and female territories with different games going on in each area. It has been argued by Fox and Hesse-Biber that this segregation is not "symmetric." It prepares children for prospective job segregation in which men (as higher status figures) are permitted to move over into women's occupations in order to upgrade them, but women are not encouraged to move into men's occupations and when they do, the prestige of the occupation is likely to diminish.[23] (A deeper critique could be made that the occupational sector does not adequately value the things that females are taught, that is, to nurture, teach, support, and facilitate.) Among children, girls are more likely to play predominantly male games more than boys are likely to enter girls' games.[24]

Sex segregation in schools, which to a significant extent is being addressed and reduced, has not been separate and equal. For fifteen years now, since the passage of Title IX of the Higher Education Act, which is a mandate for sex equity in education from preschools through higher education, attention and legal struggles have resulted in greater fairness in programs for boys and girls. Prior to 1972, for example, it was common for boys to have vastly different and better opportunities to participate in sports programs and on sports teams than girls. Girls had to "make do" with fewer athletic programs, less coaching, less convenient practice times, more out-of-pocket expenses for traveling and for uniforms, and other disadvantages.

Another educational program area with identifiable gender tracks that parallel those in the larger economy is vocational education. Surprisingly little notice by parents or by researchers has been taken of gender disparities in secondary vocational education programs resulting from "natural" selection and from deliberate tracking. According to Laws, "Research on occupations tends to presuppose college training and jobs that lie at the professional end of the spectrum. Yet when we examine occupational 'aspirations' of youth, we discover that the forgotten girls in vocational tracks faithfully reflect the dismal future that awaits them."[25]

The question of sex-differentiated curricula was an issue prompting approval of Title IX and progress has been made since 1972. Before passage it was not uncommon to find three-fourths of girls and women enrolled in government-assisted programs to be in home economics or office skills courses, and a negligible distribution of females over the potentially better-paying skilled trades or technical job areas. Furthermore, no serious effort was made to determine where labor needs and opportunities existed and to orient training toward those areas.[26] Comparison of enrollments in vocational education between 1969 and 1979 by Abrams has indeed shown a modest increase in the proportions of female enrollment in agriculture, technical, and trade and industry areas.[27] Slight but significant decreases resulted in health and consumer and homemaking categories. Even within the trade and industrial training areas, females are concentrated in traditional fields such as cosmetology, textile production, and art, whereas male students are moving toward more highly skilled and better-paid jobs.[28] Vocational education is intended to link training and skills development with post-school jobs; because of this, continuing attention should be given to the pattern maintenance of educational segregation by gender and the subsequent occupational outcomes. Roles played by families, teachers, counselors, and others in guiding students toward their occupational preparation need to become the subject of study and possible intervention strategies.

A case can be made that separating and tracking male and female students is not confined to vocational education and athletics. It pervades the academic curriculum and the college preparatory program in important ways. While it is to be hoped that sex-typing in curricula and tests has diminished (since considerable criticism and consciousness-raising has been directed toward it in the past decade), researchers in the 1960s and 1970s found biases favoring males in tests, in reading texts, and, in the 1980s, in the use of computer technology in education. Saario and her colleagues found that male pronouns predominated in achievement tests and test item content. Readers depicted stereotyped situations, e.g., girls in domestic, indoor contexts and trivial situations, and that this increased with grade level.[29] However, cultural expectations in the United States are such that girls are expected to outperform boys in reading and indeed they do, unlike the situation in some other countries where boys show higher reading achievement.[30]

There is a long history of reported differences between boys and girls in their interest and achievement in mathematics and science. Evidence of differential interest and enrollment in mathematics courses at secondary school and college levels abounds.[31] Historically, careers in science, engineering, and mathematics have been dominated by men, thus girls have limited contact with career models of the same sex. Women who choose these nontraditional careers often view themselves and are viewed by others as unusual. Such occupations have been stereotyped as unfeminine and potentially conflicting with family roles.

A number of studies have examined the development of differences in interest and achievement in mathematics. One approach uses a biological explanation to explain sex-linked differences in mathematical ability and spatial reasoning that favors males[32] while another argues that higher level math ability is associated with excess testosterone in fetal life.[33] Another approach suggests that the nature of the tasks posed in mathematics learning engages boys more so than girls. Achievement orientations may be different for the sexes in various subject areas.[34] Girls may be more likely to attribute difficulty in solving problems to their own lack of ability, boys to other situational factors. Yet another approach suggests that in the larger culture, socializing agents and media give differential information to boys and girls about gender-appropriate interests. Advertising in technological, including computing, areas is overwhelmingly male-oriented with women in more ornamental roles. For all these reasons girls come to believe that they are less able than boys in mathematics by the time they reach junior high school, and on achievement tests they earn lower scores.[35]

Related to this is the development and widespread availability of low-cost microcomputers that has changed the field of information technology and created opportunities for technically oriented careers that do not require as early commitment to math and science learning in the schools. Training opportunities on the microcomputer are widely available in schools and in settings as diverse as summer camps. Equity of access to computers and learning about them has become an important topic in education. However, the use of microcomputers in education has followed traditional lines of affluence, education, and gender bias in society. A recent study by Hess and Miura has found three times as many boys as girls enrolled in computer summer camps.[36] Parents seem to be more willing to invest in this type of training for their sons than for their daughters, possibly because they believe that such programs are more likely to increase the future earning capabilities of boys than of girls. Another perspective reasons that "computers tend to be subsumed under math or science curricula and thus take on the already existing stigma of sex differences."[37] Since the computer should be seen as adaptable to curricula generally, attention must be paid to the design of software and to the organization of classroom experiences using the computer.

The underrepresentation of female students in secondary school mathematics courses probably results from the differential interest of girls in mathematics and science and from sex-stereotypic notions held by parents, teachers, and counselors. Evidence abounds that college-bound girls drop out of the mathematics sequence in high school after geometry and girls in the general or the vocational tracks pull out even earlier. At college entry females have less frequently studied four years of high school math than have males. In Sell's study of the 1973 entering class at the University of California, Berkeley, a selective higher education institution, 8 percent of the females and 57 percent of the males had four years of high school math in their backgrounds.[38] Math is a "filter" subject necessary for about three-fourths of college and university majors, e.g., in business, medical, scientific, technical programs, and increasingly in the social sciences. Without it women are ineligible for admission into preparation programs and subsequent occupations. A single institutional case study suggests that some positive change may be occurring as a result of younger women being raised in an environment that appears to have encouraged them to do more advanced work in mathematics as compared to older undergraduate women.[39]

Attention to the school as a major arena of sex-role socialization must include recognition of the roles played by teachers, counselors, and administrators. At least two perspectives may be taken here: the structure of authority and staff arrangements in schools, and the relationships between the staff members and the students. Regarding structure, the first observation is that teaching is a feminized occupation in the United States and, contrastingly, administration of schools is defined as "men's work."[40] Sixty-nine percent of today's public school teachers are women, compared with 38 percent of the full-time, year-round work force (a figure that drops to 35 percent for working college graduates).[41] Proportionately very few administrative positions are filled by women. In the top district-level position, the superintendency, there are even fewer women incumbents than in the small proportions of the principalship held by women. If a message is conveyed by this structure of authority it is that teaching as a proletarianized profession or as a nurturing occupation is incompatible with the stereotyped image of the adult male.[42]

Numerous studies have found that teachers behave differently toward girls than boys in ways that reinforce the early sex-role socialization begun in the home.[43] Girls thrive in the elementary school in the sense that they seem to like school better, earn higher grades most of the time, and show fewer learning and behavioral problems. Girls, after all, have been socialized to seek approval, to acquiesce, and to conform to expectations. That this may be dysfunctional to their personality development, intellectual growth, occupational future, and adult competence is worth considering seriously.

However, boys receive more attention of both a positive and negative sort from teachers. When they are aggressive or disruptive, in need of directional help, or deserving of praise for giving correct answers, boys are more likely to receive an immediate response from the teacher. A cross-national review of relevant research literature suggests that these findings hold for many countries, not just for the United States.[44] The findings are open to interpretation. One prevailing explanation is that girls receive as much approval from teachers and parents for being "nice" as they do for their academic achievement. This teaches them that they can fail to achieve in school but still be successful if they are feminine, passive, and dependent. Boys learn that more is expected of their achievement, and that they can be autonomous, venturesome, and self-reliant. Some academically unsuccessful boys will find an appropriately male outlet in competitive sports. Others will drop out of school. Slightly more males than females drop out. Males are twice as likely as females to report leaving high school because of behavior problems, including not being able to get along with teachers and being expelled or suspended.[45]

School counselors are also involved in sex-role socialization, in controlling access to the various high school curricula, and in guiding students toward post–high school plans. The impact of counselors, however, is severely constrained by high student-to-counselor ratios and the domination of counselor time by required recordkeeping, scheduling, and monitoring—rather than advising students. Recent research estimates that less than one-fourth of all high school students select a curriculum with any assistance from a counselor, and only about half of all high school students receive counselor assistance in program planning.[46] Disadvantaged, rural, and minority students are less likely to receive program planning counseling than are their more advantaged and white counterparts. Students planning to attend four-year colleges probably receive more program planning counseling than do other students. The advice of counselors may be rejected if it is discrepant with perceptions of students of the reality of their future job opportunities and life status. This was the case of working-class girls in the Vancouver, British Columbia, schools studied by Gaskell.[47]

On the other hand, the potential exists for counselors to have a significant impact on women's career choices. Like parents, peers, and teachers, counselors are important people in young men's and women's lives. If sex differences in occupational aspirations are to change further than the modest movement toward convergence reported by Leuptow in 1981, counselors and others will need to be supportive of women with nontraditional career goals.[48] Some evidence suggests that counselors tend to discourage young women from training for careers usually held by men. In Houser and Garvey's study of women in nontraditional secondary school and regional center vocational training programs in California, the variable that accounted most for choice of nontraditional programs was the amount of support and encouragement women students received from the important others in their lives.[49] Guidance personnel are probably no more and no less sexist than teachers and other professionals in American society. However, because they have a special position and function in the school structure linking students to post-school career and educational paths, their influence should be considered very important.

WOMEN IN HIGHER EDUCATION

A little history is useful for appreciating how far American women have come in their quest for equal status with men in higher education. According to Solomon, colonial Americans in the 1600s "would have dismissed summarily the notion of women attaining, or even wanting a college education."[50] Even women like Abigail Adams, Anne Hutchinson, Mercy Warren, and Judith Murray in America, and Mary Wollstonecraft in England, were not ready to advocate careers for women. They believed that a liberal education would not only enable a woman better to perform the duties of wife and mother, but would also empower her to think for herself. An idea had come into being, but women would not gain access to collegiate-level schooling until after the Revolution. Teaching became an important public mission of women in the diverse and emerging schools; for this women required literacy education, if not liberal education.

Eastern academies and seminaries, a few of which incorporated the essential curriculum from men's colleges, developed some prototypes for women's institutions in the Midwest and Far West as well as the South. Coeducation on the collegiate level began at Oberlin College in Ohio in 1837 when four women asked to enroll in the "gentleman's course" rather than the less academically rigorous "ladies department." These women succeeded beyond their expectations and opened the way for other women as the faculty was won over to favor the innovation. These first women came to prepare for intelligent wifehood and motherhood, and "to the relief of many at Oberlin, all four of the first coeds were as good as engaged to Oberlin men by commencement."[51] Notwithstanding, Oberlin began to produce women missionaries, teachers, and abolitionists.

Women's own efforts enabled them to redefine the patriarchal assumptions about the marital relationship and expand the boundaries of their sphere. Their efforts to advance into higher education in the mid-1800s were aided by three forces.[52] First was the growth and spread of public education through the establishment of common schools, high schools, and, finally, colleges and universities. Second was the impact of the Civil War and Reconstruction; women students replaced males and employment opportunities were opened to women in support of the war effort, on the farms and in the factories. New expectations were generated, and the reevaluation of slavery led to reconsideration of the status of women. The third trend was the ferment and expansion in the university education, the founding of the great state universities and the Morrill Land Grant Acts that implicitly supported inclusion of blacks and women in their egalitarian purpose. By 1880 women constituted 32 percent of the undergraduate population; by 1910 almost 40 percent; by 1920 their proportion rose to 47 percent, according to Graham who also notes that women presidents, professors, and professionals reached record proportions at that time.[53] This "market share" began its slow decline and did not rise again until after 1960.

However, as Graham notes,

there was no glorious past when women professionals were ever treated equally with men. The most prestitious institutions never considered women for regular faculty positions until well after World War II. . . . When women did join the faculties of the institutions which would hire them, they were paid less than men. The years of the mid-twentieth century brought a decline for women's participation in an academic life whose past was itself hardly halcyon.[54]

What accounted for the proportionate decline in women's participation as students and as faculty? The explanation is complex. College attendance became more consistent with society's expectations for men. When the entire undergraduate population was small, and the position of women was "securely subordinate,"[55] a few exceptional women achievers did not threaten the enterprise. If the less prestigious institutions had to take in women students to remain solvent, they did not have to take on women faculty or Jewish or Catholic faculty, as even the leading institutions were essentially limiting their faculty component to white males with certain ethnic characteristics who espoused a strong interest in research. Shifts in societal expectations for women also occurred between 1920 and 1960 when the feminine ideal held women to value enhancement of youthful appearance and domestic virtuosity. Since the 1960s and the resurgence of the feminist movement and other societal changes, expectations of women's higher education attainment and pursuit of employment have shifted again, although parity with the male experience in higher education has not been achieved.

TRENDS IN ENROLLMENTS AND DEGREES EARNED

Higher education continues to be a major avenue to greater economic rewards and social mobility in the United States. Postindustrial society is marked by advancing technology and ever-increasing skills requirements for employment, the training and preparation for which have historically been inequitably distributed by race and sex.[56] Occupational and economic rewards are not simply a matter of years of schooling but also depend on the majors that students select, as the economic returns to education differ by major field. This is especially clear for women, who often obtain degrees in fields that are "feminized." Therefore, if the equity gap is to be closed, minorities and women will have to make gains in nontraditional fields.

There has been much research on women as students and as faculty members in higher education since the early 1970s. Data on enrollment trends and degrees earned are available through the National Center for Education Statistics and the American Council on Education. Disaggregation of the data is important, where possible, because "women in higher education are a composite of diverse female groups rather than a monolithic entity."[57]

Today, women make up 51 percent of all students in the United States and outlying parts.[58] They have been at parity with men or slightly above since 1978. By type of institution in 1984, women were 50 percent at four-year institutions and 56 percent at two-year institutions. Overall graduate enrollment of women in 1984 was 48 percent. This was slightly below that of men at 52 percent, but represented a significant shift since 1970 when women were 39 percent to men's 61, and 1960 when women were 29 percent to men's 71.

In more fine-grained analysis of women's enrollment from 1968 to 1978, Randour, Strasburg, and Lipman-Blumen conclude that women's enrollment rates have increased at a faster rate than men's.[59] And much of women's enrollment increase has occurred in older age groups. Fewer men are matriculating in post-secondary institutions while more and more women are attracted to higher education. What accounts for this shift? One explanation is that returns to men on post-secondary education are now lower than returns on strategies such as early labor market entry and on-the-job training. For women, however, rates of return on the college investment, particularly for those women graduates entering nontraditional fields like chemistry, engineering, and business administration, have improved.[60] Beyond the first professional level, there are no differences in the full-time/part-time enrollment statuses of women and men. However, women are more likely to attend public graduate schools and at part-time. This may indicate that women have less financial support and more family responsibilities at this stage than their male peers, a reverse of the situation that prevails in the undergraduate experience.

In terms of degrees earned, the percentages of women earning degrees are increasing at every level. In fact, in 1982–1983, the absolute number of women earning bachelor's and master's degrees exceeded that of men; nearly twice as many doctorates were awarded to men as to women, however.[61]

It is when we begin to scrutinize the fields in which women are earning degrees that women's traditional segregation within higher education translates into labor market segmentation and depressed earnings. At the undergraduate degree level, women are still found disproportionately overrepresented in education (where they earn three-fourths of the bachelor's degrees), English, modern foreign languages, music, nursing, psychology, and sociology. Examples of relatively balanced fields at present are: bacteriology, biology, botany, zoology, and even mathematics.

The percentage of doctorates awarded to women overall has increased from 10 in 1949–1950 to 33 in 1982–1983.[62] The greatest proportions of women doctorates to men are found in English (56 percent), French (70 percent), German (66 percent), Spanish (55 percent), education (50 percent), anthropology (47 percent), psychology (48 percent), and sociology (42 percent). All other percentages of women doctorates in major academic disciplines were less than 40 percent.

Although most women are still earning degrees in female-intensive fields, there have been impressive invasions of women into certain male-intensive fields since 1970. Good examples are found in law and medicine.[63] In 1970 in law, male degree earners (at the bachelor's level) outnumbered women by about fifteen to one; however in 1982–1983, the most recent year for which data are available, women degree earners made up about 42 percent of the total. In medicine in 1970, women earned 8.5 percent of the M.D. degrees; by 1982–1983 their proportion increased to 27 percent. In the engineering field, the figures are as follows: For 1982–1983, women's share of bachelor's degree was 22 percent versus 2 percent in 1970 for chemical engineering, 13 percent versus 1 percent in 1970 for civil engineering, 9 percent versus 1 percent in 1970 for electrical engineering, 26 percent versus 1 percent in 1970 for industrial engineering, and 15 percent versus 9 percent in 1970 for mechanical engineering.

By entering male-intensive fields women should expect to achieve salary parity with men. However, two results seem to occur to thwart this. When women enter (as tokens) in relatively small numbers they seem not to threaten men; however, their salaries may show disparities with those of men as in engineering where, as reported in 1975, women earned 85 percent of their male colleagues' salaries.[64] When women enter male-intensive fields in large numbers, men move out in large numbers (as historically they have from jobs as typists, teachers, and bank tellers); wages decline as the jobs become more gender-balanced or female intensive. This places working women "in Catch-22 situations."[65] While they are occupationally segregated, their wages are depressed. When they enter traditionally male fields in substantial numbers, males tend to pull out and gradually wages fall. How to achieve stably integrated occupations and parity in male to female earnings is a significant social dilemma in the United States and elsewhere.

An important observation on distribution of the men and women into different types of higher education institutions is that women have entered the two-year community colleges and earned the associate degree in unprecedented numbers, actually outnumbering men as enrollees since 1977.[66] In the two-year institutions patterns of sex segregation continue into occupational preparation curricula. For example, this means that women are found disproportionately in health services technologies and within certain subfields of other curricula such as business and commerce technologies and public service related technologies.

WOMEN FACULTY

Dramatic changes in the inclusion of women as students in higher education have not produced a dramatic increase in representation of women in the faculty ranks. As a percentage of full-time instructional faculty in all ranks, women constituted 22.3 in 1972–1973 and 26.9 in 1982–1983.[67] While the overall rate of increase may fail to impress, it does seem to be the case that women are making up a larger percentage of those currently being hired to faculty positions, e.g., in universities, 22.4 percent of the newly hired in 1980 were women as compared to 14.7 percent in 1972.[68] Faculty women are found in lower proportions than men in universities (19 percent) and are more often found in public and private four-year colleges (26.4 percent and 28 percent, respectively) and in the public two-year colleges (36.6 percent).[69]

Within institutions, patterns of distribution reveal that women faculty are concentrated in four fields: performing arts, foreign languages, health-related professions, and English. Disciplinary patterns are changing very slowly, partly as a consequence of the increased availability of women with doctorates and partly as a consequence of affirmative action policies and practices.

In the matter of salary compensation, Finkelstein's review of over fifty major studies completed in the last ten years leads to the conclusion that women are paid less than men, even after controlling for rank, institutional type, and discipline.[70] Women are less likely to hold positions at the more prestigious colleges and universities, and they have had difficulty in moving up the promotional ladder to tenure and the senior ranks. Overall, 65 percent of male faculty are tenured and 45 percent of female faculty are tenured.[71] At all institutions in 1982–1983, women constituted only 10.7 percent of the full professors (and 51.7 percent of the lecturers).[72] Women are underrepresented in top-level administrative positions as well, constituting only 8.7 percent of the presidencies of all higher education institutions.[73]

My colleague, Mary Corcoran, and I have proposed that women in academe have not enjoyed as favorable occupational socialization and accumulation of advantages which accrue to men scientists and academicians. This is sometimes known as the "Matthew effect" (advantage begets advantage).[74] We follow Lorber's suggestion that the current experience of women might be described by a modification of the Matthew effect termed the Salieri phenomenon. (In Peter Shaffer's play, *Amadeus*, Salieri, the court composer and gatekeeper for musical patronage for the Austrian Emperor Joseph, pretends to be a benefactor to young Mozart by recommending him for a post. Although Salieri seems to have opened the door of opportunity to Mozart, he in fact controls and restricts the advancement and success of the young genius by blocking the rewards and recognition which Mozart deserves.) Academic women in America have definitely gained entry, but they have hardly stormed the castle! They have not generally penetrated dominant inner circles of men faculty and administrators, nor have they risen much beyond the middle ranks.

It will take genuine commitment and direct action from those with the power to bestow and withhold rewards within the institution to ensure women's inclusion as full members in the academic community and as full recipients of its multitude of benefits and rewards.[75]

THE EXPERIENCE OF WOMEN STUDENTS AND THE REPRODUCTION OF SEXUAL INEQUALITY

Despite significant gains in the higher education of women, progress toward parity seems slow. Some social scientists and analysts have looked to early sex-role socialization in the home and school, and sex stereotyping in the societal division of labor, as chiefly accountable for reproduction of sexual inequality generally. An emerging literature in higher education investigates the climate, characteristics, and processes internal to institutions and interactive with women's experiences to explain the level of self-confidence, aspiration, and performance of women as well as effects of choice of major. Only a sample of this literature will be offered here. Much of it is controversial, not definitive.

Some feminist writers have proposed that academia in general represents a "chilly" climate for achievement-oriented women because they are either singled out or ignored because of their sex, circumstances that result in feelings of reduced confidence in their abilities and their place in the academic community.[76] Sexual harassment plays a part, but this concern is much more inclusive of subtle faculty behavior toward women. Documenting the chilly classroom climate is a task recently begun, and although the proposition has strong logic to it, the few empirical studies done to date on the classroom experience fail to substantiate the idea of a pervasive chilly climate.[77] The case is not closed, however, and future research should explore the possibility of subtle but real differential treatment of women in their various academic roles.

For a long period of time in the 1800s, "the one place where women had a guaranteed welcome was at women's college."[78] Although co-education overtook the single-sex institutions in popularity, in the post–Civil War decades several women's colleges (Vassar, Wellesley, Smith, and Bryn Mawr) evolved from seminaries to become national institutions and models for those to follow. Catholics started colleges for women just before 1900, decades after the founding of Catholic colleges for men. By the mid-twentieth century, moreover, conversion to coeducation became a popular strategy for combating shrinking enrollments in single-sex colleges. By the mid-sixties, the number of women's colleges showed a drastic decrease; critics claimed that women's colleges were anachronisms. Advocates proclaimed that women's colleges provide a supportive environment in which women are free to develop their career potential—a place where they can be resocialized away from the sex stereotypes held by society.

Research in the 1970s by Tidball contended that women's colleges produce about twice the proportion of achieving women as coeducational colleges.[79] However, studies by Lentz indicate that women enrolling in women's colleges are significantly more career salient than women enrolling in coeducational colleges.[80] Analyses by Bressler and Wendell suggest that, for women enrolled in single-sex colleges, orientations toward masculine vocations increase from freshman to senior year significantly beyond gains in like orientations of women in coeducational institutions.[81] They conclude that "sexual parity in the occupational domain might be better served if larger numbers of young women were to enroll in single-sex colleges."[82] If women are victimized by their own motivation as well as by discrimination, there may be much to gain by exposing them to the special learning environments of women's colleges. These colleges then, while relatively few in number, provide an alternative to women that seems especially encouraging of their personal development and career aspirations.

A third area of the experience of women students contributing to concerns about the reproduction of sexual inequality is choice of major, treatment of women as learners in the major field of study, and linkage between the major and the occupational stratification system. Studies of both undergraduate[83] and graduate[84] women find that women are especially attuned to the personal supportiveness of the environment of their major department. At the graduate level, women students seem to receive less encouragement from men faculty than men students do. They need faculty who are approachable as mentors. But supportive professors are really no substitute for higher occupational payoffs and rewards following graduation. Men tend to opt for unsupportive departments conferring higher rewards (engineering), whereas women tend to opt for supportive departments with lower rewards (food science, home economics, human development).[85] Increasing the personalized support from individual faculty in those areas yielding higher rewards/payoffs may give women who choose nontraditional majors the edge they need to compete with men in discriminatory job markets.

CONCLUSIONS

The ideal of equal opportunity for women is compromised at birth by patterns of sex-role socialization and sex typing begun in the home and continued later in the schools. Through this process, women learn the expectations appropriate to their gender-based status and group memberships. A consequence of these learned patterns of response is the depressed position of women in the labor force.

Raising gender-aschematic children in a gender-schematic world is a daunting challenge for parents who wish to prepare their daughters as fully for future opportunities as their sons. The dominant ideology about sex roles affects well-intentioned parents in their own sex-stereotyped behavior, pervades cultural messages carried by the media, and is everywhere evident in society. Strategies for helping children interpret a sexist world while defining sex in biological rather than social terms are needed. Some resources are at hand.

Schools soon join and reinforce the socializing process and link it to occupational outcomes. Reproduction of social inequality in school is carried out (largely) through informal practices and traditions. Sex segregation is especially evident in the subject matter of vocational curricula, effectively tracking non-college bound students into genderized occupations. Academically oriented girls have not been enrolling in advanced mathematics and science courses and using computers to the same degree as boys. The imagery of books, texts, and readers depicts boys and men as active and achieving, girls and women as more passive and unremarkable. The schools' structure of authority and power is arranged with men in charge and women in subordinate worker roles as teachers. Where counselors are available to students in their planning, they may contribute to reinforcement of traditional cultural expectations of women. However, one must take care to point out that teachers and counselors may also provide the encouragement and support needed to enable women to break the gender-expected patterns. Considerable social change has occurred and these socialization agents have frequently aided it.

In higher education, women have made obvious gains. Their presence in higher education generally, and in the traditionally male areas specifically, is impressive. Many of these gains were made in the 1970s during an era of intense social and political awareness, favorable legislation and judicial rulings. However, when the higher education data are disaggregated, it must be concluded that some of women's greatest gains have been made at the lowest levels of degree programs and in gender-segregated fields. The predominance of women in community college programs raises questions about perpetuation of the social class structure, albeit moved to a higher level. Changes in the representation of women faculty in higher education have not been as impressive as those involving women students. Again, when the data are disaggregated academic women are found at the base of the faculty and administrative pyramid, not at its apex.

Women faculty, students, and workers are caught in a national political scene that appears to be unsympathetic if not indifferent to their struggles for equity. There is a general societal notion that equity has been achieved. Many young women hold this view. The feminist movement, like so many other movements of the 1970s, is frequently described as dormant or dead in the 1980s. On the more positive side is evidence of strategies adopted by institutions to increase and enforce affirmative action, and the expansion of women's networks in their professional/disciplinary associations and at the instructional level. Women's studies as a new field of feminist scholarship and study is thriving. On the less positive side is the notable lack of progress in formulating policies supporting provision of child care for women faculty and students.

Finally, researchers have begun to look at relatively intractable areas (sex-segregated academic program majors) in new ways, since majors are linked to the external socioeconomic system. Women students seem to be responsive to intrinsic rewards and internal major department features such as a high level of faculty concern for undergraduate students. Therefore, it might be worthwhile to increase the personal supportiveness of major departments that are more male-oriented and extrinsic. This strategy might reduce the attrition of women from male-dominated fields of study—a current problem. By helping women feel that, say, being a scientist is appropriate and not unfeminine, by improving their self-confidence and depersonalizing difficulties with courses and by increasing environmental support, women may increase their commitment to science fields and science careers.[86] Of course, strategies to increase women students' comfort, commitment, and motivation to broaden educational and occupational aspirations are necessary, but not sufficient. Complementary to these important interventions are more direct political strategies that increase available opportunities. To create and maintain work options for women requires enforcement of provisions prohibiting sex discrimination in education and employment in a more vigorous way than has been demonstrated to date. American women are using both institutional change and political strategies to increase equity in education and employment.

NOTES

1. J. T. Mortimer and R. Simmons, "Adult Socialization," *Annual Review of Sociology* 4 (1978):421–54.

2. J. L. Laws, *The Second X: Sex Role and Social Role* (New York: Elsevier North Holland, Inc., 1979), 240–46.

3. Ibid.

4. R. Stoller, *Sex and Gender* (New York: Science House, 1968).

5. G. Elder, *Adolescent Socialization and Personality Development* (Chicago: Rand McNally, 1968).

6. M. F. Fox and S. Hesse-Biber, *Women at Work* (Palo Alto, Calif.: Mayfield Publishing Co., 1984).

7. C. Safilios-Rothschild, "Sex Differences in Early Socialization and Upbringing and Their Consequences for Educational Choices and Outcomes," in *Girls and Women in Education* (Paris: OECD, 1986), 30–56.

8. J. Rubin, F. Provenzano, and Z. Luria, "The Eye of the Beholder: Parents' Views on Sex of Newborns," *American Journal of Orthopsychiatry* 44 (1974): 512–19.

9. H. L. Reingold and K. V. Cook, "The Concepts of Boys' and Girls' Rooms as an Index of Parents' Behavior," *Child Development* 46 (June 1975):459–563.

10. M. Lewis, "State as an Infant-Environment Interaction: An Analysis of Mother-Infant Behavior as a Function of Sex," *Merrill-Palmer Quarterly* 18 (1972):95–121.

11. H. A. Moss, "Sex, Age and State as Determinants of Mother-Infant Interaction," *Merrill-Palmer Quarterly* 13 (1967):19–36.

12. S. Goldberg and M. Lewis, "Play Behavior in the Year-Old Infant: Early Sex Differences," *Child Development* 40 (1969):21–31.

13. F. A. Pederson and K. S. Robson, "Father Participation in Infancy," *American Journal of Orthopsychiatry* 39 (1969).

14. Safilios-Rothschild, "Sex Differences," 32.

15. S. L. Bem, "Gender Schema Theory and Its Implications for Child Development: Raising Gender-Aschematic Children in a Gender-Schematic Society," *Signs* 8 (Summer 1983):598–616.

16. E. E. Maccoby and C. N. Jacklin, *The Psychology of Sex Differences* (Stanford: Stanford University Press, 1974).

17. S. K. Thompson, "Gender Labels and Early Sex Role Development," *Child Development* 46 (1975):339–47.

18. See synthetic reviews of these sex-role socialization studies in previously cited works by Laws, Maccoby and Jacklin, and by Safilios-Rothschild.

19. Maccoby and Jacklin, *Psychology of Sex Differences*.

20. J. Stockard and M. M. Johnson, *Sex Roles: Sex Inequality and Sex Role Development* (Englewood Cliffs, N.J.: Prentice-Hall, 1980).

21. B. R. Clark, ed., *The School and the University* (Berkeley: University of California Press, 1985).

22. C. Joffe, "As the Twig Is Bent," in *And Jill Came Tumbling Down*, ed. J. Stacey, S. Bereaud, and J. Daniels (New York: Dell, 1974), 91–109.

23. Fox and Hesse-Biber, *Women at Work*.

24. J. Lever, "Sex Differences in the Games Children Play," *Social Problems* 23 (April 1976):478–87.

25. Laws, *The Second X*.

26. P. Roby, "Vocational Education and Women" (Unpublished paper, University of California, Santa Cruz, Calif., 1975).

27. M. Abrams, "Title IX—A Modest Success," *Graduate Woman* 76 (January/February 1982):23–25.

28. C. Rieder, "Work, Women and Vocational Education," in *Taking Sexism Out of Education*, ed. National Project on Women in Education (Washington, D.C.: U.S. Department of Health Education and Welfare, 1978), 69–79.

29. T. N. Saario, C. N. Jacklin, and C. K. Tittle, "Sex Role Stereotyping in the Public Schools," *Harvard Educational Review* 43 (August 1973):386–416.

30. P. Kelly, "The Influence of Reading Content on Students' Perceptions of the Masculinity or Femininity of Reading," *Journal of Reading Behavior* 15 (1986):243–56.

31. B. R. Taylor, "Equity in Mathematics: A Case Study," *Mathematics Teacher* 76 (1983):12–17.

32. Maccoby and Jacklin, *Psychology of Sex Differences*.

33. G. Kolata, "Math Genius May Have a Hormonal Basis," *Science* 222 (1983):1212.

34. B. Licht and C. Dweck, "Sex Differences in Achievement Orientations: Consequences for Academic Choices and Attainments" (Unpublished paper, 1982).

35. S. Tobias, *Overcoming Math Anxiety* (New York: Norton, 1978).

36. R. D. Hess and I. T. Miura, "Gender Differences in Enrollment in Computer Camps and Classes," *Sex Roles* 13 (1985):193–203.

37. J. Hawkins, "Computers and Girls: Rethinking the Issues," *Sex Roles* 13 (1985):165–80.

38. L. Sell, "High School Math as a Vocational Filter for Women and Minorities" (Unpublished paper, University of California, Berkeley, 1974).

39. S. Blackman, "The Masculinity-Femininity of Women Who Study College Mathematics," *Sex Roles* 15 (1986):33–41.

40. M. Apple, "Teaching and 'Women's Work': A Comparative Historical and Ideological Analysis," *Teachers College Record* 86 (Spring 1985):455–73.

41. C. E. Feistritzer, *Profile of Teachers in the United States* (Washington, D.C.: National Center for Educational Information, 1987).

42. A. P. Parelius and R. J. Parelius, *The Sociology of Education* (Englewood Cliffs, N.J.: Prentice-Hall, Inc., 1978), 204–07.

43. For a review of studies from an international perspective, see Safilios-Rothschild, "Sex Differences," 30–56.

44. Ibid.

45. R. B. Ekstrom, M. E. Goertz, J. M. Pollack, and D. A. Rock, "Who Drops Out of High School and Why? Findings from a National Study," in *School Dropouts: Patterns and Policies*, ed. G. Natriello (New York: Teachers College Press, 1987), 52–69.

46. V. E. Lee and R. B. Ekstrom, "Student Access to Guidance Counseling in High School," *American Educational Research Journal* 24 (Summer 1987):287–310.

47. J. Gaskell, "Course Enrollment in the High School: The Perspective of Working Class Females," *Sociology of Education* 58 (January 1985):48–59.

48. L. B. Leuptow, "Sex-Typing and Change in the Occupational Choices of High School Seniors: 1964–1975," *Sociology of Education* 54 (1981):16–24.

49. B. Houser and C. Garvey, "Factors That Affect Nontraditional Vocational Enrollment among Women," *Psychology of Women Quarterly* 9 (March 1985):105–17.

50. B. M. Solomon, *In the Company of Educated Women* (New Haven: Yale University Press, 1985), 1.

51. M. D. Merrill, "Oberlin's 'Highest Glory in History,' " *Oberlin College Observer* 29 (October 1987):1, 5.

52. Solomon, *In the Company of Educated Women*.

53. P. A. Graham, "Expansion and Inclusion: A History of Women in American Higher Education," *Signs* 3 (Summer 1978):759–73.

54. Ibid., 765–66.

55. R. L. Coser, Review of Jaon Huber, ed., "Changing Women in Changing Society," *Science* 182 (November 2, 1973):471.

56. W. T. Trent, "Equity Considerations in Higher Education: Race and Sex Differences in Degree Attainment and Major Field from 1976 through 1981," *American Journal of Education* 92 (May 1984):280–305.

57. M. L. Randour, G. L. Strasburg, and J. Lipman-Blumen, "Women in Higher Education: Trends in Enrollments and Degrees Earned," *Harvard Educational Review* 52 (May 1982):189–202.

58. C. A. Ottinger, *1986–87 Fact Book on Higher Education* (New York: American Council on Education, Macmillan Co., 1987).

59. Randour, Strasburg, and Lipman-Blumen, "Women in Higher Education," 192.

60. R. B. Freeman, *The Overeducated American* (New York: Academic Press, 1976`

61. Ottinger, *1986–87 Fact Book*, 147.

62. Ibid., 167.

63. Ibid., 183–84.

64. United States Department of Labor Women's Bureau, *1975 Handbook on Women Workers* (Washington, D.C.: United States Government Printing Office, 1975).

65. Randour, Strasburg, and Lipman-Blumen, "Women in Higher Education," 198.

66. Ottinger, *1986–87 Fact Book*, 74.

67. Ibid., 119.

68. A. Simeone, *Academic Women Working Towards Equality* (South Hadley, Mass.: Bergin and Garvey, 1987), 29.

69. Ottinger, *1986–87 Fact Book*, 119.

70. M. J. Finkelstein, *The American Academic Profession* (Columbus: Ohio State University Press, 1984).

71. Ottinger, *1986–87 Fact Book*, 116.

72. Ibid., 119.

73. Ibid., 130.

74. S. M. Clark and M. Corcoran, "Perspectives on the Professional Sociali-zation of Women Faculty: A Case of Accumulative Disadvantage?" *Journal of Higher Education* 57 (January/February 1986):20–43.

75. Simeone, *Academic Women*, 118.

76. R. M. Hall and B. Sandler, "The Classroom Climate: A Chilly One for Women?" (Project on the Status of Women, Washington, D.C.: Association of American Colleges, 1982).

77. J. F. Heller, C. R. Puff, and C. J. Mills, "Assessment of the Chilly Cli-mate for Women," *Journal of Higher Education* 56 (July/August 1985): 446–61.

78. Solomon, *In the Company of Educated Women*, 47.

79. M. E. Tidball, "The Search for Talented Women," *Change* 6 (1974):51–52, 64.

80. L. Lentz, "The College Choice of Career-Salient Women: Coeducational or Women's?" *Journal of Educational Equity and Leadership* 1 (1980):28–35.

81. M. Bressler and P. Wendell, "The Sex Composition of Selective Colleges and Gender Differences in Career Aspirations," *Journal of Higher Education* 51 (November/December 1980):650–63.

82. Ibid., 662.

83 J. C. Hearn and S. Olzak, "The Role of College Major Departments in the Reproduction of Sexual Inequality," *Sociology of Education* 54 (July 1981):195–205.

84. H. M. Berg and M. A. Ferber, "Men and Women Graduate Students," *Journal of Higher Education* 54 (November/December 1983):629–48.

85. Hearn and Olzak, "Role of College Major Departments," pp. 195–205.

86. N. C. Ware, N. A. Steckler, and J. Leserman, "Undergraduate Women: Who Chooses a Science Major?" *Journal of Higher Education* 56 (January/Febru-ary 1985):73–84.

3 WOMEN, MOTHERS, AND WORK

James P. Smith

Throughout all Western countries, revolutionary changes have taken place in women's economic role. Strongly held stereotypes about where the proper "place" for women was and what jobs were "women's work" have been forced to give way to new demographic and economic realities. Increasing numbers of women—in all marital and family situations—have flocked to the labor market in response to a steadily increasing demand for their services. While this revolution had its origins in economic changes in the job market, its repercussions were widespread, touching on social and psychological relations between the sexes and within the family.

In this chapter, I discuss the changing economic situation of women in the United States and draw some parallels between the American experience and that in Japan. I show, first, that economic forces have largely induced the rising fraction of American women who were in the labor force. These economic forces have eliminated marriage and then childbearing as total barriers to women's paid market work. Because of the interaction of these economic forces with women's schooling, the choice between a career and the home has become a far more difficult one, with many women now casting their votes for the job. Second, I discuss some of the consequences of childbearing on American women's labor market outcomes. The outcomes I highlight are labor supply, asset accumulation and family consumption, child care, and women's wages. Finally, I make forecasts about what will happen to American women's wages throughout the remainder of the twentieth century. It turns out that the labor market future American women face is a far brighter one than most observers predict.

Throughout this chapter, the conclusions I draw will largely rely on results from research projects on the status of American women that I and my colleagues at RAND have been involved with for some time. Although the purpose of this chapter is not to conduct a comparative study, I will draw parallels I see between the American and Japanese experiences. Because there are important cultural and historical differences between the two countries, there is a tendency to emphasize the distinctive nature of the labor force experiences of women. I will argue here that the differences are more apparent than real. There is a great deal to learn on current labor force trends of Japanese women from the twentieth-century history of American women.

AMERICAN WOMEN AT WORK

One of the most far-reaching changes in the American labor market during this century is its growing feminization.[1] The traditional division of labor within the family, with men concentrating on market work and women specializing in household work, has been eroding steadily. For example, at the beginning of this century, fewer than one woman in five was a member of the labor force; by 1981 more than six in ten were. These trends were even more dramatic among married women. Less than 5 percent of married American women worked in 1900. Today a married woman is more likely than not to be in the labor force.

Although most attention has been concentrated on postwar developments in the United States, this process has its antecedents well before World War II. For example, during the first forty years of this century, participation rates for married women increased fivefold. However, the rate of growth in the female labor force did speed up after the war. Female labor force participation rates increased by 50 percent from 1950 to 1970 and continued to grow at an accelerated pace during the 1970s and early 1980s.

What were the principal determinants of this rapidly changing economic role of American women? A number of RAND research projects have been aimed at uncovering the causes of the long-term increase in the fraction of women who work. In these projects, we also identified some important consequences of the increased participation of women in the labor market. This research indicates that economic forces largely dictated the rising proportions of American women who worked. To understand why the numbers of working women expanded, it is necessary to identify the nature of these economic forces.

The long-term growth in women's market work passed through three distinct stages. In each stage, a strong barrier existed that virtually precluded any formal market work by large subgroups of women. As these barriers were overcome, labor force participation for this subclass of women began a process of rapid expansion.

Our research dealt only with the twentieth century. But the work of others indicates that the seeds of this revolution were actually sown in the nineteenth century. The initial barrier was broken when large numbers of young single women joined the labor market in the nineteenth century. The expanding manufacturing and factory system thrived on the employment of young single women and children.[2] Relatively small scale factory production grew rapidly, leading to a substantial improvement in the relative wages of women. According to Goldin and Sokoloff, the relative wages of working women rose from 42 percent of men's in 1832 to almost 58 percent in 1885. As a consequence of this rapid rise in relative wages, labor force participation rates of single women expanded sharply. Starting essentially from zero, single women's participation rates rose to almost 40 percent by the end of the nineteenth century.

The intrinsic nature of this factory work—its long hours, geographic location, and wage depreciation—conflicted strongly with family responsibilities. As a result, the labor market in 1900 was not hospitable to working married women. In that year, marriage virtually precluded work by white women, with only 2 percent of such women in the labor force. One reason was that the wages married women could earn were far lower than those of single women—30 percent lower, by my estimates.[3] Their wages were low because in choosing a job consistent with their home and family responsibilities, married women in 1900 paid a considerable price in forgone wages. The majority of married women who did work in 1900 were employed as domestic servants, jobs that offered at least some compatibility with their homemaking responsibilities.

Another important characteristic of the 1900 labor market was that those women who worked were mostly less-educated women or those women whose husbands had low incomes or were unemployed. While even contemporary American women are less likely to work as their husbands' income rises, all studies since 1940 show that the likelihood of women working increases with their education. Since this was not the case in 1900, the character of the labor market confronting women must have altered in some fundamental way that reversed the association of work with schooling.

The other deterrents to market work in 1900 were more conventional. Even in 1900, having large families reduced the likelihood of women working. So did living in families that extended across generations (e.g., with grandmothers and older daughters at home). Finally, women who lived on farms were less likely to be members of the paid labor force, and in 1900 more than one-third of women lived on farms.

The second major historical development was the elimination of marriage as a total barrier to women working. This 1900 labor market, which proved to be so inimical to married women's work, changed significantly in succeeding decades. Our analysis points to several important structural changes in the labor market that women faced during this century. The most important was a sharp increase in women's wages between 1900 and 1920. Across these years, women's wages increased 16 percent faster than wages of men. At the same time, the 30 percent wage penalty for married women was gradually eliminated.

The catalyst for the improving wages of married women was the emergence of a large clerical sector. In the first two decades of this century, clerical jobs went from a relatively minor part of the female work force to one employing more than one-third of all new female workers. The clerical sector opened up a whole new set of jobs that lessened the conflict between work and marriage. As we said above, previously domestic work was the only realistic option. The advantage of the new clerical sector was that skills did not depreciate significantly during the long absences of married women when their children were young. For example, the now familiar labor market reentry of married women after their childbearing began was primarily into clerical jobs.

Other factors also spurred the long-term increase in the number of women working. Coincident with the time period of the most rapid increase in female employment was a significant rise in school completion among women, largely due to a sharp rise in their high school attendance. The emerging clerical sector reversed the previous negative association of work and education. Women's schooling (particularly a high school degree) proved to be very valuable in clerical work. As a result, the propensity for women to work was now positively related to their schooling.

This reversal in the correlation of women's schooling and work would have profound consequences. Previously, work by women was associated with low status, almost an embarrassment to the traditional male role of provider. However, as the association of women's education and work strengthened, the notion of women as only secondary workers weakened and the idea of an independent woman's career grew.

Our research also identified three demographic forces that contributed to the long-term growth in the female labor market: the increasing nuclearization of the American family, the urbanization of its population, and the long-term decline in fertility. In 1900, many American families were extended across generations, with grandmothers and older daughters living in the same households with mothers. In terms of the range of productive activities taking place, these homes often resembled small cottage firms. As families became more nuclear during this century, the labor available for such work diminished and many of those activities shifted out of the home.

Second, many women in 1900 lived on farms and many others resided in rural areas. Although these women often performed arduous tasks and worked long hours on the family farm, their work was so tied up with their homemaking duties that it was often impossible to

Figure 3.1
Labor Force Participation Rates by Year

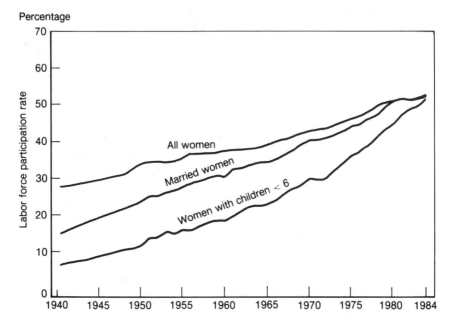

distinguish home tasks from market work. Because of this, such women were not counted as members of the paid labor force. As a result, the decline of the family farm was an important contributor to the growth in the female labor force.

With the elimination of marriage as a total barrier to women's market work, the last remaining obstacle was motherhood. Even when they worked, married women timed their participation so that it did not include the years when they were mothers of young children. In 1940, less than 6 percent of women with children under six years old were in the labor force. This concentration of market work before the birth of the youngest child and until after the youngest child was in school gave rise to the familiar double-peaked life-cycle labor force participation for women.

During the last forty years, this final barrier to women's work fell victim to the powerful historical and economic forces pulling women into the labor market. To illustrate, Figure 3.1 plots women's labor force participation rates starting in 1940. For comparative purposes, this chart plots rates for all women, all married women, and mothers with children under six years old. In all three samples, the fraction of women working rose sharply. However, the most rapid increases occurred

Figure 3.2
Labor Force Participation Rates by Age of Children

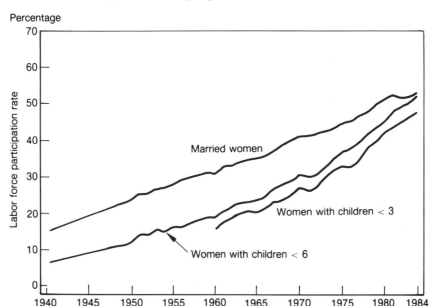

among mothers with young children. As a result, the disparities in aggregate participation levels when we stratify women by marriage or motherhood have almost been eliminated by 1984. In 1940, participation rates of married women were half as large as for all women. The rates for mothers of young children were even lower, one-quarter of the "all women" proportions. By 1984, however, there was essential parity among these three groups.

Figure 3.2 demonstrates that these spectacular increases in labor market participation among mothers also took place among mothers of toddlers. Participation rates for women with children under three have also risen rapidly. The final point to note is the sharp acceleration during the last fifteen years in the increasing numbers of American mothers of young children who work. Since 1970, it is the mothers of young children who have spearheaded the increasing numbers of American women at work.

A complex set of factors led to the elimination of motherhood as the final barrier to women's labor market work. Declining family sizes and an increase in life expectancy confronted women for the first time with a new demographic reality—an increasingly longer part of their life spans after their youngest child entered school. Work during those years (as well as earlier in the life cycle in anticipation of them) became a sound economic decision for many women. As women's wages continued to

Table 3.1
Labor Force Participation Rates of Women by
Education Level (in percentage)

	Years of Schooling		
Year	9–11	12	16+
Ages 25–34			
1940	29.6	38.0	57.7
1970	39.2	47.4	58.9
1983	49.1	66.3	82.6
Ages 35–44			
1940	25.8	31.0	48.6
1970	50.3	51.6	59.4
1983	59.5	70.6	76.5
Ages 45–54			
1940	22.9	26.6	46.9
1970	51.1	55.9	67.2
1983	53.5	64.0	74.6

Source: James P. Smith and Michael P. Ward, "Time
Series Growth in the Female Labor Force," *Journal of
Labor Economics* 3:1 (January 1985).

rise at a more rapid rate than male wages, the choice between staying
on the job and returning to the household increasingly tilted in favor
of the job. Reinforcing that decision were the low birthrates of the women
of the baby boom cohorts during the 1970s. The final element of the
story is that the bulk of the expansion of labor force participation during the 1970s took place among more educated women. This development is illustrated in Table 3.1. Especially among younger women, the
1970s were characterized by a spectacular rise in employment rates
among college-educated women. Between 1970 and 1983, labor force
participation rates jumped 23 percentage points among women twenty-
five to thirty-four years old with a college degree. The cost for these
women of dropping out of the labor market was quite high. As a result, many college-educated women in the United States now have careers that resemble those of contemporary men more than those of the
generations of women that preceded them.

Summary

The most important determinant of the growth in women's work
during this century was the increase in their wages. The rapid growth

in the American economy throughout this century increased the demand for women workers. American economic expansion produced a steady century-long growth in women's wages that exceeded male wage growth. In addition to this steady wage growth, there were two episodes of radical restructuring of the American work force that produced sharp and sudden acceleration in women's wages. The first was the onset of the factory system in manufacturing in the nineteenth century. This expanding factory system led to a sharp rise in the wages of single women, driving unprecedented numbers of young unmarried American women into the labor force. The second major restructuring event took place during the first two decades of this century. The rapid growth of clerical jobs opened up the prospect of paid market work for married women. Because of this growth of clerical jobs relative to male wages, women's wages increased rather sharply—16 percent—from 1890 to 1920. These relative wage increases were particularly large among married women. Wage progress was less explosive but continued at a steady pace after 1920. Between 1920 and 1980, the wages of women increased 20 percent faster than the wages of men.

These higher women's wages encouraged work for two reasons. The rewards from work are greater when women earn more and higher women's wages encourage smaller families. Our estimates indicate that an increase in a woman's wages decreases the number of children she has. This decrease in family size also leads to more work by women.

Parallels to Japan

Does my description of the economic forces that led to the entry of large numbers of American women into the work force carry any lessons for understanding the Japanese experience? Because there are some surface differences between the two countries, an initial response may well be in the negative. But I believe a more careful inspection demonstrates real parallels.

To make these parallels, one must keep in mind the distinction between chronological time and economic time. Because postwar economic growth rates in Japan were so large, Japan has essentially compressed a century-long U.S. experience into thirty years. Since 1940, personal income per capita grew 2.3 percent per year in the United States compared to about 8 percent per year in Japan.

Since World War II, in terms of economic time, Japan has moved three and a half years for every year in the United States. If we convert economic time into chronological time, the appropriate comparison of changes in Japanese women's labor market between 1950 and 1986 would be changes in the U.S. labor market between 1860 and today. The changes in the Japanese economy have been so profound and rapid that one sees the contemporary coexistence of economic systems in Ja-

Table 3.2
Labor Force Employment Rates of Japanese Women
(in percentage)

Year	Total	Self-Employed	Family Worker	Paid Employees
1960	53.7	8.5	23.3	21.9
1975	45.5	6.4	11.5	26.8
1984	47.4	6.2	9.6	31.6

pan that the slower American economic growth placed into separate chronological eras.

The most obvious surface difference between the United States and Japan is that over the last few decades female labor force participation rates have actually been declining in Japan. For example, 54.5 percent of Japanese women were in the labor force in 1960 compared to only 49 percent in 1984.[4] Similarly, Bowman and Osawa state that total participation rates of married Japanese women fell from 49 to 46 percent between 1950 and 1980.[5] Participation rates of Japanese women did not begin to rise until 1975. This pattern obviously stands in sharp contrast to the U.S. experience.

The resolution of the conflict lies in the coexistence of two disparate series in Japan. In Table 3.2, I list the proportion of Japanese women in the labor force in three categories: self-employed, family workers, and paid employees. As pointed out by a number of Japanese scholars, the relatively stable total female employment rates hide two very different trends.[6] The proportion of women who were family workers, particularly in agriculture, fell sharply between 1960 and 1984 as the Japanese economy was transformed from primarily agriculture based to one oriented around the manufacturing and service sectors. The paid employees series is, however, much closer to U.S. trends. Between 1960 and 1984, the percentage of women in paid jobs in the modern sector rose by 10 percentage points. Bowman and Osawa report a similar rise in the fraction of Japanese married women in paid employee jobs.[7]

Post-1960 Japan represents a process that took place over a century in the United States. As economic development proceeded, American women first moved off the family farm and into more urban settings. However, because of reporting conventions by the U.S. Census Bureau, American women who worked on their family farms were not even reported as members of the labor force. Consequently, the American labor force series captures only the growing numbers of women in paid jobs. If we counted American women working on the family farm as members of the labor force, as the Japanese do, two divergent series in the United States would also emerge. The first series would capture the falling fraction of American women working in family farm work. Subsequently, we would observe a rising proportion of women in paid modern sector work. With the spectacular rates of economic growth of women, these two developments, which were largely sequential in the United States, occurred simultaneously in Japan.

To make meaningful comparisons between the United States and Japan, we should be contrasting the contemporary Japanese experience with that of the United States in earlier decades of this century. For example, Bowman and Osawa report that labor force participation of Japanese married women rose from 8.8 percent in 1960 to 26.1 percent in 1980.[8] These rates are quite comparable to the rise among American married women from 5.6 percent in 1900 to 27.7 percent in 1955. If the past is truly prologue, during the next twenty years Japanese women will be replicating the U.S. experience from 1955 to the year 2000. By the year 2000, Japanese and American women could very well have similar labor force lives.

The coexistence at a point in time of these Japanese diverse trends confounds many comparisons to the United States. For example, the positive association of women's education and their labor force participation emerged in the course of American economic development. In the first few decades of this century, it was more likely that less-educated American women were in paid jobs. These chronologically distinct U.S. events once again exist simultaneously in Japan. Osawa reports that there is a negative association between education and female employment among older Japanese women. However, a positive correlation has emerged among younger Japanese women.[9] The aggregate relationship which combines these two age groups shows little relation between Japanese women's education and their propensity to work. As Osawa effectively points out, many of these young highly educated Japanese married women have moved into the rapidly growing Japanese clerical sector—similar to the U.S. experience decades earlier.

THE CONSEQUENCES OF CHILDBEARING ON WOMEN'S LABOR MARKET OUTCOMES

Earlier, I summarized some recent RAND research that explored the reasons why the numbers of women in the labor market have been rising at such a spectacular rate. In our research, we also examined the other side of this coin—the effect of children on a variety of economic aspects of a woman's and her family's well-being. The four dimensions that I will review here include the effect of childbearing on women's labor supply, a family's ability to save and accumulate assets, the care arrangements that children require, and a mother's ability to command

Table 3.3
Labor Force Participation Rates of Women 18–44 by
Age of Youngest Child (in percentage)

	1982	1977	Changes in Proportion of LFPR Between 1977–1982
Less than 1 year	41.4	31.9	9.5
1 year	47.7	37.2	10.5
2 year	51.0	44.4	6.6
3 year	50.8	44.0	6.8
4 year	54.3	50.0	4.3

a high wage in the labor market. In each of these four dimensions, our research indicates that children are a fundamental determinant of the economic reality that women must face.

Women's Labor Supply

The most well-established labor market consequence of children is the reduction in their mother's labor market work. The constraints that young children place on American mothers' ability to work have been diminished but not eliminated in recent decades. Some recent trends are documented in Table 3.3, which lists labor force participation rates of mothers, evaluated at the age of their youngest child. These rates are presented for the years 1977 and 1982 so that some sense of recent secular changes can emerge.

As an indication that motherhood still matters, the lowest labor force participation rates in 1982 were among mothers with children less than a year old. Only 41 percent of such mothers worked in 1982. Table 3.3 shows that the fraction of mothers who worked increases rapidly as the child ages. By the time the youngest child is four years old, more than half of American mothers are in the labor force.

The final column in Table 3.3 calculates the changing proportion of working women in the five years between 1977 and 1982. At each child's age, a much larger proportion of women were working by 1982 than five years earlier. However, the size of the increase is systematically related to the age of the youngest child. The largest change occurred among mothers of one-year-olds, a proportion that grew by 10.5 percentage points. The secular growth in participation rates declined steadily with mothers of four-year-olds registering the smallest increment of 4.3 percentage points.

Figure 3.3
Proportion Employed

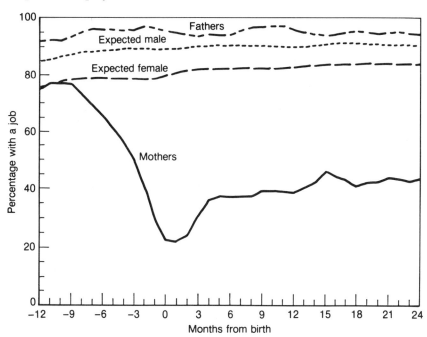

There clearly has been an explosion in the last decade in the number of American working women with young children. Moreover, the biggest increase in the proportion of working mothers with young children has taken place among more-educated women, particularly those with a college degree.

The key to understanding the labor supply adjustments of mothers centers on the period immediately surrounding pregnancy. In addition to the physical demands of the pregnancy itself, young children make particularly time-intensive demands on their parents. In another RAND project, Waite, Haggstrom, and Kanouse intensively studied the timing of the employment activities for a sample of 2,800 young ever-married women between the years 1972 and 1979.[10] The quality of their data allowed them to place in time the exact months of pregnancy and labor force activities.

The key result from the Waite et al. study is illustrated in Figure 3.3. The figure depicts the proportion of mothers employed from the year before the birth of a child until twenty-four months after the birth. The employment of mothers is plotted with the solid line. For comparative purposes, they also plot the employment rates these women could expect if they had remained childless.

Figure 3.4
Proportion of Workers Holding a Full-Time Job

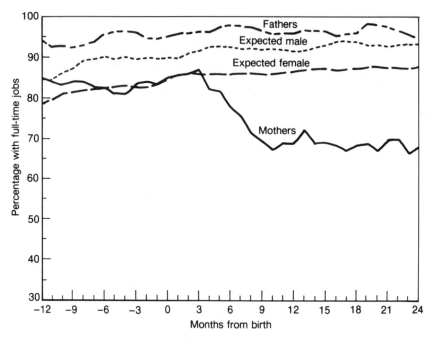

The labor supply adjustment induced by motherhood apparently begins at the point of conception. Before pregnancy began, approximately three-quarters of these prospective mothers were employed. Only half of the mothers-to-be remained in the labor force six months into the pregnancy. Not surprisingly, the lowest employment rates take place in the month of birth, but one in five women still continues to work during this month. After the birth, the process of returning to work begins immediately. A large number of women return to their jobs right away. Within three months of the birth, an additional 15 percent of mothers have returned to work. Two years after the birth, approximately 45 percent of these new mothers were workers. This proportion is double the trough rate during the birth month, but half the proportion that would exist if they had remained childless.

The working habits of American fathers are not immune to the influence of children. The top two lines in Figure 3.3 demonstrate that fathers work more than other men. This greater work effort of fathers, however, is not affected by the timing of the birth. Fathers worked more throughout the entire time span contained in Figure 3.3.

Although many American women return to their jobs soon after the birth of their child, many do so in a limited capacity. This point is illustrated in Waite et al.'s Figure 3.4, which depicts the proportion of working mothers holding full-time jobs. It may come as a surprise that right to the month of birth, these women who remain in the labor force continue to work full time. After birth, however, mothers take a different course compared to the pre-pregnancy period, as a much larger proportion of working mothers now work in part-time jobs.

The Waite et al. study investigated the timing of participation rates of mothers during the early 1970s.[11] If their study was replicated for the 1980s, we would most likely find that the fall in participation around the birth of a child would be much smaller and the return to work after the birth more common and much quicker.

Savings, Assets, and Family Consumption

The next consequence examined in our RAND research was the impact of children on a family's ability to accumulate assets.[12] In addition to their effect on a woman's labor supply, the presence of children in the household requires a complex set of financial adjustments by the family. Out-of-pocket expenses may rise and we all know what profound effects children may have on what kinds of goods we may buy and when and where we consume them. The number of children a couple has, the average spacing between siblings, and the timing of births within a marriage have all been alleged to have important impacts on family savings.

To understand the ultimate effect of children on a family's financial well-being, we traced the principal channels through which the impact of children might occur. The key channels we identified were (1) changes in husbands' and especially wives' hours of work affecting family income, and (2) changes in household consumption.

Children have complex effects on total family consumption. Since children consume, it is traditionally assumed that they must of necessity cause the household to consume more. Obviously the needs of the children must be met and the demand for commodities complementary with children will increase. But parents' consumption may also change as the wife spends more time at home. This increase in non-market time by women will typically allow the family to substitute her time for goods previously purchased in the marketplace. To give just two examples, the amount the family spends on living space and household durable goods probably increases when children are present, while restaurant meals, vacations, and other forms of market entertainment will probably fall. If the wife can now substitute her time for many previously purchased goods, total family consumption may fall when children are present.

In our research, we found the effect of children on a family's finan-

Table 3.4
Estimated Effect of Young Children on Family Assets, Income, and
Consumption (in dollars)

Number of Children Under 5 Years Old	Net Worth	Financial Assets	Durables	Family Consumption	Wife's Hours	Wife's Income
First year of marriage	−1181	−1255	74	−414	−534	−1597
After nine years of marriage	325	676	−351	−1138	−335	−815

cial well-being depended critically on two factors. The first was how old the youngest child was. The second was how many years the couple had been married. For young children, i.e., those under five years old, length of marriage mattered a lot. Because of this, I summarize our results for young children in Table 3.4 by listing the effects of adding a young child to the family at two points in the life cycle of a marriage. The first case captures those families with a child in the first year of marriage, and the second represents the effect of having a child for couples who have been married at least nine years, the "long run" marriage effect. The effect of children when they were over four years old did not vary with marriage duration. Therefore, Table 3.5 contains a single set of financial adjustments induced by having another child over four years old.

In our work we wanted to trace out all the avenues through which a family makes its financial adjustments to having a child. With this in mind, Tables 3.4 and 3.5 show us the changes in a family's net worth as well as the separate impact of children on financial assets and du-

Table 3.5
Estimated Effect of Older Children on Family Assets, Income, and
Consumption (in dollars)

Number of Young Children	Net Worth	Financial Assets	Durables	Family Consumption	Wife's Hours	Wife's Income
Number of Children Age 5 or Older	−21	−286	265	−106	−97	−163

rable assets. These savings effects are then broken down into their separate consumption and income components.

First, let us consider older children. The number of children over four years old has a negligible effect on total family savings. First, the reduction in wives' working hours is one-fifth as large as that due to preschool children. This smaller hours decline translates into a considerably smaller reduction in female earnings—a drop of $163 compared to $815 for young children. Finally, even this effect on savings is partly offset by a $106 reduction in family consumption. Thus, families with older children compensate for the loss in mother's income by using the added mother's time at home to reduce the purchases of some market goods.

Although the number of older children has a minor influence on total savings, they do alter the composition of savings. Older children significantly increase durable assets and reduce assets in financial form. This recomposition is not surprising if children increase the demand for housing and other durable goods.

Now let's turn to the effect of young children. Young children present early in marriage have a much more pronounced effect on family savings. For example, we found that a new child in the first year of marriage reduces savings by $1,181. This lower savings is reflected entirely in a decline in financial assets. Since children require household durable goods, young families are forced to run down their liquid assets and increase their borrowings. However, this straightforward effect belies an entire set of independent effects which can be traced through the income and consumption equations. On the income side, it is well established that young children are a strong deterrent to market work of women. This reduction in working hours is significantly larger earlier in marriage. This larger hours reduction due to the presence of a child results in a larger decline in female earnings among young married couples. As a partial offset to lower female earnings, family consumption declines by $414. Family consumption declines because the increased female home time is substituted for some goods normally purchased in the market.

These large effects of young children decay with marriage duration until, by the ninth year of marriage, young children actually have a slight positive effect on savings. This reversal in the effect of young children is caused by a smaller decline in female earnings and working hours due to the presence of young children, and a larger reduction in total family consumption.

Why does total family consumption decline so much more when a couple has a baby later in marriage? By the time a family has been married for nine years, the family probably already owns a house and other consumer durable goods that children require. In older mar-

Table 3.6
Percentage Distribution of Principal Type of Child Care Arrangement of Mothers 18 to 44 Years Old for Their Youngest Child under 5 Years, by Employment Status: June 1977 and June 1982

Marital Status of Mother and Principal Child Care Arrangement	1982 Employed		1977 Employed		1965 Employed		1958 Employed	
	Full Time	Part Time	Full Time	Part Time	Full Time	Part Time	Full Time	Part Time
Care in child's home	27.1	41.2	28.5	41.7	47.2	47.0	56.6	(NA)
By father	10.9	21.3	9.7	22.2	10.3	22.9	14.7	(NA)
By other relative	10.9	13.3	12.7	12.1	18.4	15.6	27.7	(NA)
By nonrelative	5.4	6.6	6.1	7.3	18.5	8.6	14.2	(NA)
Care in another home	46.3	35.7	47.7	30.4	37.3	17.0	27.1	(NA)
By relative	20.8	16.4	21.0	14.1	17.6	9.1	14.5	(NA)
By nonrelative	25.4	19.3	26.7	16.4	19.6	7.9	12.7	(NA)
Group care center	19.9	7.9	14.8	9.2	8.2	2.7	4.5	(NA)
Mother cares for child while working	6.5	15.1	7.5	17.3	6.7	32.3	11.2	(NA)
Other arrangements	0.3	0.1	1.2	0.7	0.7	0.9	0.6	(NA)
Total	100.0	100.0	100.0	100.0	100.0	100.0	100.0	100.0

Source: U.S. Bureau of the Census, *Current Population Reports,* Series P-23, No. 117, 1982, p. 6; No. 129, 1983, p. 4. The percentages are normalized to exclude the "Don't know/no answer" category. Component numbers may not sum to 100 percent because of rounding.

riages, the birth of a child affects total family consumption mainly through reducing the consumption of market goods through which the wife can substitute her time.

Child Care

An important recent development has been the rapidly expanding proportion of mothers of very young children who are in the labor force. However, children remain relentless demanders of time and attention. With their expanding job responsibilities, however, American mothers are finding alternative ways to care for their children. Because of its emerging importance, this issue is the topic of a current project by two RAND researchers, Arleen Leibowitz and Linda Waite.

American families with working mothers are coping with child care in a variety of ways with no one solution dominating the alternatives. To illustrate this variety and the way it has been changing over the last few decades, Table 3.6 lists the distribution of type of child care chosen

Table 3.7
Percentage of Children Cared for
Outside the Home, for Fully
Employed Women

Year	
1982	56.2
1977	62.5
1965	45.5
1958	31.6

Table 3.8
Percentage of Children Receiving
Care by Non-Relatives

Year	
1982	50.7
1977	47.8
1965	46.3
1958	31.4

for selected years between 1958 and 1982. Because the type of child care sought depends critically on whether the mother is working full time or not, all statistics in Table 3.6 are stratified by the full-time/part-time status of the mothers. Consider, first, the type of care utilized by mothers in the most recent year available, 1982. Among women employed full time, 27 percent of mothers provide care for their children inside the home. In most cases, this in-home care is now provided by a relative. With the decline in domestic service as an important occupation for American women, it is now quite rare to have a non-relative come into the home to care for children.

Table 3.6 also points to a number of important long-term changes over time in child care arrangements. I highlight the two most important trends in Tables 3.7 and 3.8. These tables list the proportion of fully employed women whose children receive care outside the home and who are cared for by non-relatives.

In the last few decades, child care in the home declined sharply. Only one-third of children received child care outside the home in 1958. By 1982, this proportion had doubled with two out of three children receiving care outside the parent's home. Alongside this shift to care outside the home, the percent of children in the care of non-relatives also expanded rapidly. In 1958, two-thirds of children of fully employed mothers were still cared for by some relative. By 1982, children were about equally likely to be cared for by a non-relative. Only part of this movement to non-home care by a non-relative reflects the growth of formal day care centers. Group day care has expanded, almost doubling its market share in the last twenty years. However, it still remains very much a minority choice with only one in five fully employed mothers selecting it as an option.

Wages

The strong negative effect of young children on a woman's current hours of labor market work has long-run effects that are often over-

Figure 3.5
Expected Reductions in Market Work

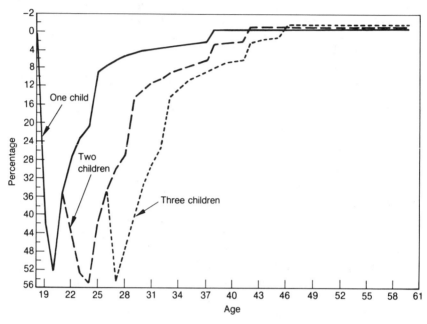

looked. Skills typically increase with added years on the job and many women forgo developing these skills by leaving the labor market when their children are born. In addition, the critical period of intense investments in worker skills often conflicts with a woman's normal childbearing years. In another RAND project, Cogan and Berger estimated the long-run impact children had on mothers' ability to command wages in the labor market.[13]

The negative effects of children on American women's ability to earn turn out to be large. These effects were calculated by first estimating the cumulative impact of children on women's lifetime hours worked. In Figure 3.5, reproduced from Cogan and Berger, I present life-cycle reductions in women's work time for three typical families—those with one, two, and three children, respectively. In this graph the vertical axis represents the percentage reduction in work time compared to work time for a woman without children. For each family size, the deterrent effects on women's labor market work are largest during the child's birth year. The life-cycle reduction in hours worked becomes smaller as the child ages through his preschool years. Women's hours worked continue to rise, leveling off to their normal level without children as children finish their schooling. The birth of a second child starts the

Figure 3.6
Number of Children and Life-Cycle Wages

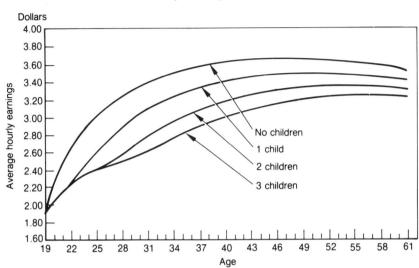

process off anew, leading to additional reductions in mother's work time over her life cycle.

For all three families, the lifetime reduction in work time was substantial, especially during the ages when the children were young. In fact, working hours of these mothers did not approach the levels of a childless woman until the women were in their thirties. American women lost a substantial amount of valuable work time during their twenties because they decided to become mothers. The loss of this work time is especially critical, because it took place precisely at the time in the life cycle that men were investing heavily in getting ahead in their careers.

The number of children a woman rears, then, has an important deterrent effect on her accumulated work experience. To quote Cogan and Berger, "A woman who has one child will work, on average, about 2.5 years less over her lifetime than a woman with no children. A second child results in an additional two years withdrawn from the labor force, and a third one additional year." Since American women typically raise two children, these women will have lost, on average, 4.5 critical years of labor market work.

Through its effect on accumulated work experience, child rearing has a substantial impact on women's wages. Cogan and Berger illustrate the impact in Figure 3.6, which plots the typical wage profile of women with alternative numbers of children in the family. Because they deter lifetime work, each additional child lowers a mother's life-cycle wage profile. For example, at age 30 a woman with no children would earn a 30 percent higher wage than a woman who had three children. After the childbearing years, the cost of children in terms of lower women's wages becomes smaller, averaging about 13 percent. Motherhood has many benefits, but the Cogan-Berger study indicates that it has real costs in the limit it places on the ability of women to earn high wages.

THE FUTURE WAGE PROSPECTS OF AMERICAN WOMEN

Fortunately, the large wage penalties women pay for having children has its optimistic side. We have seen that labor force participation rates have risen most rapidly among women with young children. As women's education levels have risen and as their families have become smaller, the amount of time they have spent out of the labor force has been diminishing. The income cost to many educated women from dropping out of the labor force has simply become prohibitive. We know that the amount of work experience that American women will forgo in the future will be much less than in the past. What, then, will the future of women's wages be in the United States?

To answer this question, it is first necessary to understand the past path of the sex wage gap in America. In the United States, women's wages stayed at 60 percent of those of males for decades, according to virtually all government sources. The constant wage gap was seen as confirmation of a very pessimistic view of the labor market realities that American women must face. Many economists argued that the tremendous increases in the number of women who work must have translated into more market skills for women. And as the job skills of women increased, their wages should have been rising and much faster than those of men. However, the constant wage gap of 60 percent suggests that this did not happen.

In the face of this apparently unchanging wage gap, it is also easy to see why many people are so pessimistic about the future of American women's wages. A recent study I did at RAND provides an antidote to this pessimism.[14] Let me forgo the technical details and tell you about the reasons for our conclusions about trends in women's wages. I will divide them into three parts—those that concern the past, the future, and the present.

To understand my results for the past, it is important to distinguish between the female work force and the female population. The reason is that as the fraction of women working increases from 20 percent levels that prevailed in 1920 to those over 60 percent that exist today, more of the female population is absorbed in the labor force and the base on which the average wage of the work force is calculated changes.

Table 3.9
Projected Years of Labor Market Experience

Year	20	25	30	35	40	45	50
				Age			
Women in the Labor Force							
1910	2.53	5.34					
1920	2.62	5.57	8.74	11.80			
1930	2.34	5.55	8.97	12.04	15.38	18.51	
1940	1.98	5.05	9.54	11.08	13.55	15.85	17.54
1950	2.81	5.87	7.97	10.57	13.99	16.43	19.31
1980	3.00	6.23	9.50	11.70	14.39	16.97	20.64
1990			10.44	15.06	17.24	18.76	22.17
2000					19.63	24.07	26.57
The Female Population							
1910	1.73	3.19					
1920	1.81	3.0	4.53	5.31			
1930	1.55	3.57	4.90	5.82	6.65	7.39	
1940	1.25	3.08	4.63	6.11	7.19	7.94	8.59
1950	2.14	4.08	5.04	6.29	8.13	9.87	10.85
1980	2.47	5.27	7.85	9.46	11.40	13.35	15.04
1990			8.66	11.57	14.74	16.23	18.04
2000					15.57	19.16	22.90

The fairly stagnant wage ratio for women in the work force would surely be bad news if the experience and education of working women had been increasing all that time relative to the experience and education of working men. In fact, they have not. The assumption that working women have become increasingly skilled relative to men in recent decades is a false one. Compared to men, in the last thirty years working women, on average, lost a year of education and gained only half a year of market experience.

How could this be? The answer is simple. New entrants and reentrants into the female labor force have predominantly been women with relatively little labor market experience and lower than average education. These relatively low-skill, low-wage entrants have tended to hold down the average wage of all working women, disguising what would otherwise have been an upward trend in women's wages.

In Table 3.9, I list years of labor force experience for the female work force as well as the female population. The increasing labor force participation rates brought into the labor force women with very little prior labor force experience. As a result, the average amount of labor force experience of a 40-year-old working woman in 1980 was less than that of a 40-year-old working woman in 1930.

Thus, it is no surprise that the wages of working women have remained constant relative to men. Because of these compositional changes, it is correct to say that the level of women's skills has stayed consistently lower than that of men; so has the level of women's wages in comparison to that of men. In short, nothing new has happened to narrow the wage gap between men and women "workers" over the last fifty years.

But the story is quite different when we monitor trends for all women. As more women have entered the labor force, experience levels for the entire population of women taken together—working and nonworking—have been increasing. For example, the average 40-year-old woman in 1980 had five more years' work experience than her counterpart in 1930. The impression people have of a progressively more skilled female population is thus a correct one. However, the skills of the entire population of women should not be compared with the wages of the female work force; they should be compared with the wages of the entire population of women. This we did.

We estimated that in 1920 the average earnings of all women were 43 percent of those of all men; in 1950, 48 percent; in 1980, 53 percent. Thus, across the sixty years between 1920 and 1980, women's wages grew 20 percent faster than men's wages.

Therefore, the correct historical record shows that there has been considerable improvement in the economic status of American women. Moreover, this improvement was due largely to higher levels of the market skills women brought with them to the labor market.

Feminization of Poverty

Individual earnings alone tell us little about how well off people are. Because incomes are typically pooled among family members to set family consumption levels, all members tend to share a common economic fortune. For example, in intact families, poverty status is definitionally sex neutral because all family members are assigned as a group to their income class. Table 3.10 summarizes trends across the last forty years in the fraction of adults of either sex who were poor. To highlight the feminization of poverty, this table also lists the percent of the adult poor who were women.

In 1940, poverty was indeed sex neutral. Over 90 percent of all 1940 families included a husband and wife. As a result, the margin for any sex differential in poverty rates was very small. Unless resources were very unequally distributed within families, Table 3.10 indicates that men

Table 3.10
Women and Poverty

	1980	1970	1960	1950	1940
% Who are poor					
Women	11	11	15	23	34
Men	7	8	13	22	34
% of poor					
who are women	62	60	55	51	50

and women in 1940 shared a similar economic lot. This is no longer the case.

Although the feminization of poverty is a real phenomenon, it should not obscure the fact that poverty rates have declined substantially for both sexes. Women's poverty rates were about one in nine in 1980, a threefold advance across these forty years. The sustained and rapid growth of the post-1940 American economy carried with it impresssive benefits for men and women alike. The timing of these gains and their subsequent slowdown during the 1970s attests to the primacy of economic growth in shaping these trends. Success in reducing poverty was five times larger in the twenty years before 1960 than in the twenty subsequent years.

The second row in Table 3.10 tracks the growing feminization of poverty, a growth which correlates with the increasing breakup of the two-spouse family. With the rising incidence of unwed parenting and divorce, the fraction of female-headed families rose and did so at an accelerated rate after 1960. By 1980, women headed almost one in seven families, almost 70 percent more than in 1960. This problem reached epidemic proportions among blacks, where now more than four out of every ten families are headed by women.

Affirmative Action

Given the intentions of affirmative action policy, no assessment of women's labor market gains would be complete without some consideration of its influence on relative wages. Labor market discrimination against women still exists, and laws such as Title VII of the Civil Rights Act were put in place to combat it. But what role, if any, did affirmative action play in the changes we have been discussing? While vested interests on both sides of the political spectrum hope for uni-dimensional consequences, as usual the empirical evidence contains more of a mixed bag.

The key to assessing effects is recognition that not all sectors of the

Table 3.11
Fraction of Employment in EEO-1 Reporting Firms
(in percentage)[a]

	1970	1974	1978	1980
White Women				
All EEO-1:				
Officials and managers	30.8	33.9	34.4	32.1
All	50.2	50.2	48.1	46.9
Federal contractors:				
Officials and managers	15.4	19.2	21.8	20.9
All	28.1	28.9	29.4	29.5
Black Women				
All EEO-1:				
Officials and managers	42.5	64.5	78.7	67.8
All	63.5	74.0	71.4	74.9
Federal contractors:				
Officials and managers	22.5	38.2	53.0	45.6
All	34.6	43.6	45.6	48.7

[a]Derived from EEO-1 reported employment divided by CPS employment in potentially covered industries.

economy will be equally affected. If affirmative action is adequately enforced, women's employment should increase more in firms required to report to the Equal Employment Opportunity Commission (EEOC) than among firms that are not. Since federal contractors have more to lose, the greatest gains should take place among EEOC firms that are federal contractors.

Table 3.11 summarizes the effects by examining the changing location of women's employment. Among black women, strong positive changes are evident. As this table shows, black women were hired in force by EEOC-covered and federal contractor firms. This shift is even larger when we isolate the high-paying official and managerial positions. Among white women, by far the numerically dominant group, effects are mixed. While there were increasing numbers in the professional and managerial tiers, especially among federal contractor firms, aggregate employment of white women actually moved out of the EEOC-covered sector. Essentially, advances in the professional ranks in the covered sector were more than offset by a relative reduction of white women employed in clerical jobs. Affirmative action is always a two-edged sword. Firms must be cautious about having "observably over-qualified" women in low-paying jobs (e.g., a white, college-educated woman as a secretary).

In sum, these figures indicate that the overall impact of affirmative action on the average woman was quite small. However, there were some winners and unfortunately some losers as well. Black women have been the primary beneficiaries, most likely because they allow firms to fill two quotas for the price of one. To a lesser extent, college-educated white women gained as firms covered by affirmative action placed women in managerial and professional jobs where they had previously been quite scarce. In contrast, covered firms also responded by reducing their employment of white women in traditionally female occupations, particularly clerical jobs. The net result was a wash with no significant effect on wages for the average working woman.

Parallels to Japan

Do these wage trends in the United States have any implications for understanding the post–World War II history of the women's labor market in Japan? On this issue, I believe once again that there exists a great deal of similarity between the two countries. The overall trends in relative women's wages in Japan are more similar to those in the United States than they are to most Western European countries. Compared to men, working women's wages are even lower in Japan than in the United States. (The wage ratio is lower in the United States than in Western Europe.) Wages of Japanese working women are roughly 55 percent of those of Japanese men.[15] More important, this wage ratio has stabilized at this level throughout the 1970s and early 1980s.[16] The United States and Japan stand out as two countries in which working women's wages apparently made the least progress compared to men's.

Why has the sexual wage gap stabilized during the last fifteen years in spite of the large growth in Japanese women's labor force participation in paid work? In an important recent paper, Osawa puts forth a compelling explanation.[17] She demonstrates that there are sharp parallels between the U.S. and Japanese experience on the issue of trends in women's wages.

Osawa shows that in order to understand the overall trend it is first necessary to separate the trends in the young women's labor market from trends in the labor market of older Japanese women. During the last fifteen years, these stable aggregate relative wages of Japanese women have hidden two divergent series. Wages of younger Japanese women (those under age 30) actually continued to rise during the 1970s while those of older Japanese working women declined relative to men's. For example, Osawa reports that between 1975 and 1985, wages of Japanese women compared to wages of men who were 45–59 years old fell from 54 percent to 46 percent. In contrast, between 1970 and 1980 relative wages of Japanese women 25–29 years old rose from 61 percent to 72 percent.

The explanation Osawa offers for these divergent experiences rests once again on the distinction between the work force and population. On the education side, there was a rapid general postwar increase in education levels of women relative to men in Japan. But those gains were not uniform across age groups. The increases in participation among younger women (largely into clerical jobs) were greater for the more educated, leading to a larger increase in the skill of young female workers than of male workers (consistent with the continued rise in their wages). However, among older Japanese women, increases in labor force participation (into production jobs) came largely from less-educated women, making the increase in the education of the female work force larger than the increase in education of the population of women.

The main emphasis in Osawa's paper, however, is on work experience. Her results are dramatic. Among older women the increases in labor force participation were largely for women with low education and with little prior labor force experience. The consequence was that these compositional changes actually lowered the average amount of work experience of working women in these older age groups. To use the most dramatic case, the actual labor force experience of the work force of women dropped six years between ages 30–35 (and calendar years 1970–1975) for the 1940 birth cohort. Osawa estimates that the typical working woman had twelve years' experience in 1970. By 1975, with the influx of so many new women with little experience, the average working woman worked only six years. While this is an extreme case, Osawa reports similar stability or declines in the amount of work experience of the typical older Japanese working woman.

The situation was very different among younger Japanese women. Osawa reports that the rapid increases in participation increased the average work experience of the female work force and population among younger women. For example, for women born in 1950 there was a three-year increase in work experience of women in the work force between 1970 and 1975.

Osawa's work demonstrates that what happened in the United States to artificially hold down the growth in women's wages also operated in Japan. The optimistic side of the study is that as the older Japanese women workers leave the labor force over the next decades, we should also see a rapid rise in Japanese women's wages relative to men's.

CONCLUSIONS

In this chapter, I have attempted to describe and interpret some major changes in the American women's labor market. I have argued that sustained economic growth and some structural changes in the U.S. economy produced the rapid rise in the numbers of American women in the labor market. These forces interacted with rising women's education levels to eventually dissipate the barriers that marriage and then motherhood placed on American women entering the labor market. Historically, an important cost of motherhood to women was the reduction in their labor supply which in turn reduced their lifetime accumulated amounts of labor market experience. These fewer years in the labor market substantially depressed the wages American mothers could earn in the job market.

Rising women's schooling levels and their wages eventually made the real cost of leaving the labor market quite high. In response, many American mothers are increasingly reluctant to leave the job market when they have their children. The consequences of this change are profound. American working women will be achieving far higher levels of work experience than their mothers did. The end result is that during the next two decades women's wages will increase much faster than wages of men. My work suggests that half the wage gap between American men and women will be eliminated by the year 2000.

NOTES

1. This section is based in part on J. P. Smith and M. P. Ward, "Time Series Growth in the Female Labor Force," *Journal of Labor Economics* 3 (January 1985, Supplement): S59–S90.

2. C. Goldin and K. Sokoloff, "The Relative Productivity Hypothesis of Industrialization: The American Case, 1820–1850," *Quarterly Journal of Economics* 99 (August 1984): 461–87.

3. Smith and Ward, "Time Series Growth," 559–90.

4. Japan Institute of Labor, *Problems of Working Women*, Japanese Industrial Relation Series, No. 8, 1986, Figure 3, p. 9.

5. M. J. Bowman and M. Osawa, "Developmental Perspectives in the Education and Economic Activities of Japanese and American Women" (Unpublished paper, 1985).

6. For excellent analysis, see H. Shimada and Y. Higuchi, "An Analysis of Trends in Female Labor Force Participation in Japan," *Journal of Labor Economics* 3 (January 1985, Supplement): S355–S374.

7. Bowman and Osawa, "Developmental Perspectives."

8. Ibid.

9. M. Osawa, "The Wage Gap in Japan: Changing Patterns of Labor Force Participation, Schooling and Tenure" (Unpublished paper, 1986).

10. Their analysis was based on the National Longitudinal Study of the Class of 1972. See L. J. Waite, G. H. Haggstrom, and D. E. Kanouse, "Changes in the Employment Activities of New Parents," *American Sociological Review* 50 (April 1985): 263–72.

11. Ibid.

12. See J. P. Smith and M. P. Ward, "Asset Accumulation and Family Size," *Demography* 17 (August 1980): 243–60.

13. J. F. Cogan and F. Berger, *Family Formation, Labor Market Experience, and the Wages of Married Women*, R-2310-NICHD, The RAND Corporation, May 1978.

14. Smith and Ward, "Time Series Growth," 559–90.

15. Osawa, "The Wage Gap."

16. Ibid.; Shimada and Higuchi, "An Analysis of Trends," S355–S374.

17. Osawa, "The Wage Gap."

4 CAUSES AND CONSEQUENCES OF TEENAGE PREGNANCY AND CHILDBEARING

Frank F. Furstenberg, Jr., and J. Brooks-Gunn

All societies devise means of managing sexuality in order to regulate reproduction. The task is rarely accomplished without some strain. Control of youthful sexuality was considered a problem in American society long before the 1960s, when the so-called sexual revolution occurred. Nonvirginity at marriage was common at the beginning of the century, and by the 1950s it was estimated that a quarter of all marriages involved pregnant teenage brides.[1] Since the 1960s, however, adolescent pregnancy increasingly has aroused public concern.[2] This chapter reviews recent evidence on the causes and consequences of childbearing among adolescents, especially those under eighteen, and assesses what is presently known about preventive and ameliorative strategies. Our summary draws upon our own research and also makes use of several excellent existing source books. Since we cannot give full treatment to many important topics, readers may wish to consult these references for more detailed information.[3]

CHANGING PATTERNS OF ADOLESCENT PREGNANCY AND CHILDBEARING

Adolescent fertility has decreased in recent decades but most authorities probably would view the issue with greater concern today than two decades ago when the incidence of early childbearing was much higher. This apparent contradiction is illustrated by the different indicators of trends in adolescent fertility (see Table 4.1). The data are shown by race because a substantial and disproportionate share of early childbearing occurs among blacks. In absolute numbers, fewer teenage females among both whites and nonwhites are becoming mothers today than a decade ago. Since 1960, just after the peak of the baby boom, rates of early childbearing have been declining. Even among teens un-

Table 4.1
Adolescent Fertility by Race, 1955–1986

Age/Race	1955	1960	1970	1980	1983	1984	1986
			Number of Births (in thousands)				
15-19							
Total[a]	484	587	645	552	489	470	462
White	373	459	464	388	338	321	311
Black	111[b]	129[b]	172	150	137	134	135
18-19							
Total	334	405	421	354	317	303	292
White	269	329	320	260	229	216	206
Black	65[b]	76[b]	95	84	79	77	77
15-17							
Total	150	182	224	198	173	167	169
White	104	130	144	128	110	105	105
Black	46[b]	53[b]	77	66	58	57	58
< 15							
Total	6	7	12	10	10	10	10
White	2	3	4	4	4	4	4
Black	4[b]	4[b]	7	6	5	6	6
			Birthrates (per thousand women)				
15-19							
Total	90.3	89.1	68.3	53.0	51.7	50.9	50.6
White	79.1	79.4	57.4	44.7	43.6	42.5	41.8
Black	167.2[b]	156.1[b]	147.7	100.0	95.5	95.7	98.1
18-19							
Total	—	—	114.7	82.1	78.1	78.3	81.0
White	—	—	101.5	72.1	68.3	68.1	69.8
Black	—	—	204.9	138.8	130.4	132.0	141.0
15-17							
Total	—	—	38.8	32.5	32.0	31.1	30.6
White	—	—	29.2	25.2	24.8	23.9	23.4
Black	—	—	101.4	73.6	70.1	69.7	70.0
10-14							
Total	0.9	0.8	1.2	1.1	1.1	1.2	1.3
White	0.3	0.4	0.5	0.6	0.6	0.6	0.6
Black	4.8[b]	4.3[b]	5.2	4.3	4.1	4.3	4.6
		Rates of out-of-wedlock births (per thousand unmarried women)					
15-19							
Total	15.1	15.3	22.4	27.6	31.6	32.6	
White	6.0	6.6	10.9	16.2	20.5	21.5	
Black	77.6[b]	76.5[b]	96.9	89.2	88.8	89.9	

Table 4.1 (continued)

Age/Race	1955	1960	1970	1980	1983	1986
	Ratio of out-of-wedlock births (per thousand births)					
15-19						
Total	143	148	295	476	580	608
White	64	72	171	330	446	481
Black	407[b]	421[b]	628	851	897	900
18-19						
Total	102	107	224	398	507	536
White	49	54	135	270	380	415
Black	324[b]	337[b]	521	792	855	860
15-17						
Total	232	240	430	615	703	733
White	102	116	252	452	578	611
Black	524[b]	543[b]	760	928	953	953
<15						
Total	663	679	808	887	919	425
White	421	475	579	754	824	835
Black	801[b]	822[b]	935	985	987	990

[a] All totals include all nonwhites, which exceed the sum of whites and blacks.
[b] Including all nonwhites, not only blacks.

Sources: K. A. Moore, M. C. Simms, and C. L. Betsey, *Choice and Circumstance: Racial Differences in Adolescent Sexuality and Fertility* (New Brunswick, N.J.: Transaction Books, 1986); W. Baldwin, "Adolescent Childbearing Today and Tomorrow," updated statement prepared for U.S. Senate Human Resources Committee, June 14, 1987; U.S. Bureau of the Census, *Current Population Reports*, Series P-20, No. 385, *Marital Status and Poverty Status of Families and Persons in the United States: 1983* (Washington, D.C.: U.S. Government Printing Office, 1984); National Center for Health Statistics, Advance Report of Final Natality Statistics, 1983, *Monthly Vital Statistics Report*, 34:6 (suppl.) (Hyattsville, Md.: Public Health Service, 1985); and National Center for Health Statistics, Advance Report of Final Natality Statistics, 1986, *Monthly Vital Statistics Report*, 37:3 (suppl.) (Hyattsville, Md.: Public Health Service, 1988).

der 18, the rates have decreased although the decline is much less dramatic among whites than blacks.

A major difference with earlier periods is that the majority (61 percent in 1986) of teens who bear children today do so out of wedlock. Most teens who became mothers in the 1950s and 1960s were married before or soon after they became pregnant. Indeed, the incidence of nonmarital childbearing among the young has increased over the past several decades as is shown in the bottom panel of Table 4.1. Twenty-four percent of black and five percent of white unmarried adolescents born in the late 1950s became mothers by the end of their eighteenth year.[4] Were it not for the legalization of abortion, the incidence of early childbearing would be much higher.[5] About half of all pregnancies among teenagers under the age of eighteen are terminated voluntarily.[6] The incidence of abortion has not increased in the past few years, but the overall number of abortions among teenagers is an area of major political concern.[7]

Two conspicuous demographic changes largely account for the growth of abortion and the rising proportion of out-of-wedlock births. Starting in the 1960s and accelerating in the decade of the 1970s, a sharp increase took place in the incidence of sexual activity among adolescents.[8] The proportion of young women who had experienced intercourse rose by two-thirds during the 1970s. The increase was especially large for whites and younger teens because they started from a lower baseline. By 1979, close to half of all teen females were sexually active, and about a third of those between 15 and 17 were nonvirgins.[9] Almost no change occurred in the 1980s.[10]

The increase was accompanied by other changes in the life-style of youth, increased drug and alcohol use and probably greater tolerance for nonconforming behavior in general.[11] Some of these changes can be traced to the emergence of "youth culture" in the Vietnam era, to the cultivation of a huge youth market by commercial interests, and to the gradual decline of restrictive sexual standards in the adult population. The availability of oral contraception and legalized abortions may have contributed to the changing sexual climate, though these factors are probably best seen as both causes and consequences of the sexual transformation.[12]

Marital timing also contributed to the growth of out-of-wedlock pregnancies and childbearing among the young. During the baby-boom period, marriage age had declined significantly; in the 1960s, it reversed direction and from the 1970s to the present has continued to rise. In 1960, 40 percent of all females were married by the age of nineteen. By 1986, this proportion had dropped to 15 percent.[13] There are probably many reasons for this change: the extension of education; the poor job prospects for young adults; the entrance of women into the labor force in greater numbers; the acceptability of cohabitation and nonmarital sex; and, perhaps, the declining social value placed on marriage.[14] In the 1950s, most teenagers were able to delay having intercourse until they were of marriageable age, even if they often did not wait until they were actually married. Today, if they employed a similar strategy, they would need to wait until they were in the early or middle twenties. Thus, the once-secure connection between the onset of sexual activity and marriage has been severed, providing no anchor point for sexual initiation.

ANTECEDENTS OF ADOLESCENT PREGNANCY AND PARENTHOOD

Transition to Sexual Behavior

All studies on the antecedents of sexual activity in adolescents show that the major contributing factors to the sexual transition may differ for blacks and whites and for males and females.[15] Existing research indicates that most teens do not consciously plan to become sexually active, and they often do not foresee their first sexual experience. As such, it frequently is not experienced as a decision but rather as something that "happened."[16]

A relatively larger proportion of younger than older teens are initiated into sexual activity by friends or acquaintances than by steady dating partners.[17] Younger females are often pressured or coerced into having sex by males, who are often ill-prepared to assume responsibility should a pregnancy occur. The timing of sexual activity also is affected by the social world of the teenager.[18] Part of that world, of course, is conveyed symbolically through the mass media. The lyrics of popular music, films, MTV and television, and magazines all portray sexual experience as attractive and cost-free. The sexual standards of popular culture inevitably are channeled through the media to the social world of adolescents, affecting their attitudes and actions.

Adolescents' sexual behavior resembles the behavior of their peers and, even more, perceptions of their peers' sexual experience. In the National Survey of Children, a nationwide study of youth carried out in 1981, 47 percent of the 15- and 16-year-olds who said that they had many friends who were sexually experienced were nonvirgins as compared to 10 percent who said that few or none of their friends were sexually experienced.[19] Teenagers project their own experiences to their friends and may be more likely to select friends who have similar experiences to their own, but their actions are regulated to a great extent by the behavior of their close friends.[20] The adolescent's desire to be accepted by peers may encourage some to engage in early intercourse.

Peer influence can be controlled in part by parents.[21] Families may be able to choose to live in certain neighborhoods or send their children to schools where early intercourse is not the norm. Families with more economic resources can exercise much greater control over their teens' behavior while poorer parents, especially poor blacks, are at a great disadvantage in selecting living and school situations that may minimize the risk of early sexual activity. Parents who effectively supervise their children may be able to restrict the opportunity for early intercourse. Children are at greater risk of early sexual activity if they live in a single-parent family or if they are unsupervised in the afternoons and evenings.[22]

Parents also may restrict early coitus by explicit appeals to their children to delay intercourse. The evidence on the effect of parental communication about sexual matters is mixed, partly because most parents avoid extensive discussions about sexual matters.[23] Parents who have close relations with their children may be more effective in getting them to conform to their expectations, which typically discourage early sexual experience. Parents who communicate more easily and openly with their adolescents may also help them not be overly dependent on peers. And, there is a widespread belief supported only by inconsistent evidence that more open communication encourages sexually active teens to use contraception.[24] Newcomer and Udry have challenged the belief that parents exert much influence on their teenager's sexual behavior through social communication.[25] They contend that a generational link exists because of two inherited biological traits: the age of menarche affects the timing of intercourse and fecundity affects the probability of pregnancy. Thus, girls resemble their mothers' fertility pattern because they share biological characteristics that shape the probability of early intercourse and the risk of pregnancy. However, social influences have been shown to play a large role in onset of sexuality.[26]

Differences in sexual norms have been postulated to account for ethnic differences in sexual activity and pregnancy rates. For example, white teenagers are more likely to engage in a predictable series of precoital behaviors prior to first intercourse than black teenagers. Black girls, who are more likely to move from necking to intercourse without intermediate steps, may be less likely to be prepared for intercourse, in the sense that there is little time to think about and obtain contraceptives.[27]

Use of Contraception Among Sexually Active Adolescents

Rates of sexual activity among teens in the United States are not notably higher than rates in several countries in Western Europe. Yet, the incidence of pregnancy and childbearing in the United States, especially among younger teens, exceeds the level of most other industrialized nations.[28] This is partly due to poor contraceptive use among American youth. Case studies conducted by the Alan Guttmacher Institute (AGI) suggest that American youth are exposed to mixed messages about contraception and that birth control services are not effectively delivered to the teenage population.[29] Recent research by AGI reveals that U.S. youth are not distinctively different from adults, who also have lower patterns of contraceptive use than their European counterparts.[30]

Over half of all teenagers do not use contraception the first time they have sexual relations, and the majority do not practice birth control regularly thereafter.[31] Most teenagers who use clinic services have been sexually active for a year or more before their initial visit.[32] About a third of the teens who come to clinics do not return for the required follow-up visits.[33] One study that followed up clinic attenders found that only 40 percent used contraception every time they had intercourse over a fifteen-month period after they first received birth control.[34] Not surprisingly, teenagers who experience physical side effects from birth control are more likely to stop. Also, teenagers who have sex only occasionally and are not in steady dating relations are less likely to practice contraception faithfully. Several studies have shown that teenagers who come from better-educated families and who themselves have higher educational ambitions are better contraceptors.[35]

Some attempts have been made to develop a psychological profile of poor contraceptors.[36] In general, it is not easy to identify psychological characteristics associated with ineffective use of birth control. High-risk takers, as might be expected, are prone to discontinuation, but many other standard psychological attributes have low or no predictive ability to distinguish continuous users from dropouts.[37] Even reasonably well motivated and psychologically robust teenagers will be imperfect users given the problems we describe. Many adults face the same difficulties and react similarly. The most widely used method of contraception among adults in their thirties is sterilization.[38] Presumably mature adults resort to sterilization because they have many of the same apprehensions and problems with contraception that teenagers do. The difference is that teens do not have the option of sterilization. Still, most teens eventually practice contraception and the majority use it regularly if not absolutely consistently. Zelnik and Kantner estimate that without the practice of contraception, 680,000 additional pregnancies would occur each year.[39]

Contraceptive services for teens are relatively novel. It was not until 1970 and the passage of Title X, legislation providing subsidized family planning services for low-income women, that access to contraception for unmarried minors became widely available. But the provision of contraceptive services for the young has remained controversial. Funding cuts have forced cutbacks in the expansion of family planning programs designed to reach the young. Political, economic, and social influences have discouraged innovative and aggressive programs.

Compared to many European countries, the United States has adopted a timid and reactive approach to contraceptive services. Many critics of family planning programs believe that providing birth control to teens promotes sexual activity. While there is no evidence for this contention, and some evidence to the contrary, it is an assertion that is not easily dismissed by empirical data. Present policy seems to be a compromise course, permitting but not promoting contraception.

The Resolution of Pregnancy

Close to 1.1 million teenagers become pregnant each year, about two-fifths of them below the age of eighteen. The vast majority of teenage pregnancies are unintended. In the Zelnik and Kantner survey, less than a fourth of the teens indicated that their pregnancy was planned; most were initially upset when the pregnancy occurred. These expressions of sentiment are consistent with the figures on abortions. Among women under the age of eighteen, nearly one of every two pregnancies is voluntarily terminated.[40] If abortion services were easier to obtain, the proportion would, no doubt, be even higher. Nonetheless, many teenagers who did not want to become pregnant elect to have the child because they disapprove of abortion. A common response in one study which asked teenagers about their attitudes toward abortion was "It's not fair to make the baby pay for the mother's mistake."[41]

Only a small fraction of whites and an even smaller fraction of blacks use adoption as a way of avoiding early parenthood. By all accounts this proportion has been declining in recent decades, especially among whites. No doubt, the availability of abortion is a factor. Also, as adoptions have decreased, the practice may receive less peer group and family encouragement. Among blacks there was never a large "market" for formal adoptions though many teens, in fact, allow their child to be informally adopted by relatives or friends.[42] The small group of teenagers who keep their infants are probably quite different from those who do not. In a comparison study of single mothers who chose adoption and those who kept their infants, the former were younger, more likely to be white, Catholic, primiparous, economically independent, and to have not planned their pregnancy.[43]

With the rise of marriage age, the growing tolerance for out-of-wedlock childbearing, and changing economic opportunities for youth,[44] "shotgun" weddings have all but disappeared among black teenagers and diminished sharply among whites.[45] Interestingly, blacks may have been pacesetters for the population at large. As marriage rates for white teens have been declining rapidly and nonwanted births rising sharply, the proportion of first births occurring out of wedlock is over 50 percent. Less information is available for Hispanics. In a recent analysis of 1982 data from the National Longitudinal Study, young Hispanic women with Mexican and Puerto Rican origins had similar proportions of births as did young black women.[46] However, most Mexican and white first births occurred in the context of marriage, while most black and Puerto Rican births did not. Interestingly, later generations of Mexican-origin women had proportionally more premarital births than more recent immigrants, suggesting that as the traditional norms become more distant, marriage and childbearing are not as tightly linked.[47] Clearly, changes in norms within and across cultural subgroups have resulted in great increases in young unmarried mothers, and differences between ethnic subgroups can be expected to decline even further.

Some claim that the availability of welfare discourages marriage and may even encourage some adolescents to begin early childbearing. There is little evidence, however, that more generous welfare payments deter marriage or promote earlier parenthood.[48] Most empirical tests of this hypothesis find that the direct link between welfare and family formation among the very young is weak or nonexistent.[49] Few teenagers who have children believe that welfare will provide adequate support for their children. Most expect to work and probably overestimate their ability to find steady employment. The majority look to their immediate family for temporary relief. And most studies of the accommodation to early parenthood show that parents of teenage childbearers do, in fact, shoulder much of the economic burden. A major reason young black women are able to keep children is that their parents and siblings frequently share the child-rearing responsibilities. The availability of public assistance may contribute to the support furnished by the extended family, but parents seem to be willing to lend assistance whether or not they receive welfare supplements.[50]

THE CONSEQUENCES OF ADOLESCENT CHILDBEARING

The Adolescent Mother

Existing research has consistently shown that early childbearing reduces a woman's chances of achieving her educational goals. Teenage mothers are much more likely to drop out of high school, even when compared to peers of similar socioeconomic backgrounds and academic aptitude.[51] How much of the educational decrement is due to childbearing itself and how much can be explained by the fact that early childbearers are more prone to drop out because they are less academically committed and competent is still an open question.[52] It seems likely that if childbearing could be postponed, many young mothers would achieve more school than they otherwise do, although some would find other reasons to discontinue their education.

A generation ago, pregnancy was grounds for expulsion from school. As school systems have become more accommodating to young mothers, more have remained in school.[53] Still, a large proportion cannot handle the dual responsibilities of being a mother and a student. Some of these women eventually return to school or obtain a degree by passing a high school equivalency test (GED). A seventeen-year follow-up of a sample of young mothers in Baltimore revealed that about one woman in six completed high school in her twenties or early thirties. This result suggests that some of the shorter-term follow-ups may underreport the educational achievement of teenage mothers and therefore overstate the difference between early and later childbearers, but even so the disparity in schooling level is significant.[54]

Partly because of their educational deficit, teenage mothers are less likely to find stable and remunerative employment and more likely to rely on public assistance than women who begin childbearing later in life. Several studies have discovered a significant difference in job status and income, which seems to be attributable to the timing of parenthood.[55] Again, that difference can be only partially explained by differences in socioeconomic background and abilities.

Many teenage mothers who use public assistance in their late teens to cope with the economic strains of early parenthood eventually return to work when their youngest children reach school age. In the Baltimore study, the proportion on welfare dropped substantially between the three-year and seventeen-year follow-up. Thus, the gap between early and later childbearers may diminish over time, especially when later childbearers drop out of the labor force to have children in their late twenties and early thirties. Nonetheless, most studies indicate that early childbearers will not achieve complete economic parity with women who postpone parenthood until they are adults.

A major reason for the residual difference is that later childbearers are more likely to enter stable marriages than women who have children in their early teens. Women who marry early in life have a much higher risk of divorce, especially if they marry as a result of pregnancy.[56] And, many of those who delay marriage and elect to become single parents may never marry at all. Few married-couple households live in poverty while more than a third of single-parent households are poor.[57]

We suspect that the payoff in postponing childbearing is significantly lower for blacks than whites. The labor market is dismal for young blacks; so, too, the opportunities for marriage. In economic terms, marriageable age is very late for blacks. Accordingly, many are willing to reverse the sequence of marriage and parenthood, deciding to have children before they marry.[58] Because they can rely on family support, blacks often have children and remain in the parental household. If they are fortunate enough to have a mother, aunt, or older sister who will care for the child, they probably will return to school. Compared to whites, black women are much more likely to complete high school after becoming mothers and may, therefore, suffer relatively less disadvantage.[59] After all, their peers who postpone parenthood have only modest prospects of entering a stable marriage, given the poor economic chances of black males in their early twenties.[60] Still, evidence from the seventeen-year follow-up in Baltimore revealed that blacks who bear children in their teens are significantly less likely to be married and, therefore, economically secure in later life than black women who postponed parenthood.

Another condition diminishing the difference between early and later childbearers is the availability of contraception and abortion. A generation ago, family size varied greatly for women who began childbearing as teenagers and those who waited until their twenties. A difference still exists among recent cohorts but it is probably narrowing. Teenage parents generally do not want larger families than older childbearers, but they are at greater risk of having children in excess of their desires because of their early start. Increasingly, however, many are using contraception or abortion to limit their family size. In the Baltimore study, 20 percent of the sample with two or more children reported that they had aborted a pregnancy, and 64 percent were sterilized by the time of the seventeen-year follow-up. These young mothers may have been exceptionally well equipped to regulate their fertility because they all had access to family planning at the time of their initial pregnancy. Nonetheless, their receptivity to family planning services suggests that young mothers may recognize the necessity of limiting their family size to achieve some measure of economic well-being.

Managing the Transition to Motherhood: The Baltimore Study

An intriguing and important question receiving little empirical attention is why some young mothers manage the transition to parenthood while others do not. We addressed this issue in the Baltimore study, originally an evaluation of a comprehensive prenatal care program for pregnant, primarily black adolescents and ultimately a seventeen-year follow-up. The results of the five-year follow-up (1972) suggested that a certain amount of variation in the life courses of the women would be evident in the seventeen-year follow-up (1984). However, the extent of diversity and the degree of improvement seen between 1972 and 1984 was totally unexpected. Characteristics of both the teens' family of origin and of the teens themselves were significant predictors of economic success in later life. Teens whose parents had higher levels of education, smaller family sizes, and no welfare assistance were more likely to succeed as adults. In contrast, other familial factors such as teens' mothers' marital or employment status or age did not relate to the teens' long-term outcome.

Three characteristics of the teens themselves predicted economic success in later life: educational attainment and ambition, family size, and marital status. Whether or not the adolescent had repeated a grade by the time of the pregnancy was a powerful determinant of her future economic position. Her educational ambitions also were predictive of later economic outcome, independent of parental education and her own grade repetition. Limiting the number of additional births was strongly related to economic success. An important additional pathway away from economic dependency for the teen mothers was stable marriage. Those women who were married at the time of the five-year follow-up were much more likely to have succeeded economically, presumably because of their husbands' income, than those who had never married. However, this was a risky strategy because so many early marriages ended in divorce. At the same time, women who remained with their families of origin for at least five years after their first child was born were less likely to be economically secure and more likely to be on welfare in adulthood. Thus, while living with one's parents for the first year or two promoted school attendance and employment, such an arrangement over the long term posed obstacles to independence and self-sufficiency in adulthood.[61]

The Adolescent Father

Much less is known about teenage fatherhood, in part because of traditional beliefs about father involvement in child care more generally and negative social sanctions against paternal participation among unmarried young men more specifically.[62] The majority of the partners of adolescent mothers are probably older than the mothers. However, we have little information on this point. Paternal age is missing in one-third of the birth certificates of children born to teenage mothers, perhaps because of the high rates of out-of-wedlock births.[63] In one study of teenage births in 1981, 47 percent were to fathers over twenty, 19 percent to fathers under 20, and one-third to fathers of unspecified age.[64] Even if all of these unknown cases were males under age 20, one-half of the fathers would not be teenagers.

Young fathers seem to be less adversely affected by early parenthood than young mothers.[65] However, men's educational careers are influenced by the occurrence of an early birth, even if they do not marry their pregnant partner.[66] For example, high school drop-out rates are higher for teenage fathers than other youth and are not affected by marital status. The effects are more pronounced for whites and Hispanics than blacks.[67] It is unclear whether early fatherhood precedes or follows school drop-out. Early entry into the work force also is linked to teenage fatherhood.[68] Some teenage fathers never acknowledge parenthood. In the Baltimore study, a much lower proportion of adolescent males report that they have ever impregnated a woman than females report ever having been pregnant.[69] Part of this difference is no doubt due to the fact that at least one-half of all children born to teen-age women are fathered by men over age 20. However, a substantial minority of fathers do not admit their paternity, either because of ig-norance, disbelief, or refusal to accept the obligations fatherhood im-plies. Qualitative evidence collected from fathers in the Baltimore study indicates that many doubt their capacity to provide support and are ill-prepared to lend emotional support to the mother or parental nurtur-ance to the child. In a study of 272 adolescent mothers and their part-ners only about one-third of the men and women said that their part-ner was one of their two main sources of emotional support *even* when they were married. The percentage was even lower for unmarried cou-ples.[70]

The minority of fathers who become involved are generally in more committed relationships with the mother or in a better position to fur-nish economic aid to the child. Approximately a quarter of the Balti-more fathers living outside the home continued to see their child at least on a weekly basis five years after the delivery. A sixth of the biological fathers living outside the home were still as involved in rais-ing the child at the seventeen-year follow-up. Never-married fathers generally were no less active in child rearing than the previously mar-ried men. In either case, only a small minority of fathers played an important role in supporting or raising the children though they re-mained significant figures to the children so long as they retained at least occasional contact.[71] One clinical observation is that teenage fa-thers frequently are seen as competitors by the parents of the adoles-cent girl. Having to choose between an insecure relationship with a male and a secure one with the family, most teenage mothers opt to cut off ties with the father.[72]

The Adolescent Mother's Family

Teenage mothers typically elect to remain with their family during the transition to parenthood, but the limited data available suggest that co-residence is temporary for most young mothers. In the Baltimore study, the majority left the parental household when they were ready to marry, have a second child, or when they became self-supporting. By the seventeen-year follow-up, fewer than one in ten were residing with a parent, and many of these women had returned to the family of origin after a marital separation.

A great deal of variation exists in the styles of parental collaboration between the young mother and her immediate family regardless of whether the mother continues to reside with her parents. At one ex-treme, the grandmother assumes major responsibility for child rearing and the mother and child become quasi-siblings. At the other extreme, the grandmother and other relatives are supportive figures but the mother assumes the primary responsibility for child care. The weight of evidence suggests that collaborative child care in general works to the benefit of both the mother and child.[73] Children have more favorable developmental outcomes when the mother is not the sole parent figure. Presumably the skill and support of a more experienced figure, usually the grandmother, provides an on-site mentor for the young mother.

The Teenage Mother's Children

Only a handful of studies have been conducted on the relationship of early parenthood to child development, and most of these are confined to the period of infancy and early childhood.[74] However, the limited evidence, based largely on the Collaborative Perinatal Project, suggests that children in the preschool and early school years born to teenage mothers are at a developmental disadvantage compared to children born to older mothers. Small but consistent differences in cognitive functioning between offspring of early and later childbearers appear in preschool and continue into elementary school.[75] These decrements are observed in the sons but not the daughters of early childbearers. Larger effects are reported for psychosocial than cognitive development. For example, children of teenage mothers, as early as their infant years, are rated as being more active and as possessing less self-control. By preschool, they are rated as more aggressive as well. Again, these differences in children of early and late childbearers are characteristic of boys but not girls.[76] Such cognitive and psychosocial differences may set the stage for later school and social difficulties.

By adolescence, school achievement among the offspring of adolescent mothers is markedly lower. For example, in the Baltimore study and in the National Survey of Children, about half of the adolescents born to teenage mothers had repeated a grade. In comparison, in the National Survey of Children, only 20 percent of those adolescents born to later childbearers had repeated a grade. School misbehavior, an indication of lack of interest and learning problems, is also twice as high in the adolescents whose mothers were teenagers at their birth than in those whose mothers were older.[77]

The question still remains as to what factors account for these differences. The strongest empirical evidence involves the adverse social and economic effects of early parenthood on children. Teenage mothers are generally more likely to be poor and less educated, and their children are likely to grow up in disadvantaged neighborhoods, attend low-quality schools, and experience high rates of family instability. To the extent that teenage parenthood elevates the risks of these events occurring, it definitely contributes to the likelihood of unfavorable outcomes. However, child differences do not entirely disappear when family background is held constant.[78] One reason may involve the higher likelihood of residing in a single-parent household, if one has a teenage parent. Both the economic and psychological benefits of living in a two-parent household may be especially important to teenage children. An ongoing extension of the Baltimore study is testing this proposition.

Over and above the residential and economic instability associated with early childbearing, teenage parents may be less experienced and/or less adequate in their parenting. However, we have little information on teenagers' parental practices with the exception of their treatment of infants. While few differences between teenage and older mothers have been found, the one that has, vocalization, may be directly linked to depressed cognitive scores in preschool and childhood.[79] Practitioners expect a higher incidence of child abuse, learning disabilities, delinquency, and sexual promiscuity among children of teenage parents, but the empirical record is very unclear. It remains for researchers to establish whether, how much, and why early childbearing complicates the development of children. Equally important is learning how some children manage to escape these risks. We have begun to address these issues in the Baltimore study by examining whether variability in the children's outcomes could be understood in terms of the timing and sequencing of maternal life events. As in other studies, continuity in academic and behavior problems was found across the years.[80] Once a trajectory was begun, it was likely to continue. The seventeen-year follow-up results also demonstrated that children's performance at ages 5 and 17 was related to concurrent maternal characteristics, specifically, educational attainment, marital status, welfare status, and family size. Such an examination of the association between maternal and child characteristics is similar to approaches in other cross-sectional and longitudinal designs.[81]

The Baltimore study is unique in its attempt to link changes in the mothers' life courses with changes in the children's development. What types of changes at what points in time affected child outcome? Effects of changes depended upon specific maternal characteristics, for specific child outcomes, at specific ages. For academic performance as an outcome, mother's change in welfare status (i.e., moving off welfare after the child's preschool years) significantly reduced the likelihood of the child's subsequent grade failure. Similarly, mothers who entered a stable marriage and advanced their educational standing by the time of their children's adolescence had teens with school performance superior to that of teens whose mothers had not brought about these improvements. In contrast, mothers' early fertility behavior negatively affected preschoolers' performance, but later fertility did not affect adolescents' school achievement. Rapidly increasing family size during the child's early years may have had negative effects because of the intensity of child-rearing demands in the first years of life. Births occurring later seem not to affect adolescent performance, perhaps because the child-rearing demands are spaced out over time.

PREVENTION AND INTERVENTION STRATEGIES

Many strategies for preventing teenage pregnancy and for ameliorating the negative consequences of early childbearing for teenage mothers and their children have been proposed. Some see the problem as moral breakdown in the family and the solution as restitution of the social order, and others accept family changes and want to institutionalize them by building new supports for the contemporary family. Somewhere in the middle are those who are less certain about the desirability or inevitability of change but who are prepared to accommodate to the current reality. We shall consider several major intervention strategies, keeping in mind that different constituencies favor different solutions.[82]

Prevention

Postponing Sexual Activity. Some have long argued that the most effective strategy for preventing early childbearing is to encourage delay of sexual activity until adulthood, preferably until marriage. Strong advocates of family planning have countered that such a strategy is ineffective and potentially counterproductive. They contend that teenagers will continue to have sex but will be unprepared to use contraception because of a greater reluctance to acknowledge their sexual activity.[83]

Sex education programs do seem to increase short-term knowledge and, in some instances, affect attitudes about sexuality and heterosexual relations. However, programs do not seem to raise or lower the level of sexual activity, to promote more effective contraceptive use, nor to decrease the incidence of pregnancy.[84] However, many of these interventions did not focus on behavior change and were limited in scope.[85] But if these model programs do not affect behavior, then sex education, by itself, is not likely to be a powerful instrument in prevention of sexual initiation. While program evaluations have not produced much evidence for a strong impact on behavior, two separate surveys which asked adolescents if they had received sex education did find more encouraging results. In one survey, younger teens who reported classroom instruction were less likely to have had intercourse.[86] In the other survey, they were as sexually active as students who had not received sex education but more likely to practice contraception.[87] Neither of these studies confirms the impression of critics of sex education that school-based programs promote sexual activity among the young. A more recent study, based on the data collected in the National Longitudinal Survey, provides a less reassuring picture of the effects of sex education programs.[88] Youth who reported receiving sex education were likely to have had intercourse at earlier ages though no more likely to have become pregnant. Further research is clearly indicated to establish what effects, if any, result from exposure to sex education.

Contraceptive Programs. Advocates of family planning programs contended for many years that greater access to family planning by teens would have a marked impact on the rate of pregnancy and childbearing among adolescents. In the 1970s, declines in the birth rates were due in a large part to increases in abortions. However, recent evidence is more encouraging. From 1980 to 1983, the declines in birth rates were not mirrored by an increase in the abortion rate. This suggests that contraceptive use may be increasing.[89] However, too many sexually active teenagers still find their way to services too late, use contraception ineffectively, or shy away from the most reliable methods.

It is believed by some that the greater availability of contraception may reinforce a more tolerant climate toward nonmarital sexual behavior. However, in the last fifteen years, the growth of contraceptive programs was a response to, rather than a precipitant of, changing patterns of behavior among the young. Rates of pregnancy and childbearing began to rise in the early 1970s, before contraception was widely available to teens. In any case, it seems unlikely that many teenagers decide to become sexually active because of contraception as few avail themselves of contraception before beginning to have sex. Additionally, the percentage of sexually experienced teenage never-married women has not risen dramatically in the 1980s; indeed, for black women, the percentage of those who have ever had intercourse actually declined from 1980 to 1983 (59.3 percent to 57.8 percent).[90]

Despite a decade of experience with contraceptive programs for adolescents, we are still learning how to make them more effective. In the past, family planning programs tried to tailor clinics to suit youthful tastes by providing rock music in the waiting room, offering rap sessions, or employing peer counselors. None of these measures had much effect on clinic continuation or contraceptive compliance. Teenagers are probably attracted to the same standards that appeal to adults seeking contraception: convenience, confidentiality, competence, and humane treatment. Community outreach programs also may be an important determinant.[91] Whether teenagers need more is not firmly established although one study has shown that young women attending family planning clinics respond well to authoritative advice.[92] Teenagers require more aggressive outreach to get them into programs and more support to continue than older women.

Several school-based contraceptive programs have been developed in the past few years. This seems like a promising approach for providing easy access, reasonable confidentiality (when the programs offer general health services as well), and an efficient means of follow-up. Whether these programs work better than clinics situated in Planned Parenthood affiliates, hospitals, health centers, or through services provided by private physicians is being studied.[93] A recent evaluation of a school-based health clinic in Baltimore is very encouraging.[94] Cross-national studies suggest that there are many different approaches to delivering contraception to young people.[95] The lesson to be learned from these international comparisons is that given a reasonable amount of societal commitment, young people can and will use contraception. The United States seems to be something of an anomaly in the Western world, perhaps because the reality of premarital sex among young people has not been accepted.

Abortion Services. So long as adolescents are sexually active and use contraception with difficulty or not at all, pregnancy rates will remain high. In 1981, 1.3 million teenagers between the ages of 15 and 19 became pregnant. Almost four in ten of these pregnancies were ended by an abortion. After *Roe v. Wade*, the Supreme Court decision that eliminated most barriers to legalized abortion, the incidence of abortion among teens, as well as older women, rose sharply. In the past few years, however, rates have leveled off and may even be declining as pregnancy rates drop.

Of all age groups, except for women over 40, teens have the highest ratio of abortions to pregnancies. In 1981, teens obtained 28 percent of all abortions.[96] Despite their frequent use of abortion, teens, especially those under 18, face special problems in obtaining abortions. Younger teens may deny the symptoms of pregnancy or even fail to recognize them and, consequently, delay action until it is too late to obtain a first-trimester abortion. Lack of resources also may restrict access; many teenagers cannot or will not ask their family for help and are reluctant to approach the father of the child who may not support their decision. Desire to keep the pregnancy confidential hampers their ability to get economic assistance and social support for terminating the pregnancy. Finally, teenagers not living near an abortion facility may find it difficult to locate and travel to a service outside of their immediate community. Most counties in the United States, especially nonmetropolitan areas in the middle of the country, do not offer local services. Abortion rates for teenagers in New York, Massachusetts, and the District of Columbia are about three times the rate for teenagers living in Utah, Mississippi, and West Virginia.

Adoption Services. Only a small percentage of teens who decide to bear children place them for adoption. Most estimates suggest that it is fewer than one out of ten. Adoption has become less popular as adolescents have either elected abortion or single parenthood. Under the current administration, the Office of Adolescent Pregnancy has vigorously promoted adoption as an alternative to abortion or single parenthood for teenagers. Efforts have been made to provide more information to pregnant teens about this alternative and to make it financially easier for teens to bear children for subsequent adoption, although it is too soon to evaluate the success of these efforts.

Services for Teenage Parents. Beginning in the late 1960s, a wide variety of health and welfare services were developed for teenage parents and their children such as prenatal and postnatal medical care, educational and vocational counseling, and programs aimed at preventing school dropout and increasing job experiences, family planning services, day care, and parent education. These services now are often packaged together in comprehensive programs. It is assumed that programs that address a range of needs will be more efficient and effective in attracting teens and sustaining their involvement.[97]

Regrettably, many of these comprehensive service programs have not been carefully evaluated.[98] Klerman and Jekel, in an early assessment of one of the first such programs, concluded that the impact of the intervention did not seem to last any longer than the program.[99] So long as teenagers received services, they seemed to benefit from the assistance provided, but the effects did not last after the programs were terminated. The Baltimore study had more encouraging findings. A hospital-based family planning and medical care program had modest effects in postponing second pregnancies. Postponing the next pregnancy increased the probability of not being on welfare seventeen years later.[100] In a recent review of programs offering services targeted toward parenting skills and child care, as well as maternal education, fertility limitation, and job skills, the results suggest that more integrated services may be most effective.[101] This finding is also reinforced by the results of a five-year follow-up of a carefully designed experiment to provide comprehensive services to teen parents. The evaluation of Project Redirection, a multi-site service program, revealed lasting economic benefits for teens who participated in an educational training program.[102]

In general, insights from program evaluations include the following. First, serving adolescent parents is a formidable challenge to providers. Teenage mothers, not to mention teenage fathers, generally have a large number of educational and economic deficits. The most competent and highly motivated can make use of regular programs, but the majority require intensive interventions with varied remedial services. Even well-delivered comprehensive programs will not appeal to many adolescent parents. A large number of teen parents will not have the commitment, the ability, or the necessary support to remain in school and care for their young children at the same time. On-site day care has helped many mothers.[103]

No single program will appeal to all teen mothers. Most teen parents are prepared to continue in school but many are not. The school-resistant may accept vocational training or classes to prepare for a GED, though some young mothers are not eligible for special educational programs until they are older. One of the greatest difficulties of providing occupational training to adolescent parents is that so few teens can expect to find remunerative employment. Data from the seventeen-year follow-up in Baltimore showed that many teen mothers did not begin to work at a regular job until they were in their early or late twenties. At this point, many mothers were able to find employment and leave welfare. Significantly, educational and family planning services which the Baltimore teens received during pregnancy and just after delivery did have a noticeable impact on reducing their chances of being on welfare and having three or more children later in life.

In sum, our reading of the data is that for teenage parents, programs are probably worthwhile, but they are likely to have only a modest impact in ameliorating the consequences of early parenthood. But this is truly an area where an ounce of prevention is worth a pound of cure.

Implications for Programs

Primary prevention programs aimed at delaying sexual activity or promoting more effective contraceptive use are relatively new. Existing programs of sexual education have not as yet demonstrated their capacity to change the sexual practices of adolescent youth. They may be too little and may occur too late, but it is equally plausible that they, like many other preventive programs directed at adolescent populations, are not forceful enough to alter peer-supported behavior. To do so requires sharper age boundaries to discourage young adolescents from engaging in intercourse much as we now attempt to discourage younger teens from using alcohol or drugs.

Family planning programs have had only modest success in preventing unwanted pregnancies. They could be more effective if they were openly supported by the larger society. At present they still have a secretive and, sometimes, intimidating image which deters adolescents from using them. In countries where premarital sexual activity is widely accepted, youth seem to be willing to use contraception more responsibly. American society will have to abandon the goal of premarital chastity, at least among older adolescents, to increase contraceptive compliance. To do so requires the adoption of a more open policy toward family planning: promoting contraceptive advertisements in the mass media, working with family physicians to encourage contraceptive practice among the sexually active, building a more extensive network of easily accessible contraceptive services, and other like measures.

Contraception will remain difficult to use for young people. No method other than the pill or condom is well suited to the irregular and unpredictable sexual patterns typical in the adolescent population. The pill and IUD may have undermined the use of the condom and discouraged males from assuming contraceptive responsibility. It is not obvious what concrete measures might be taken to promote greater responsibility on the part of males. Programs that have attempted to involve males have encountered resistance.[104] But the risk of AIDS in the teenage heterosexual population may dramatically erode the resistance to use of condoms.[105] As public attention focuses on the health benefits of condom use, contraceptive practice among teenagers (and adults as well) may shift from pill use to prophylactic. If this were to happen, it could have important effects on pregnancy and childbearing rates. Abortion is likely to remain a measure of last resort for many teenagers. It is increasingly less accessible for the very young and the very poor. If present restrictive policies toward abortion continue, we can expect to see a modest decline in the rate of abortions and perhaps a rise in the rate of unintended births among adolescents.

We briefly reviewed programs designed to ameliorate the impact of early childbearing. While it is too soon to give a definitive assessment of these services, the preliminary evidence suggests that they have only a modest impact on the lives of participants. Some teens will benefit from the assistance provided, but these programs are too limited in scope and duration to offset the disadvantages associated with premature parenthood for both young mothers and their offspring.

Given this bleak prognosis, we return to an earlier point. Preventive strategies are undoubtedly cheaper and probably more effective, but they are also imperfect. But even if we make small inroads in the incidence of early childbearing, the benefits can be considerable. If early childbearing begins to decline, social sanctions against adolescent parenthood may rise; this could have an additional dampening effect on the rate. In order for this "snowball effect" in public opinion to occur, local communities that currently regard early childbearing as inevitable, if undesirable, will have to assume greater responsibility for changing the social definition of adolescent childbearing. Recently, the Urban League and the Children's Defense Fund have undertaken programs of community education about the adverse effects of teenage parenthood. And the Girls Clubs have launched a campaign to prevent premature parenthood. These actions may signal a willingness of community-based organizations to participate in primary prevention efforts. Like early marriage, teenage parenthood may, in communities where it is presently tolerated, be treated with greater public opprobrium. The challenge is to alter opinion without eliminating services to those who do become pregnant. This strategy is consistent with the recommendations of the recent report of the National Academy of Sciences Panel on Pregnancy and Childbearing. Their goals include reducing the rate of unintended pregnancy, while offering alternatives to adolescent childbearing and pregnancy and services to those teens who become parents.[106]

Our survey of existing strategies for reducing the rate of early childbearing or ameliorating its negative consequences offers little comfort to policymakers who are searching for a quick fix. We believe that many of the existing programs are constructive, but they must be strengthened or extended in order to make more of a difference. The lack of systematic evaluation of existing services is a serious deterrent to making wise decisions about which programs should be retained and expanded and which should be dropped or radically altered.

In the 1970s, there was a good deal of experimentation but rather few of the innovative efforts survived, in part because it was difficult to distinguish the successes from the failures. There is a clear lesson to be drawn from this experience for practitioners who want to address the problems associated with adolescent fertility in the 1980s. Social scientific theory and methods must be used more effectively to assess the value and the viability of both preventive and ameliorative services. If we are correct that different teens will benefit from different types of interventions at different points in the life course, the need for careful evaluation becomes all the more evident. The spirit of fiscal caution in the 1980s may stifle promising and potentially productive programs. But it could have one salutary feature if it resulted in a more deliberate attempt to increase the payoff of existing programs and lay the groundwork for a strategy of intervention in the 1990s.

POLICY PRIORITIES

The results of the Baltimore study, as well as our review of research and programs directed toward teenage pregnancy and childbearing, are consistent with the National Academy of Sciences Panel's recent summary on Early Childbearing.[107] We would like to paraphrase their recommendations here.[108] The Academy Panel was convened as a response to the personal and societal costs of early childbearing and the fragmented nature of existing services for sexually active and pregnant teens, both of which we have highlighted in this chapter. Three overarching policy goals were spelled out by the Panel. They are as follows (in order of priority):

1. Reduce the rate and incidence of unintended pregnancy among adolescents, especially among school-age teenagers.
2. Provide alternatives to adolescent childbearing and parenting.
3. Promote positive social, economic, health, and developmental outcomes for adolescent parents and their children.

We concur that the delay of parenthood facilitates the chances of an individual receiving additional education and entering the labor force. In cases where parenthood does occur, support is necessary to overcome barriers to such attainment as well as to ameliorate the developmental delays often seen in the children of teenagers.

To reduce the rate of unwanted early pregnancies, the Panel recommends programs to enhance life options (school performance, role models, employment opportunities); delay sexual initiative; and encourage contraception after the sexual debut. The Panel urges that sex education include sections on contraceptive use, decision making, and assertiveness training; that medical and community services work together to provide integrated, continuous services to youth; that the media be discouraged from glorifying sex, aggression, and violence and encouraged to promote contraceptive advertising; and that more school-based clinics be developed and evaluated. The provision of alternatives to adolescent childbearing and parenting (Goal 2) may be implemented by making abortion available to all teenagers, encouraging early pregnancy testing and counseling, and strengthening adoption services. The last goal, that of promoting healthy outcomes for those who become teenage parents, includes program initiatives for adequate antenatal care, postpartum services for additional family planning, nutrition, pediatric care, and obstetric care. Programs to enhance parenting skills, to provide day care services, and to provide educational and employment opportunities are crucial, as is enforcing child support.

As we have shown in this chapter, and as the Academy Panel's report underscores, no easy answers exist. Additionally, the proposed strategies are not new. They do make clear that more integration among services must be achieved and these services must be made available to those in need.

NOTES

1. A. C. Kinsey, W. B. Pomeroy, C. E. Martin, and P. H. Gebhard, *Sexual Behavior in the Human Female* (Philadelphia: W. B. Saunders, 1953); C. N.

Degler, *At Odds: Women and the Family in America from the Revolution to the Present* (New York: Oxford University Press, 1980).

2. M. A. Vinovskis, *An "Epidemic" of Adolescent Pregnancy? Some Historical and Policy Considerations,* (New York: Oxford University Press, 1988).

3. A. Guttmacher, *Teenage Pregnancy: The Problem That Hasn't Gone Away* (New York: Alan Guttmacher Institute, 1981); J. Brooks-Gunn and F. F. Furstenberg, Jr., "Adolescent Sexuality," *American Psychologist* (in press); C. S. Chilman, *Adolescent Sexuality in a Changing American Society: Social and Psychological Perspectives for the Human Services Professions,* 2d ed. (New York: John Wiley and Sons, 1983); F. F. Furstenberg, Jr., J. Brooks-Gunn, and L. Chase-Lansdale, "Teenaged Pregnancy and Childbearing," *American Psychologist* (in press); F. F. Furstenberg, Jr., J. Brooks-Gunn, and S. P. Morgan, *Adolescent Mothers in Later Life* (New York: Cambridge University Press, 1987); F. F. Furstenberg, Jr., R. Lincoln, and J. Menken, eds., *Teenage Sexuality, Pregnancy and Childbearing* (Philadelphia: University of Pennsylvania Press, 1981); C. D. Hayes, ed., *Risking the Future: Adolescent Sexuality, Pregnancy, and Childbearing,* Vol. I (Washington, D.C.: National Academy Press, 1987); S. L. Hofferth and C. D. Hayes, eds., *Risking the Future: Adolescent Sexuality, Pregnancy, and Childbearing,* Vol. II (Washington, D.C.: National Academy Press, 1987); E. R. McAnarney and C. Schreider, *Identifying Social and Psychological Antecedents of Adolescent Pregnancy: The Contribution of Research to Concepts of Prevention* (New York: William T. Grant Foundation, 1984); K. A. Moore and M. R. Burt, *Private Crisis, Public Cost: Policy Perspectives on Teenage Childbearing* (Washington, D.C.: The Urban Institute Press, 1982).

4. M. J. Bane and P. A. Jargowsky, "The Links between Government Policy and Family Structure: What Matters and What Doesn't," in *The Changing American Family and Public Policy,* ed. A. J. Cherlin (Washington, D.C.: The Urban Institute Press, 1988), 219–61.

5. J. Dryfoos, "The Epidemiology of Adolescent Pregnancy: Incidence, Outcomes, and Interventions," in *Pregnancy in Adolescence: Needs, Problems, and Management,* ed. I. R. Stuart and C. F. Wells (New York: Van Nostrand Reinhold, 1982).

6. U.S. Bureau of the Census, Statistical Abstract of the United States, 108th ed. (Washington, D.C.: U.S. Government Printing Office, 1988).

7. R. P. Petchesky, *Abortion and Woman's Choice: The State, Sexuality, and the Conditions of Reproductive Freedom* (New York: Longman, 1982).

8. Brooks-Gunn and Furstenberg, "Adolescent Sexuality," *American Psychologist* (in press).

9. M. Zelnik and J. F. Kantner, "Sexual Activity, Contraceptive Use and Pregnancy among Metropolitan Area Teenagers: 1971–1979," *Family Planning Perspectives* 12, 5 (1980): 230–37.

10. Hofferth and Hayes, *Risking the Future;* S. L. Hofferth, J. R. Kahn, and W. Baldwin, "Premarital Sexual Activity among U.S. Teenage Women over the Past Three Decades," *Family Planning Perspectives* 19, 2 (1987): 46–53.

11. F. F. Furstenberg, Jr., and G. Condran, "Family Change and Adolescent Well-Being: A Reexamination of U.S. Trends," in *The Changing American Family and Public Policy,* ed. A. J. Cherlin (Washington, D.C.: Urban Institute Press, 1988), 117–33.

12. Hayes, *Risking the Future*.

13. U.S. Bureau of the Census, "Marital Status and Living Arrangements: March 1986," *Current Population Reports*, Series P-20, No. 418 (Washington, D.C.: U.S. Government Printing Office, 1987).

14. A. Thornton and D. Freedman, "The Changing American Family," *Population Bulletin* 38, 4 (1983): 3–43.

15. McAnarney and Schreider, *Identifying Social and Psychological Antecedents*; M. Zelnik, J. F. Kantner, and K. Ford, *Sex and Pregnancy in Adolescence* (Beverly Hills: Sage, 1981).

16. D. B. Frank, *Deep Blue Funk and Other Stories: Portraits of Teenage Parents* (Chicago: The Ounce of Prevention Fund, 1983); P. M. Rains, *Becoming an Unwed Mother: A Sociological Account* (Chicago: Aldine/Atherton, 1971); Chilman, *Adolescent Sexuality*.

17. Zelnik, Kantner, and Ford, *Sex and Pregnancy in Adolescence*; M. Zelnik and F. K. Shah, "First Intercourse among Young Americans," *Family Planning Perspectives* 15, 2 (1983): 64–70.

18. Hayes, *Risking the Future*.

19. F. F. Furstenberg, Jr., K. A. Moore, and J. L. Peterson, "Sex Education and Sexual Experience among Adolescents," *American Journal of Public Health* 75, 11 (1985): 1331–32.

20. J. O. Billy, J. L. Rodgers, and J. R. Udry, "Adolescent Sexual Behavior and Friendship Choice" (Carolina Population Center, University of North Carolina, Chapel Hill, 1981).

21. G. L. Fox, "The Family's Role in Adolescent Sexual Behavior," in *Teenage Pregnancy in a Family Context: Implications for Policy*, ed. T. Ooms (Philadelphia: Temple University Press, 1981), 73–130.

22. Zelnik, Kantner, and Ford, *Sex and Pregnancy in Adolescence*.

23. A. Gaddis and J. Brooks-Gunn, "The Male Experience of Pubertal Change," *Journal of Youth and Adolescence* 14 (1985): 61–69; H. D. Thornburg, "Adolescent Sources of Initial Sex Information," in *Studies in Adolescence: A Book of Readings in Adolescent Development*, ed. R. E. Grinder (New York: Macmillan, 1975), 334–40.

24. G. L. Fox, B. Fox, and K. Frohardt-Lane, "Fertility Socialization," in *The Childbearing Decision*, ed. G. L. Fox (Beverly Hills: Sage Publications, 1982) 19–49; F. F. Furstenberg, Jr., J. Shea, P. Allison, R. Herceg-Baron, and D. Webb, "Contraceptive Continuation among Adolescents Attending Family Planning Clinics," *Family Planning Perspectives* 15, 5 (1983): 211–17.

25. S. F. Newcomer and R. J. Udry, "Mothers' Influence on the Sexual Behavior of Their Teenage Children," *Journal of Marriage and the Family* 46, 2 (1984): 477–85.

26. Brooks-Gunn and Furstenberg, "Adolescent Sexuality," *American Psychologist* (in press).

27. E. A. Smith and R. J. Udry, "Coital and Non-Coital Sexual Behaviors of White and Black Adolescents," *American Journal of Public Health* 75 (1985): 1200–1203.

28. E. F. Jones, J. D. Forrest, N. Goldman, S. K. Henshaw, R. Lincoln, J. I. Rosoff, C. F. Westoff, and D. Wulf, "Teenage Pregnancy in Developed Countries: Determinants and Policy Implications," *Family Planning Perspectives* 17:2

(1985): 53–63; C. F. Westoff, G. Calot, and A. D. Foster, "Teenage Fertility in Developed Nations: 1971–1980," *Family Planning Perspectives* 153, (1983): 105–10.

29. Jones et al., "Teenage Pregnancy," 53–63.

30. E. F. Jones, J. D. Forrest, S. K. Henshaw, J. Silverman, and A. Torres, "Unintended Pregnancy, Contraceptive Practice, and Family Planning Services in Developed Countries," *Family Planning Perspectives* 20, 2 (1988): 53–67.

31. Zelnik and Shah, "First Intercourse," 64–70.

32. L. S. Zabin, J. F. Kantner, and M. Zelnik, "The Risk of Adolescent Pregnancy in the First Months of Intercourse," *Family Planning Perspectives* 11, 4 (1979): 215–22.

33. J. A. Shea, R. Herceg-Baron, and F. F. Furstenberg, Jr., "Factors Associated with Adolescent Use of Family Planning Clinics," *American Journal of Public Health* 74, 11 (1984): 1227–30.

34. Furstenberg et al., "Contraceptive Continuation among Adolescents," 211–17.

35. K. A. Moore, M. C. Simms, and C. L. Betsey, *Choice and Circumstance* (New Brunswick, N.J.: Transaction Books, 1986).

36. C. S. Chilman, "Some Psychosocial Aspects of Adolescent Sexual and Contraceptive Behaviors in a Changing American Society," in *School-Age Pregnancy and Parenthood: Biosocial Dimensions*, ed. J. B. Lancaster and B. A. Hamburg (New York: Aldine De Gruyter, 1986); B. A. Hamburg, "Subsets of Adolescent Mothers: Developmental, Biomedical, and Psychosocial Issues," in *School-Age Pregnancy and Parenthood: Biosocial Dimensions*, ed. J. B. Lancaster and B. A. Hamburg (New York: Aldine De Gruyter, 1986); D. M. Morrison, "Adolescent Contraceptive Behavior: A Review,"*Psychological Bulletin* 98, 3 (1985): 538–68.

37. B. Mindick and S. Oskamp, "Individual Differences among Adolescent Contraceptors: Some Implications for Intervention," in *Pregnancy in Adolescence: Needs, Problems, and Management*, ed. I. R. Stuart and C. F. Wells (New York: Van Nostrand Reinhold, 1982).

38. C. A. Bachrach, "Contraceptive Practice among American Women, 1973–1982," *Family Planning Perspectives* 16, 6 (1984): 253–59.

39. M. Zelnik and J. Kantner, "Contraceptive Patterns and Premarital Pregnancy among Women Aged 15–19 in 1976," *Family Planning Perspectives* 10, 3 (1978): 135–42.

40. S. K. Henshaw, N. J. Binkin, E. Blaine, and J. C. Smith, "A Portrait of American Women Who Obtain Abortions," *Family Planning Perspectives* 17, 2 (1983): 90–96.

41. F. F. Furstenberg, Jr., *Unplanned Parenthood: The Social Consequences of Teenage Childbearing* (New York: The Free Press, 1976).

42. R. B. Hill, *Informal Adoption among Black Families* (Washington, D.C.: National Urban League, 1977); C. B. Stack, *All Our Kin: Strategies for Survival in a Black Community* (New York: Harper and Row, 1974).

43. M. W. Yogman, C. Herrera, and K. Bloom, "Perinatal Characteristics of Newborns Relinquished at Birth," *American Journal of Public Health* 73 (1983): 1194–96.

44. V. R. Fuchs, *How We Live: An Economic Perspective on Americans from Birth to Death* (Cambridge: Harvard University Press, 1983).

45. M. O'Connell and C. C. Rogers, "Out-of-Wedlock Births, Premarital Pregnancies and Their Effect on Family Formation and Dissolution," *Family Planning Perspectives* 16, 4 (1984): 157–62.

46. K. F. Darabi and V. Ortiz, "Childbearing among Young Latino Women in the United States," *American Journal of Public Health* 77 (1987): 25–28.

47. F. Bean, R. L. Curtis, and J. P. Marcum, "Familism and Marital Satisfaction among Mexican Americans," *Journal of Marriage and the Family* 39 (1977): 759–67.

48. W. J. Wilson, *The Truly Disadvantaged* (Chicago: University of Chicago Press, 1987).

49. Furstenberg, Brooks-Gunn, and Morgan, *Adolescent Mothers in Later Life*; Moore and Burt, *Private Crisis*; P. J. Placek and G. E. Hendershot, "Public Welfare and Family Planning: An Empirical Study of the 'Brood Sow' Myth," *Social Problems* 21, 5 (1974): 658–73; Bane and Jargowsky, "Links between Government Policy," 219–61.

50. F. F. Furstenberg, Jr. and A. G. Crawford, "Family Support: Helping Teenage Mothers to Cope," *Family Planning Perspectives* 10, 6 (1978): 322–33; S. G. Kellam, R. G. Adams, C. H. Brown, and M. E. Ensminger, "The Long-Term Evolution of the Family Structure of Teenage and Older Mothers," *Journal of Marriage and the Family* 44, 3 (1982): 539–54; H. B. Presser, "Sally's Corner: Coping with Unmarried Motherhood," *Journal of Social Issues* 36, 1 (1980): 107–29; Furstenberg, Brooks-Gunn, and Morgan, *Adolescent Mothers in Later Life*.

51. J. J. Card and L. L. Wise, "Teenage Mothers and Teenage Fathers: The Impact of Early Childbearing on the Parents' Personal and Professional Lives," in *Teenage Sexuality, Pregnancy, and Childbearing*, ed. F. F. Furstenberg, Jr., R. Lincoln, and J. Menken (Philadelphia: University of Pennsylvania Press, 1981), 211–22; Hofferth and Hayes, *Risking the Future*.

52. R. R. Rindfuss, C. St. John, and L. Bumpass, "Education and the Timing of Motherhood: Disentangling Causation," *Journal of Marriage and the Family* 46, 4 (1984): 981–84; S. L. Hofferth and K. A. Moore, "Early Childbearing and Later Economic Well-Being," *American Sociological Review* 44 (1979): 784–815.

53. F. L. Mott and N. L. Maxwell, "School-Age Mothers: 1968 and 1979," *Family Planning Perspectives* 13, 6 (1981): 287–92.

54. Furstenberg, Brooks-Gunn, and Morgan, *Adolescent Mothers in Later Life*.

55. Hofferth and Moore, "Early Childbearing," 784–815; Card and Wise, "Teenage Mothers," 211–22. J. Trussell, "Economic Consequences of Teenage Childbearing," in *Teenage Sexuality, Pregnancy, and Childbearing*, ed. F. F. Furstenberg, Jr., R. Lincoln, and J. Menken (Philadelphia: University of Pennsylvania Press, 1981), 251–64; G. J. Duncan, *Years of Poverty, Years of Plenty* (Ann Arbor: Institute for Social Research, University of Michigan, 1984).

56. Furstenberg, Brooks-Gunn, and Morgan, *Adolescent Mothers in Later Life*; J. McCarthy and J. Menken, "Marriage, Remarriage, Marital Disruption and Age at First Birth," *Family Planning Perspectives* 11, 1 (1979): 21–30; Hofferth and Hayes, *Risking the Future*.

57. U.S. Bureau of the Census, *Current Population Reports*, Series P-60, No. 145, "Money Income and Poverty Status of Families and Persons in the United States: 1983" (Washington, D.C.: U.S. Government Printing Office, 1984).

58. Moore, Simms, and Betsey, *Choice and Circumstance*.

59. Mott and Maxwell, "School-Age Mothers," 287–92.

60. Wilson, *The Truly Disadvantaged*.

61. J. Brooks-Gunn and F. F. Furstenberg, Jr., "The Children of Adolescent Mothers: Physical, Academic and Psychological Outcomes," *Developmental Review* 6 (1986): 224–51; Furstenberg, Brooks-Gunn, and Morgan, *Adolescent Mothers in Later Life*.

62. R. D. Parke and B. Neville, "Teenage Fatherhood," in *Risking the Future: Adolescent Sexuality, Pregnancy, and Childbearing*, ed. S. L. Hofferth and C. D. Hayes (Washington, D.C.: National Academy Press, 1987); R. D. Parke and B. R. Tinsley, "Fatherhood: Historical and Contemporary Perspectives," in *Life Span Developmental Psychology: Historical and Generational Effects*, ed. K. A. McCluskey and H. W. Reese (New York: Academic Press, 1984), 203–48.

63. F. L. Sonenstein, "Risking Paternity: Sex and Contraception among Adolescent Males," in *Adolescent Fatherhood*, ed. A. B. Elster and M. E. Lamb (Hillsdale, N.J.: Erlbaum, 1986), 31–54.

64. National Center for Health Statistics, "Advance Report of Final Natality Statistics, 1981," *Monthly Vital Statistics Report*, 32 (1983).

65. Card and Wise, "Teenage Mothers," 211–22.

66. R. I. Lerman, "Who Are the Young Absent Fathers?" unpublished paper; W. Marsiglio, "Teenaged Fatherhood: High School Completion and Educational Attainment," in *Adolescent Fatherhood*, ed. A. B. Elster and M. E. Lamb (Hillsdale, N.J.: Lawrence Erlbaum Associates, 1986).

67. Marsiglio, "Teenaged Fatherhood," 67–87.

68. Card and Wise, "Teenage Mothers," 211–22.

69. Furstenberg, Brooks-Gunn, and Morgan, *Adolescent Mothers in Later Life*.

70. M. E. Lamb, A. B. Elster, L. J. Peters, J. S. Kahn, and J. Tavare, "Characteristics of Married and Unmarried Adolescent Mothers and Their Partners," *Journal of Youth and Adolescence* 15 (1986): 487–96.

71. Furstenberg, Brooks-Gunn, and Morgan, *Adolescent Mothers in Later Life*.

72. Stack, *All Our Kin*.

73. W. Baldwin and V. S. Cain, "The Children of Teenage Parents," *Family Planning Perspectives* 12, 1 (1980): 34–43; S. G. Kellam, M. E. Ensminger, and R. J. Turner, "Family Structure and the Mental Health of Children: Concurrent and Longitudinal Community-Wide Studies," *Archives of General Psychiatry* 34 (1977): 1012–22.

74. Baldwin and Cain, "Children of Teenage Parents," 34–43; Brooks-Gunn and Furstenberg, "Children of Adolescent Mothers," 224–51; J. Brooks-Gunn and F. F. Furstenberg, Jr., "Continuity and Change in the Context of Poverty: Adolescent Mothers and Their Children," in *The Malleability of Children*, ed. J. J. Gallagher and C. T. Ramey (Baltimore: Brookes Publishing Company, 1987) 171–88; Hofferth and Hayes, *Risking the Future*.

75. S. H. Broman, "Longterm Development of Children Born to Teenagers," in *Teenage Parents and Their Offspring*, ed. K. Scott, T. Field, and E. Robertson (New York: Grune and Stratton, 1981); J. Maracek, "Economic, Social, and Psychological Consequences of Adolescent Childbearing: An Analysis of Data from the Philadelphia Collaborative Perinatal Project," Final Report to NICHD, 1979; J. Maracek, "The Effects of Adolescent Childbearing on Chil-

dren's Cognitive and Psychosocial Development" (Unpublished manuscript, 1985).

76. Broman, "Longterm Development of Children;" Maracek, "The Effects of Adolescent Childbearing."

77. Brooks-Gunn and Furstenberg, "Children of Adolescent Mothers."

78. Broman, "Longterm Development of Children."

79. T. Field, "Early Development of the Preterm Offspring of Teenage Mothers," in *Teenage Parents and Their Offspring*, ed. K. Scott, T. Field, and E. Robertson (New York: Grune and Stratton, 1981); H. Sandler, P. Vietze, and S. O'Connor, "Obstetrics and Neonatal Outcomes Following Intervention with Pregnant Teenagers," in *Teenage Parents and Their Offspring*, ed. K. Scott, T. Field, and E. Robertson (New York: Grune and Stratton, 1981); Brooks-Gunn and Furstenberg, "Children of Adolescent Mothers," 224–51.

80. Kellam, Ensminger, and Turner, "Family Structure and the Mental Health of Children," 1012–22.

81. N. Garmezy and M. Rutter, *Stress, Coping and Development in Children* (New York: McGraw–Hill, 1983); J. Kagan and H. A. Moss, *Birth to Maturity* (New York: John Wiley, 1962); Kellam, Ensminger, and Turner, "Long-Term Evaluation," 539–54; M. Rutter, "Maternal Deprivation, 1972–1978: New Finds, New Concepts, New Approaches," *Child Development* 50 (1979): 283–305.

82. Hayes, *Risking the Future*; Hofferth and Hayes, *Risking the Future*; Brooks-Gunn and Furstenberg, "Adolescent Sexuality"; Furstenberg, Brooks-Gunn, and Chase-Lansdale, "Teenaged Pregnancy and Childbearing," *American Psychologist* (in press).

83. A. M. Kenney, J. D. Forrest, and A. Torres, "Storm Over Washington: The Parental Notification Proposal," *Family Planning Perspectives* 14, 4 (1982): 185–97.

84. D. Kirby, *Sexuality Education: An Evaluation of Programs and Their Effects* (Santa Cruz, Calif.: Network Publications, 1984).

85. M. A. Vinovskis, *An "Epidemic" of Adolescent Pregnancy?*

86. Furstenberg, Moore, and Peterson, "Sex Education and Sexual Experience among Adolescents," 1331–32.

87. M. Zelnik and Y. J. Kim, "Sex Education and Its Association with Teenage Sexual Activity, Pregnancy and Contraceptive Use," *Family Planning Perspectives* 14, 3 (1982): 117–26.

88. W. Marsiglio and F. L. Mott, "The Impact of Sex Education on Sexual Activity, Contraceptive Use and Premarital Pregnancy among American Teenagers," *Family Planning Perspectives* 18, 4 (1986): 151–62.

89. B. J. Maciak, A. M. Spitz, L. T. Strauss, L. Morris, C. W. Warren, and J. S. Marks, "Pregnancy and Birth Rates among Sexually Experienced U.S. Teenagers—1974, 1980, and 1983," *Journal of American Medical Association* 285, 15 (1987):2069–71.

90. Ibid.

91. Hofferth and Hayes, *Risking the Future*.

92. C. A. Nathanson and M. H. Becker, "The Influence of Client-Provider Relationships on Teenage Women's Subsequent Use of Contraception," *American Journal of Public Health* 75, 1 (1985): 33–38.

93. J. Dryfoos, *Review of Programs to Foster Responsible Sexual Behavior on the*

Part of Adolescent Boys, Report to the Carnegie Corporation of New York, 1985; D. Kirby, *School-Based Health Clinics: An Emerging Approach to Improving Adolescent Health and Addressing Teenage Pregnancy* (Washington, D.C.: Center for Population Options, 1985).

94. L. S. Zabin, M. B. Hirsch, E. A. Smith, R. Street, and J. B. Hardy, "Evaluation of a Pregnancy Prevention Program for Urban Teenagers," *Family Planning Perspectives* 18 (1986): 119–26.

95. Jones et al., "Teenage Pregnancy in Developed Countries."

96. Henshaw et al., "A Portrait of American Women," 90–96.

97. B. C. Clewell, J. Brooks-Gunn, and A. A. Benasich, "Child-Focused Programs for Teenage Parents: Anticipated and Unanticipated Benefits," *Family Relations* (in press).

98. Vinovskis, *An "Epidemic" of Adolescent Pregnancy?*

99. L. V. Klerman and J. J. Jekel, *School-Age Mothers: Problems, Programs and Policy* (Hamden, Conn.: Linnet Books, 1973).

100. Furstenberg, Brooks-Gunn, and Morgan, *Adolescent Mothers in Later Life.*

101. Clewell, Brooks-Gunn, and Banasich, "Child-Focused Program," *Family Relations* (in press).

102. D. F. Polit, J. C. Quint, and J. A. Riccio, *The Challenge of Serving Teenage Mothers: Lessons from Project Redirection* (New York: Manpower Demonstration Research Corporation, 1988).

103. Clewell, Brooks-Gunn, and Benasich, "Child-Focused Program," *Family Relations* (in press).

104. S. D. Clark, Jr., L. S. Zabin, and J. B. Hardy, "Sex, Contraception and Parenthood: Experience and Attitudes among Urban Black Young Men," *Family Planning Perspectives* 16,2 (1984): 77–82.

105. J. Brooks-Gunn, C. B. Boyer, and K. Hein, "Preventing HIV Infection and AIDS in Children and Adolescents," *American Psychologist* 43, 11 (1988): 958–64.

106. Hayes, *Risking the Future.*

107. Ibid.

108. Ibid.

5 DIVORCE, FEMALE HEADSHIP, AND CHILD SUPPORT

Irwin Garfinkel, Sara McLanahan, and Dorothy Watson

This chapter discusses divorce and child support in the United States. By child support we mean the transfer of income to a custodial parent for care of a child with a living noncustodial parent. Transfers paid for by the noncustodial parent are referred to as private child support. Those financed by government are referred to as public child support. Although our specific focus is on divorced mothers with children, neither divorce nor child support can be understood well without reference to the broader context of conditions and policies affecting all single mothers.[1] Never-married and separated mothers are part of the recent growth in single parenthood and these mothers are also potentially eligible for child support. Consequently, this discussion of divorce will be placed in the broader context of the growth of mother-only families.

First we describe and explain the increase in divorced and mother-only families. Then we analyze the relationship between economic insecurity and divorce or single parenthood. Next, mothers' adaptations to divorce are discussed. We then describe the evolution and weaknesses of the private and public systems of child support, discuss the new child-support-assurance system being piloted in the state of Wisconsin, and summarize the major findings of the chapter.

THE GROWTH OF DIVORCED AND MOTHER-ONLY FAMILIES AND ITS CAUSES

In 1985, there were about 6 million families headed by single mothers in the United States, representing about 19 percent of all families with children.[2] Among whites, these families accounted for 15 percent of all families and among blacks they accounted for about 50 percent. These figures are based on cross-sectional data and understate the proportion of women and children who will ever live in a female-headed family. Demographers estimate that about 45 percent of the white children and about 84 percent of the black children born in the late 1970s will live for some time with a single mother before they reach the age of eighteen. The median duration in a female-headed family is six years for children of formerly married mothers and even longer for children born to never-married mothers.[3]

Of the 6 million mothers who headed families in 1985, 2.7 million, or 46 percent, were divorced. Families headed by divorced mothers represent 8.8 percent of all families with children—8.3 percent among whites and 12.5 percent among blacks.[4]

Trends in the proportion of families headed by both divorced and all single women are depicted in Figure 5.1 for the period 1940 to 1985. Trends for divorce and single motherhood and for blacks and whites are quite similar, although single motherhood has always been more common among blacks.

Historically, widowhood was the most common form of single parenthood. Since World War II, divorce and premarital birth have become increasingly important factors. The composition also varies considerably by race, with a much higher proportion of black single-mother households resulting from out-of-wedlock births than white. An analysis of the demographic components of the growth in single parenthood, however, indicates that in one critical respect the pattern for blacks and whites is similar: most of the growth in single parenthood is due to changes in marital behavior. The difference is that whites marry and increasingly divorce, whereas blacks are increasingly likely never to marry at all.

The distinction among the different types of single-parent families and the changing composition is important because these groups differ considerably with respect to access to economic and social resources. Widows have much higher incomes and experience less social disapproval than other groups, whereas never-married mothers have the fewest resources of all single mothers and are most likely to become dependent on government welfare assistance.

Numerous explanations have been put forward to account for the growth of female-headed families in the United States, and there is a vast literature of empirical studies that attempt to test many of these arguments. We examine the five explanations most frequently propounded. The first three are economic explanations in that they focus on the effects of welfare and employment opportunities of men and women on the relative economic gains from marriage for each of the partners. The last two explanations are more sociological and historical in nature in that the first traces the increase in divorce to changing values while the second accepts the argument that the increase in divorce is attributable to the increased employment opportunities of women and then seeks to explain the latter in terms of broader shifts in society arising from industrialization and urbanization.

Figure 5.1
The Proportion of Mother-Only and Divorced Mother-Only Families,
1940-1985

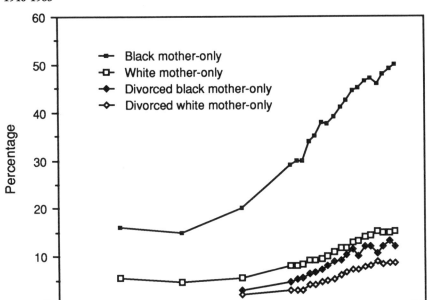

Sources of data for mother-only families: The 1940, 1950, and 1960 data are taken from the Public Use Sample of the U.S. Bureau of the Census. Data for 1968-1984 are from "Household and Family Characteristics," *Current Population Reports,* series P-20, Table 1 for each respective year. Rates are computed by dividing the number of families with a female head of household and children under age eighteen by the total number of families with children under age eighteen. The counts used to compute the 1980-1985 rates include unrelated subfamilies, since prior to 1980 unrelated subfamilies were counted as families.

Sources of data for divorced mother-only families: The 1960 data are from "Characteristics of the Population," *Census of the Population,* Volume 1, Part 1 (Washington, D.C.: GPO, 1961). Other data are from U.S. Bureau of the Census, "Household and Family Characteristics" for each respective year. Data were not available to add unrelated subfamilies to families for the years 1980-1985.

Increase in Welfare Benefits

A few analysts have argued that increases in welfare benefits are responsible for the growth in single parenthood. Higher benefits increase the ability of single mothers to afford to establish their own households and thereby to become household heads. They enable a single mother to choose to keep her baby rather than have an abortion or have the baby adopted. They also increase the ability of poor single mothers to refrain from marriage and the ability of poor married mothers to choose divorce rather than remaining in a bad relationship. In short, increases in benefits should increase single motherhood, all else being equal. The question is, How big will any of these effects be?

Numerous studies have examined the relationship between welfare and single motherhood. Some researchers have compared welfare benefits across states with the "stock" of mother-only families (the proportion of families headed by women).[5] Others have compared benefit levels with flows into and out of single motherhood, e.g., marital disruption and remarriage rates, illegitimacy rates, and the propensity to establish independent households.[6]

In general a correlation has been found between the level of benefits and the proportion of single mothers. This relationship has been attributed chiefly to the effects of benefits on living arrangements and remarriage rates.

Using what appear to be the most reliable studies, Garfinkel and McLanahan estimate that the increase in benefits led to a 9 to 14 percent increase in the prevalence of single motherhood between 1960 and 1975. In view of the fact that the prevalence increased approximately 100 percent during this period, increases in welfare benefits account for no more than one-seventh of the overall growth.[7] In short, although increased benefits may have led to a measurable increase in prevalence, they account for only a small portion of the total growth in mother-only families.

The effect of welfare on the growth of divorce in particular must be even smaller than its effect on the growth of single parenthood in general. For a large proportion of the divorcing population, welfare benefits are simply too low and/or too stigmatizing to have any possible influence on their decision making. Finally, the fact that divorce rates have increased as rapidly among women with high as compared to those with low educational backgrounds suggests that welfare cannot be the major explanation for increases in divorce.[8]

Increase in Women's Employment

Most analysts believe that the increase in single parenthood is at least intimately related if not due directly to the large increase in the labor force participation of married women with children that has occurred since World War II. Some believe that the increase in employment has created an "independence effect," which arises from increased opportunities for women.[9] Others, who focus on divorce alone, emphasize the "role conflict" that accompanies the renegotiation of traditional husband/wife roles when a wife becomes employed. Clearly financial security from employment competes with marriage and economic dependence on the husband. It also affects traditional ideas about husband/wife roles by reducing the amount of time available for women to spend on housework and child care.

The empirical research in this area is nearly as large as the literature on welfare. Sam Preston and Alan Richards, for example, examined the 100 largest metropolitan areas in the United States in 1960 and found that job opportunities, women's earnings, and unemployment rates for men were all good predictors of the marital status of women in the population.[10] Several studies have found that married women who work or who have higher earnings potential are more likely to divorce than more dependent women. Ross and Sawhill found that a $1,000 increase in wife's earnings was associated with a 7 percent increase in separation rates.[11] Similarly, Cherlin found that the ratio of wife's earnings capacity to husband's earnings was a strong predictor of marital disruption.[12] Taken together, these studies indicate that increased economic opportunities for women may account for a substantial part of the increase in single motherhood among whites. For black mothers, who have traditionally been employed in larger numbers than white mothers, the change in employment opportunity is much smaller, and the overall effect appears to be weaker.

Decrease in Men's Employment

A third explanation for the growth of female-headed families is the decline in male employment opportunities, particularly in the black population. Changes in marital relationships as a result of unemployment were first documented in research on the Great Depression.[13] More recently, Liebow has presented a vivid picture of how unemployment or underemployment undermined marital relationships and attitudes toward marriage among the black men who hung out at "Talley's Corner."[14] Quantitative research reinforces these findings in several areas. For example, researchers have shown that unemployment lowers psychological well-being and increases marital conflict and even family violence.[15]

Senator Daniel Patrick Moynihan, one of the first social scientists to graphically document the relationship between cyclical unemployment and marital instability, argued in the early sixties that unemployment among black men was causing a breakdown of the black family.[16] William Julius Wilson and his colleagues find that there is a similar relationship today across regions among blacks.[17] Their indicator, the "index of marriageable males"—the ratio of black employed males per 100 black females of similar age in the population—takes into account not only unemployment but nonparticipation in the labor force and sex differences in mortality and incarceration rates. All these factors lessen the size of the "marriageable pool" of black men. Wilson and his colleagues point to the decline in unskilled jobs in cities such as New York, Philadelphia, and Baltimore. These regions also showed the greatest growth in female-headed families. They conclude that the loss of such jobs in the central cities is a major factor in the growth of female-headed families. Based on this review of the evidence, Garfinkel and McLanahan hypothesized that the principal culprit in the decline in marriage among young blacks was the decline in male employment opportunities.[18]

Changes in Values

The fourth explanation for the increase in mother-only families is that values with regard to divorce, premarital sex, and single parenthood have become increasingly permissive. Evidence on attitudes toward divorce suggests that changes in values follow rather than cause changes in behavior. In his book on marriage and divorce, for example, Cherlin notes that attitudes about divorce apparently changed very little until the late 1960s, but changed a great deal between 1968 and 1978.[19] In both 1945 and 1966 the most common response (34–35 percent) to the question of whether divorce laws were too strict or not strict enough was "not strict enough." Thereafter attitudes changed substantially. In 1968, 60 percent of the people interviewed thought that divorce should be more difficult to obtain. But by 1974 and 1978 only about 42 percent thought so. Cherlin concludes that changes in attitudes could not have caused the initial increase in divorce.

On the other hand, there is another sense in which changes in values may have played a role in the long-term rise in divorce during the twentieth century. The increasing emphasis on individualism certainly predates the 1960s, and individual fulfillment may conflict with the institution of marriage.

Furthermore, even if changes in attitudes cannot account for the long-term rise in divorce during the twentieth century or for the acceleration of the trend in the 1960s, there are two reasons to think that values may have played an important role in sustaining the trend. First, as single parenthood has become more common and more acceptable, the stigma associated with the status probably declined. Thus parents who might have stayed together in the past for social approval have become more free to divorce and establish separate households. Second, as the risk of marital disruption increases, young mothers are more likely to make career choices that enhance their economic independence; such choices, in turn, make it easier to divorce in the event that the marriage is unsatisfactory.

Industrialization and Urbanization

Of the first four explanations for the growth in divorce, the increase in employment opportunities for women is the strongest. But why have employment opportunities for women increased? The answer would appear to be that an increase in employment opportunities for women is a by-product of industrialization and urbanization.

Industrialization reduces the importance of physical strength in work and thereby increases the comparative advantage of women in market work. In the twentieth century this trend has become pronounced as an increasing proportion of mature economies have shifted from manufacturing to services. Similarly, industrialization in the twentieth century has lightened the burden of housework and thereby increased the ease with which women can combine market and home work.

THE CAUSES OF ECONOMIC INSECURITY

Female-headed families face a much higher risk of poverty than other demographic groups. Roughly 45 percent of mother-only families with children under age eighteen are poor, according to the official government definition of poverty. The proportion of families headed by divorced mothers that are poor is lower—only 26 percent.[20] Figure 5.2 shows trends in the prevalence of poverty for female-headed families, two-parent families, aged persons, and disabled persons for the years 1967 through 1983. It is important to note that these measures of poverty take into account the assistance provided by the major government income support programs, such as Aid to Families with Dependent Children (AFDC), Social Security, and Disability Insurance. They do not include, however, the value of in-kind benefits such as food stamps and Medicaid. Women and children in female-headed families are the poorest of all these groups. And the gap has been widening, not because of an absolute deterioration in the position of female-headed families, but rather because the economic position of other groups improved during the past two decades.[21]

Poverty is but the most extreme form of economic insecurity. Most single-mother families who escape poverty still suffer from severe economic insecurity. Many barely escape poverty. As the first row in Table 5.1 indicates, in 1982 the average income of families headed by a divorced white mother was only $13,845. The comparable figure for blacks was $11,187. Equally important, of those who are fortunate enough to escape poverty, nearly all have experienced large drops in income. Duncan and Hoffman find that one year after divorce, the average income of the most fortunate half of single mothers is equal to only 60 percent of their predivorce income.[22]

Figure 5.2
Trends in Poverty Rates for Mother-Only Families, Two-Parent Families, Persons over 65, and Disabled Persons, 1967-1983

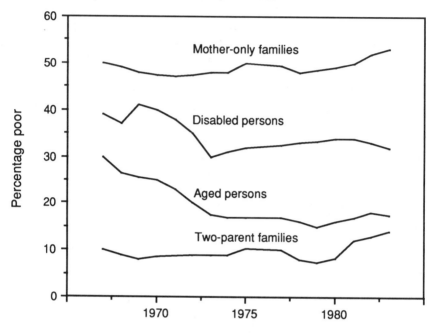

Source: C. Ross, "Trends in Poverty, 1965-1983," paper prepared for the Conference on Poverty and Policy: Retrospect and Prospects, sponsored by the Institute for Research on Poverty, University of Wisconsin-Madison, and the U.S. Department of Health and Human Services, December 1984.

The Extent of Economic and Social Instability Following Divorce

Following a divorce, women and children undergo numerous other changes in roles and social position that involve loss of social status as well as loss of family and friends. Changes in residence are perhaps the most common form of social instability in newly formed mother-only families. One study shows that about 38 percent of divorced mothers and their children move their residence during the first year after a divorce.[23] Subsequently household moves drop off rapidly to about 20 percent a year on average—still about one-third higher than the rate for two-parent families. Changes in residence not only require adjustment to new neighborhoods and living conditions; they may also mean the loss of important social networks and support.

Changes in employment are also common. In an effort to recoup

Table 5.1
Average Income Receipts of Two-Parent, All Mother-Only, and Divorced Mother Families in 1982, by Race

	Whites			Blacks		
	Married-Couple Families	Mother-Only Families	Divorced Mother-Only Families	Married Couple Families	Mother-Only Families	Divorced Mother-Only Families
Total cash income	$30,814	$12,628	$13,845	$23,913	$9,128	$11,187
Head's earned income	21,932	7,666	9,556	13,508	5,363	7,660
Other's earnings	6,377	928	874	8,096	827	888
Alimony and child support	227	1,246	1,797	253	322	613
Social Security, pensions, other unearned income	2,171	1,782	834	1,720	907	765
Public assistance and food stamps	174	1,399	1,083	1,838	2,573	1,877

Source: I. Garfinkel and S. McLanahan, Single Mothers and Their Children: A New American Dilemma (Washington, D.C.: Urban Institute Press, 1986), 18-21.

some of their income loss, many divorced and separated mothers enter the labor force for the first time or increase their working hours. Duncan and Hoffman found that the proportion of mothers who worked 1,000 or more hours per year increased from 51 percent before divorce to 73 percent after divorce. The average divorced mother earned $8,937 in 1981 dollars the year after divorce, compared with $5,829 the year before divorce.[24] When a mother makes a substantial change in her working hours, this change in itself is stressful for her as well as her children. If her children are young, child care arrangements must be made, and both mother and child are likely to experience anxiety about the new situation.

In addition to experiencing changes in residence and working hours, divorced and separated mothers are more likely to experience job changes, changes in their household composition, and unemployment than are the fathers in two-parent families. According to data from the Michigan Panel Study of Income Dynamics (PSID), unemployment was three times more common among single mothers during the first three years after a divorce or separation than among fathers in two-parent households, and job changes were about one and a half times more common. Family composition changes, such as another adult or child moving in or out, also were about one and a half times more common among mother-only families, even five years after marital disruption.[25]

Social and economic instability have direct implications for the mental health of these families. Research on stressful life events indicates that changes in social roles or status may lead to increases in psychological distress and anxiety.[26] Undesirable and involuntary changes are thought to be the most stressful, particularly when they involve the disruption of social networks and support systems. Not surprisingly, epidemiological surveys show that single mothers report substantially higher rates of anxiety and depression than do married women and men; and facility utilization statistics show that mother-only families with children consume a disproportionate share of community mental health services.[27] According to Guttentag and her colleagues, the mental health service utilization rates of preschool-age children in mother-only families are four times as great as those of children in two-parent families; for children between the ages of seven and eighteen, the rates are twice as high. Much of the variation in psychological distress appears to be caused by differences in income and economic instability. The Michigan PSID data also indicate that single mothers are much more likely to experience declines in psychological well-being than are married men with children and that most of the relative decline could be explained by differences in income.[28]

A comparison of the sources of income available to different family types suggests three reasons why divorced and mother-only families

are especially likely to be poor: lower earnings of the family head, inadequate child support from the second parent, and meager public
transfers. After considering each of these in turn, this section concludes with a brief note on the division of assets at divorce.

The Causes of Economic Insecurity

Low Earnings of Single Mothers. The major source of income for all
family types apart from those headed by widows is the earnings of the
household head. Earnings account for approximately 60-70 percent of
total income. The ability of single mothers to earn income, therefore,
is a critical determinant of their economic status. Table 5.1 shows the
average income from different sources received by married-couple, all
mother-only, and divorced families. Female breadwinners in general
and divorced mothers in particular bring in much less than married
fathers, 35 percent as much for white single mothers and 44 percent as
much for white divorced mothers. For blacks the proportions are 40
and 57, respectively. This is partly because they work fewer hours and
partly because they have lower hourly earnings.

Much of the difference in poverty rates between different family types
is due to the fact that single mothers work fewer hours than married
fathers. David Ellwood has shown that only about 6 percent of single
mothers who worked full time year round during the previous decade
were poor in any given year as compared with more than 70 percent
of nonworking women.[29]

These findings should not be interpreted to mean that if all single
mothers worked full time, only 6 percent of them would be poor. To
some extent the apparent advantage of working mothers reflects the
selection process that channels women with higher earnings capacity
into the labor force and women with lower earnings capacity into
homemaker and welfare status. On this point, Sawhill found that most
of the women on welfare in the late 1960s had very low earnings capacity and that even if they worked full time, more than half would
still earn less than their welfare grants.[30]

The lower wages of women, then, are probably as important as their
lower labor force participation rates in explaining the high incidence of
poverty in mother-only families. Despite the massive increase in the
labor force participation of women, the wage gap between women and
men has not narrowed, and occupational segregation is still widespread.

Inadequate Private Child Support. The second reason for the greater
poverty of mother-only families is that in most cases only one parent
contributes to the family income. In two-parent households, the earnings of white wives account for about one-fifth of family income and

the earnings of black wives account for about one-third of family income (Table 5.1). In mother-only families, alimony and child-support payments from noncustodial fathers account for only 10 percent of family income for whites and 4 percent for blacks. For the divorced, the situation again is somewhat better. Child support accounts for 13 and 5 percent of total family income for these families.

When a family splits, it loses the economies of scale that result from living together in one household. Two residences must be maintained rather than one. Even if all noncustodial fathers paid a reasonable amount of child support, such payments would not compensate fully for the costs a separation entails. Yet most noncustodial fathers do not pay reasonable amounts of child support.

National data on child support awards indicate that in 1986 only about 61 percent of the 8.8 million single mothers with children under twenty-one years old were awarded child support. Of these only about 48 percent received full payment, 26 percent received partial payment, and 26 percent, no payment at all.[31] Marital status makes a big difference to the likelihood of having a support award: 82 percent of divorced women, 43 percent of separated women, but only 18 percent of never-married women had a support award.[32]

Even among those who obtain child support, the mean amount received in 1985 was only $2,215. For whites and blacks the amount was $2,294 and $1,754, respectively. For divorced mothers the mean amount was $2,538.[33] These payments are much lower than the contribution of fathers in two-parent families and also lower than the contribution of the other adults in two-parent families. Thus, even though women's earnings capacity is lower than men's, and even though the contribution of the second parent is needed more in mother-only families than in two-parent families, absent fathers contribute a smaller proportion to child support in the former than mothers do in the latter.

Inadequate Public Child Support. A final cause of poverty in female-headed families is the inadequacy of the public transfers these families receive. The United States is the only industrialized nation in the world that does not provide public cash allowances for all children. The government also provides much less health care and day care than most other industrialized nations. Widows in this country receive Survivors Insurance (SI), whether or not they are poor. Other single mothers receive nothing unless they are poor, in which case they are eligible for welfare. Welfare benefits, however, are much smaller than those received under SI. We are virtually unique in relying so heavily upon welfare to aid female-headed families.

The Division of Assets at Divorce

Most divorcing couples don't have many assets. Weitzman found that in California 60 percent of divorcing couples had less than $20,000 worth of assets.[34] Seltzer and Garfinkel found that 50 percent of divorcing couples in Wisconsin had $8,200 or less in property to be divided.[35] Yet relative to child support awards and payments, property settlements are important. If a 10 percent rate of return is used to calculate the income value of the property awarded to mothers, the value of the property settlement is equal on average to 40 percent of the child support award.[36] This percentage increases with the predivorce income of the couple from 32 percent for those with less than $15,000 to 68 percent for those with predivorce incomes in excess of $45,000. The relative importance of property settlements is even greater than these numbers suggest when one takes account of the widespread failure to pay all child support that is owed, the cessation of child support when the child reaches age 18 or so, and the emotional value of the most important asset—the family home. In short, how property is divided is less important than differences in earnings ability and child support, but still quite important.

The division of property on divorce was originally a process by which a court sorted out which spouse owned what.[37] The ownership by spouses of property accumulated during a marriage differs depending on the marital property rules of that state. In a few states with a marital property regime called community property, all property accumulated during the marriage belongs equally to both spouses and on dissolution of marriage by death or divorce each spouse owns one-half of the assets. In most jurisdictions, however, separate property rules govern: the assets accumulated during the marriage are owned by the spouse who contributed the money to purchase them. A spouse who devotes his or her energies to the care of the home and family rather than to earning money may receive property from the income producer as a gift but does not earn any right to that property. Given that men have traditionally been the principal income producers in marriage, they have come out of marriage on divorce with most of the assets in separate property states.

Today most states, recognizing the unfairness of a system which gave no compensation for provision of care for a home and child, have gone to a system, known as equitable division, under which property owned by the spouses is distributed between them at divorce, not on the basis of ownership but on the basis of certain equitable factors, such as the length of the marriage, the contribution of each party to the marriage, the ages and health of the parties, the employability of the parties, and, in some jurisdictions, fault.[38]

Just what is an "equitable division" differs from state to state and case to case. Although there appears to be a trend in judicial opinions to describe marriage as an economic partnership, fifty-fifty property divisions on divorce are the exception, not the rule. However, several states have enacted legislative rebuttable presumptions favoring a fifty-fifty property division.[39] This would seem to suggest that the share of property going to women is increasing.

On the other hand, the widespread enactment of no-fault divorce may be leading to a decrease in the share of property going to women. When the principal ground for obtaining a divorce was the fault of a spouse, many states provided that fault be considered in making the property division. Lenore Weitzman found that, prior to 1970, when the law in California required that more than half the assets be awarded the innocent party, women received 91 percent of the property of the marriage in San Francisco and 78 percent in Los Angeles. After the enactment of the California no-fault divorce statute, which mandated a fifty-fifty division of property, the shares going to the wife declined to 62 percent and 54 percent, respectively.[40] Whether the decline can be attributed to no-fault divorce and whether these findings are generalizable to other states are both controversial.[41] In balance, therefore, the trend in division of property upon divorce remains unclear.

ADAPTATIONS TO THE INSECURITY OF DIVORCE

The strategies that divorced mothers adopt to cope with insecurity include relying upon income from private or public child support, working more, returning to school to increase one's earnings ability, moving to less expensive housing, sharing household expenses with a friend or relative, and remarrying. In the first part of this section, we discuss particular coping strategies. In the second section, we discuss a problem that is common to almost all of the strategies: what to do with the children.

Alternative Coping Strategies

The strategies are not mutually exclusive. Few divorced mothers rely entirely on either private or public child support. Many combine earnings and private child support. Some work more and remarry. Some depend on welfare for a short period of time and then either remarry or go to work, or do both.

A portion of divorced mothers rely on private and public child support. About half of divorced mothers receive some private child support. Few, however, rely very heavily upon child support. Even for white divorced mothers with above-average incomes (for the divorced-mother population) the average child support payment the year after divorce is only $3,712, and that falls to $1,085 by the fifth year following divorce.[42] About one-third of divorced mothers receive welfare. During the months that they receive welfare, most divorced mothers are nearly completely dependent on it. Yet most divorced mothers leave welfare within two to three years.

Most divorced mothers work. Over three-quarters work at least 1,000 hours per year.[43] About 20 percent of divorced mothers acquire more education after divorce.[44] A critical question for these mothers and more broadly for society as a whole is, "Who cares for the children?"

In addition to seeking to increase their incomes by working more or increasing their education, divorced mothers cope with economic insecurity by cutting expenses. As noted above, about 40 percent of divorced mothers move to less expensive housing in the year following their divorce. A much smaller proportion—about 15 percent—share expenses at some point with a relative, friend, or other adult.[45]

Finally, remarriage is a very common method of coping with the insecurity that accompanies divorce. Divorced men remarry faster than divorced women, but within two years about 20 percent of divorced mothers have remarried and by five years about one-half of divorced mothers have remarried.[46] Remarriage differs from the other coping strategies of divorced mothers in two fundamental ways. First, unlike work and the other adaptations discussed above, the effects of remarriage on the plight of the divorced mothers and their children are not reflected in statistics on the economic insecurity of divorced mothers. The reason is simple: remarried mothers are no longer single mothers. Second, remarriage has a profound effect on economic insecurity. Whereas five years after their divorce, the average income of mothers who do not remarry equals only about 60 percent of their predivorce income, the average income of those who remarry is actually greater than their predivorce income. On the other hand, Duncan and Hoffman find that the potential gains from remarriage for those who haven't remarried are much smaller than the gains for those who have remarried. This is particularly true for black divorced mothers because the earnings ability of unmarried black men is abysmally low.[47]

The Problem of Day Care

One of the problems for mothers who decide to work or return to school is the availability, adequacy, and affordability of child care.

The types of child care arrangements of all working mothers—married and divorced—vary by the age of the child. Care in their own home (31 percent) or in someone else's home (37 percent) are the most common form of primary day care arrangements for preschool-age children (0-4 years).[48] Day care centers or preschools are the primary child care arrangement for an additional 23 percent of children in this age group. When care is provided in the children's home while the mother works, the usual provider is the father. When care is provided in some-one else's home, it is usually by a nonrelative. Not surprisingly, school is the most common form of child care for grade-school-age children (age 5 to 14 years old). About three-quarters of these children are in school most of the time their mothers are working.

The pattern of care differs between the children of married and non-married mothers, mainly because of differences in the availability of fathers for child care. Nineteen percent of the children of married women are cared for by their fathers while the mothers work as compared with only 2 percent of the children of unmarried women. Nonmarried women depend more on the children's grandparents for care in the child's home (16 percent) than do married women (3 percent).

There is also some variation according to whether the mother works part or full time. Care at home by the father is more common if the woman works part time (24 percent of the children). Mothers who work full time rely more on care in the home of a nonrelative or on orga-nized child care facilities.

From 1977 to 1982 the most significant change in child care patterns was an increase in the percentage of women using organized child care. This rose from 13 to 16 percent. A similar increase occurred from 1982 to 1984–1985.[49] These numbers suggest that organized child care is slowly displacing care by relatives or in family day care homes.

Day care is expensive. Only about 20 percent of all mothers who work are able to obtain free child care. (And it is not clear what the nonmonetary costs of this free care are.) In 1985 families who paid for the care of a child under age 5 spent an average of $36.69 per week. The cheapest source of day care, a relative, was nearly as much as the most expensive, a day care home provider—$34.57 vs. $38.80, because families use fewer hours of the more expensive forms of care. Expen-ditures on day care represent a substantial portion of the budgets of single mothers who pay for day care—about 17 percent.[50] They are an even higher proportion of the budgets of the poor—23 percent. For low-income single mothers, the most problematic aspect of day care is undoubtedly its high cost.

Although the federal government provides subsidies for day care ex-penditures, the bulk of the subsidization goes to middle- and upper-middle income families in the form of the dependent care tax credit in the federal income tax. Under the tax credit, families can subtract from their tax liability between 20 and 30 percent of child care expenditures up to a maximum of $480 for one child and $960 for two or more chil-dren. In 1986, this program accounted for about $3.5 billion of the $5.5 billion in federal expenditures on day care. That leaves only about $2 billion in expenditures that subsidize the day care expenditures of low-income families.[51]

Finding suitable day care can also be a problem. Some of the best day care centers have long waiting lists. There are also waiting lists for government-subsidized day care. Judging the quality of day care settings is also difficult, and the location of available day care may be problematic. Philip Robins found that single mothers who lived in public housing projects that provided day care were much more likely to work than those who lived in projects that did not provide day care.[52]

Finally, parents worry about the quality of the day care their children receive. Although most of the research appears to indicate that good-quality day care is not harmful to children's development and may even have positive effects, not all day care is of high quality.[53] As Edward Zigler, one of the foremost experts in the area, notes, "The lousy centers won't let a researcher near the place."[54] In short, for the divorced mother who works or attends school, day care is expensive, often difficult to arrange, and frequently a source of concern.

PUBLIC ENFORCEMENT OF PRIVATE SUPPORT

The U.S. child support system is undergoing profound changes. The evolution of this system is best characterized as a movement away from judicial discretion toward the routinization associated with taxation and social insurance.

The private child support system in the United States has historically been a state prerogative implemented through the judicial branch, and until the Family Support Act of 1988 is fully implemented, the system will continue to operate as described here. In most states, the obligation of absent parents to pay child support is explicitly stated in statute, although in some states the obligation is only implied.[55] The court determines the amount of child support to be paid by the noncustodial parent on an individualized basis, and the payment is made by that parent directly to the custodial parent.

With respect to establishing awards and setting amounts, several problems can arise. First, there is often a failure to establish any award at all. Nationally, only 61 percent of mothers eligible for child support have awards.[56] Although about eight out of ten divorced mothers receive child support orders, less than half of separated mothers and less than one in five never-married mothers have orders.

Second, the setting of an award on a case-by-case basis by a judge in a judicial hearing is very expensive, in time and cost to the parents as well as in delays for the children needing support. The time of judges and other court personnel makes the procedure expensive to the public also.

Third, the case-by-case determination of the amount of the award often results in unfairness. Numerous studies documented that the child support system treats equals unequally.[57] Data for Wisconsin indicate that child support awards range from zero to over 100 percent of the noncustodial father's income. The system is also regressive. Child support obligations represent a greater proportion of the incomes of low-income parents than of those who are well off.

Child support awards are also considered to be inadequate.[58] What is not so clear is the extent to which they are low because the initial awards were low or because they have not been updated to reflect changes in the cost of living or earnings ability of the noncustodial parent. Data from Wisconsin suggest the entire problem is due to the failure to update.[59]

Aside from the difficulties associated with the establishment of an award and the setting of an amount, the system also has problems in the collection of support once the award is made. The standard procedure has been for the court to order the noncustodial parent to pay, with the actual collection left to the beneficiary of the order—the custodial parent. This means that if the absent parent fails to pay, the custodial parent has to initiate a legal action, usually by citing the non-paying parent for contempt. This proceeding is fraught with difficulties for the custodial parent. It requires legal counsel—a substantial financial burden for a parent already not receiving support—and often involves difficult fact determinations because of the lack of adequate records of direct payments to the custodial parent.

In a few states, such as Michigan and Wisconsin, private child support must be paid to a government agency, which not only serves the entire community by documenting whether support is paid or not, but also has the authority to initiate legal action when obligations are not met.

Jail is the ultimate sanction for those who do not pay. According to David Chambers, jailing, when combined with an effective monitoring system, deters nonpayment.[60]

The most effective tool for collecting child support is a wage assignment.[61] A wage assignment is a legal order to the employer of the child support obligor to withhold a specified amount from the employee's wages.

The legal system for collecting child support is generally regarded as ineffective.[62] Nationally, only half of the parents with awards receive the full amount due them and about one-quarter receive nothing.[63] Yet the enforcement of private child support was viewed as strictly a state and local problem until the late 1940s, when congressional interest in absent fathers grew as children with living but absent parents replaced orphans as the most numerous recipients of Aid to Families with Dependent Children (AFDC), a government subsidy to poor children living with one parent, funded jointly by the states and the federal government. Congress enacted the first federal legislation regarding private child support in 1950. State welfare agencies were required to notify law enforcement officials when a child receiving AFDC benefits had been deserted or abandoned. Further legislation, enacted in 1965 and 1967, allowed states to request addresses of absent parents from federal social security records and tax records. States were also required to establish a single organizational unit to enforce child support and establish paternity.

In 1975 Congress added Part D to Title IV of the Social Security Act, establishing the Child Support Enforcement (IV-D) program. This legislation established a federal Office of Child Support Enforcement and required each state to establish a corresponding agency to help enforce child support in all AFDC cases and, since 1980, in non-AFDC cases, should assistance be requested from the custodial parent. It also required states to maintain a parent locator service that tied in with a federal service. In short, the 1975 act created the public bureaucracy to enforce private child support obligations.

By 1985 collections reached $2.7 billion, including $1 billion for AFDC recipients. This represents an increase of 282 percent in collections for AFDC families between 1976 and 1985.[64] There is good reason to believe that child support collections will continue to grow, for the 1985 figures do not reflect the effects of significant new legislation in 1984 and 1988.

The 1984 child support legislation was passed by a unanimous Congress. It addressed most of the major shortcomings of the private child support system: the failure to obtain a child support award from the courts, the inequity and inadequacy of awards, and the failure to collect support even though the payer is delinquent.

On the issue of obtaining orders, the states were required to adopt expedited procedures for obtaining support orders either through the judicial system or in an administrative agency. To increase the number of awards among never-married mothers, states were also required to allow the initiation of paternity action any time prior to a child's eighteenth birthday. Paternity suits in the past typically permitted only two to six years of delay after the child's birth. On the issue of equitable and adequate support orders, all states were required to establish child support guidelines for judges and other officials to use. These guidelines, however, need not be binding upon the judiciary. And there were no provisions to ensure the updating of awards. On the issue of the effective collection of child support, the 1984 amendments encouraged the states through federal fiscal incentives to monitor payments in all child support cases. Moreover, the amendments required the states to adopt automatic income withholding for child support to take effect after one month of nonpayment.

By 1988, many states had gone beyond the 1984 federal law. Several states had established standards that are nearly binding upon the judiciary in that the standard becomes the presumptive child support award from which the judge or hearing officer can depart only with a written justification, which may be reviewed by a higher court. Similarly, several states had adopted income withholding laws to take effect automatically when an obligation was established rather than only in response to a delinquency in payment. Indeed, Massachusetts had gone so far in the direction of a tax model for child support collections as to turn over responsibility for collections to the state revenue department.[65]

The Family Support Act of 1988 also goes even further than the 1984 legislation in strengthening child support enforcement. The guidelines that states were required to adopt in 1984 become the presumptive child support obligation from which judges can depart only if they make a written justification for doing so. Instead of waiting for a delinquency before withholding child support obligations from wages and other sources of income, the 1988 legislation requires income withholding from the outset in all cases. In short, the trend is clear. The United States is moving away from judicial discretion toward the routinization associated with taxation and social insurance.

Both states and the federal government have been strengthening legislation to assure that paternity is established. Between 1979 and 1986 the proportion of never-married cases with child support awards increased dramatically, from 11 percent to 18 percent.[66] In view of the fact that nearly all of the improvement came from the flow of new cases into the system, the efficacy of current procedures is substantially underestimated by the 18 percent figure. Furthermore, both states and the federal government are continuing to enact legislation that facilitates the establishment of paternity. It seems likely therefore that, within a decade, paternity will be established in at least a majority of new out-of-wedlock births. If so, the United States will begin to look more like other industrialized countries that are members of the Organisation for Economic Co-operation and Development (OECD). Compared to Sweden, however, which establishes paternity in 95 percent of out-of-wedlock cases, the United States still has a long way to go.[67]

Several features of the Family Support Act of 1988 are designed to increase the number of cases in which paternity is established. The act establishes performance standards for the states with respect to establishing paternity. If the states fail to increase the proportion of out-of-wedlock births in which they establish paternity, they face fiscal penalties. At the same time, the federal government will provide greater fiscal assistance to the states for establishing paternity. For example, the federal government will pay 90 percent of the costs of laboratory tests associated with the establishment of paternity.

THE PUBLIC CHILD SUPPORT SYSTEM

Public support is a significant feature of the U.S. child support system. Public transfers to poor families with children eligible for child support substantially exceed private child support transfers to all U.S. children. Whereas slightly over $7 billion in private child support was paid in 1985, AFDC expenditures on families eligible for child support were equal to about $8 billion. If the costs for food stamps ($5 billion), housing assistance ($3 billion), and Medicaid ($8 billion) are included, public transfers equaled nearly $24 billion, or more than three times private child support transfers.[68] In general, the public system substitutes for the private system where the latter has broken down. About half of all children living in female-headed households are on AFDC, and only slightly over 10 percent of these households receive any financial support from the absent parents.[69]

The AFDC program, commonly referred to as welfare, was established in 1935 for quite different purposes from those it now serves. It was intended to provide support for the families of deceased fathers in a society in which it was considered undesirable for mothers with children to work. Today the program is primarily for children who have a living absent parent legally liable for their support and a custodial parent who increasingly is expected to work.

By the 1960s, the prevailing belief that cash welfare programs should enable poor single mothers to stay home and rear their children had begun to erode. At first, in 1967, the federal government tried to induce AFDC mothers to work by creating work incentives within AFDC. When this failed to have much impact on either work or caseloads, the Congress in 1972 began legislating requirements for mothers to work when they had no children under age six. In 1977, the Carter administration proposed a combination of a guaranteed-jobs program and assistance, which would have, in effect, required mothers without preschool-age children to work. In 1981, the Reagan administration rejected the approach of creating work incentives within the AFDC program in favor of a pure work requirement. It sought to cut off benefits to those who were already working a substantial amount and to require those who received benefits to work for them. In the early 1980s, Congress agreed to much, but not all, of this strategy. The Family Support Act of 1988 contains both strengthened work requirements and the provision of services such as training and day care to facilitate work.

As structured, the current public system of child support encourages welfare dependency. It imposes a high tax on the earnings of welfare mothers, which discourages work, and it offers nothing outside of welfare to supplement the incomes of poor single mothers who have a low earnings capacity. Like any social assistance program, AFDC is designed to aid only the poor, and therefore benefits are reduced when earnings increase. After four months on a job, a woman on AFDC faces a reduction in benefits of a dollar for every dollar of net earnings. It is not surprising that the majority of mothers on welfare do not work during the months they receive benefits.

As mentioned earlier, welfare mothers have a very low earnings capacity. This suggests that some form of transfer is necessary to provide an adequate standard of living for their families. The only way to alleviate their poverty without creating total dependency is to supplement rather than replace their earnings. Some of this money can come from improved collections of private child support. The rest must come from public transfers. How much of each is not known at this time.[70]

We have described above a number of federal reforms designed to strengthen the enforcement of private child support obligations. Increased child support payments from parents of children on AFDC will generate savings in AFDC expenditures. These savings can be used to reduce taxes or to increase the economic well-being of children eligible for child support, or some combination of both. In view of the fact that children potentially eligible for child support and the mothers who care for most of them are among our poorest citizens, using these funds to improve the economic well-being of these families is at the very least the compassionate thing to do. It is also wise. One-half of our next generation will be eligible for some child support before reaching adulthood. Investing in them is therefore investing in our future. Furthermore, sharing some of the increased revenues with these families will encourage the mothers to cooperate in establishing the paternity of noncustodial fathers—one of the weakest links in the current system.

Congress and the present administration have already approved two alternative methods of sharing some of the AFDC savings with families eligible for child support. All states are now required to ignore the first $50 per month of private child support (a $50 set-aside) in calculating the amount of the AFDC benefit. Two states, Wisconsin and New York, are permitted to use the federal share of AFDC savings to help fund an assured child support benefit as part of a comprehensive child support assurance system (CSAS).

Which method is preferable: sharing the gains inside or outside of welfare? This question is addressed in the section below, which describes the Wisconsin Child-Support-Assurance System.

THE WISCONSIN CHILD-SUPPORT-ASSURANCE SYSTEM

Under a child-support-assurance system all parents who live apart from their children are required to share their income with their children. The sharing rate is proportional, according to the number of children owed support. The obligation is collected through paycheck withholding, as Social Security and income taxes are. All children with a living noncustodial parent are entitled to benefits equal to either the child support paid by the absent parent or a socially assured minimum benefit, whichever is higher. Should the absent parent pay less than the assured benefit, the difference is financed out of general revenues, and the custodial parent is subject to a small surtax up to the amount of the public subsidy.

In addition to the assured benefit, custodial parents in Wisconsin with one child will be paid a work-expense offset of $1 per hour worked. Custodial parents with two or more children will receive $1.75 per hour worked. This work-expense offset has a sliding scale feature so that it is not paid to custodial parents with incomes greater than $16,000.

A few words about the rationale for the three major features of this new system are warranted. First, why establish child support obligations by legislation rather than judicial discretion? The principal argument is that because of the large financial obligation already borne by the state, the apportionment of support for poor children among the custodial parent, the absent parent, and the public is more appropriately a legislative function. Moreover, a legislated formula would reduce inequity. Finally, the use of courts is too costly to society and the families affected.

Second, why use the withholding system in all cases? Because wage withholding is the most effective collection tool we have, and effective and efficient collection of child support is essential.

Third, why use general revenues to supplement inadequate child support payments from absent parents? The answer is that doing so will insure children against the risk that their noncustodial parent's income declines or is permanently low and will also promote work and independence among those now dependent on AFDC.

Both the benefits and the costs of a child-support-assurance program will depend upon the level of the assured benefit, the contribution rates on noncustodial and custodial parents, and the effectiveness of child support collections. In Table 5.2 estimates of net savings or costs and reductions in poverty and AFDC caseloads are presented for a national child-support-assurance program with four different assured benefit levels. The assured benefits for the first child range from $2,000 to $3,500. Assured benefits for the second, third, fourth, fifth, and sixth child,

Table 5.2
Estimated Costs or Savings and Effects on Poverty and AFDC Caseloads of
Alternative Child Support Insurance Programs in 1983 Dollars

Minimum Benefit Level for First Child	Net Savings or Costs (billions)	Reduction in Poverty Gap	Reduction in AFDC Case Loads
100% collection effectiveness			
$2000	$2.37	39%	48%
2500	1.72	43	54
3000	0.87	48	59
3500	-0.18	53	64
80% collection effectiveness			
$2500	$0.59	40%	49%
3000	-0.33	45	56
70% collection effectiveness			
$2500	-$0.06	38%	48%
3000	-1.83	43	54

Source: The estimates are derived from the *1979 Current Population Survey-Child Support Supplement* (CPS-CSS). The CPS-CSS is a match file which contains data from both the March annual demographic and income survey and the April 1979 child support supplement. On the basis of the March survey, 3,547 women who were eligible to receive child support were identified and interviewed in April. In order to estimate savings or costs and reductions in poverty and AFDC caseloads, it was necessary to impute noncustodial parent incomes. Estimates of the noncustodial fathers' income are derived from regressions relating wives' characteristics to husbands' incomes. For a more detailed description of the data and methodology, see D. Oellerich and I. Garfinkel, "Distributional Impacts of Existing and Alternative Child Support Systems," *Policy Studies Journal* 12 (September 1983): 119-29.

respectively, are equal to $1,500, $1,000, $500, $500, and $500. The contribution rates for noncustodial parents are 17 percent for one child, 25 percent for two children, 29 percent for three children, 31 percent for four children, 32 percent for five children, and 33 percent for six or more children. Contribution rates for custodial parents are equal to one-half those for noncustodial parents. No work-expense offset is included in these simulations. The estimates in the top panel of Table 5.2 assume 100 percent collection effectiveness.

The most striking finding is that if we collect 100 percent of the non-custodial parents' child support obligation, three of the four child-support-assurance program plans would actually save money. That is, the extra dollars paid out under the new program would be more than offset by increased child support collections and consequent reductions in welfare expenditures. Even the most generous plan costs less than one-quarter of a billion dollars. (The cost estimates are too low because children living with custodial fathers are not identified in the CPS [Current Population Survey] child support survey used for the cost estimates.)

At the same time, all the plans would reduce the poverty gap (the difference between the income of a poor family and the income the family would need to reach the poverty line) and the number of families on welfare. The reductions in the poverty gap for families eligible for child support are quite large, ranging from a low of 39 percent to a high of 53 percent. Similarly, reductions in welfare caseloads are very large, ranging from 48 to 64 percent.[71] In short, all of the child-support-assurance program plans would substantially reduce poverty and welfare dependence and three of four would actually save money.

No matter how efficient the collection system is, less than 100 percent of potential revenue will be collected. Consequently, the second and third panels in Table 5.2 present estimates of the effects of the two middle plans if we collected only 80 percent and 70 percent, respectively, of the noncustodial parents' child support obligation. If we collect only 70 percent of potential revenue, both plans cost more, though the extra cost of the $2,500 plan is very small. Note also that collecting less than 100 percent of the noncustodial parent obligation also reduces the effectiveness of a child-support-assurance program in reducing poverty and welfare dependence. The effects are not so large as on costs, however, because for poor families the minimum benefit makes up for most of the loss in private child support.

The Status of the Wisconsin Demonstration

The state of Wisconsin is implementing the child-support-assurance system in stages. The percentage-of-income standard was made an option for the courts to use in 1983 and became the presumptive child support obligation as of July 1987. (The percentages, however, are still being used to arrive at fixed-dollar child support orders rather than being expressed in percentage terms.) Immediate withholding was piloted in ten counties in 1984 and also became operational statewide in July 1987. The assured benefit is scheduled to be piloted in mid-1989.

NOTES

1. No children are involved in 47 percent of divorces. See "National Center for Health Statistics: Advance Report of Final Divorce Statistics, 1984," *Monthly Vital Statistics Report*, vol. 35, no. 6 (Hyattsville, Md.: U.S. Public Health Service).

2. U.S. Bureau of the Census, "Household and Family Characteristics, March 1985," *Current Population Reports*, series P-20, no. 411 (Washington, D.C.: U.S. GPO, 1986).

3. L. Bumpass, "Children and Marital Disruption: A Replication and Update," *Demography* 21 (February 1984): 71–82. See also S. L. Hofferth, "Updating Children's Life Course," *Journal of Marriage and the Family* 47 (1985): 92–116.

4. U.S. Bureau of the Census, "Household and Family Characteristics, March 1985."

5. See M. Honig, "AFDC Income Recipient Rates and Family Dissolution," *Journal of Human Resources* 9 (1973): 303–22; H. Ross and I. Sawhill, *Time of Transition: The Growth of Families Headed by Women* (Washington, D.C.: Urban Institute, 1975); S. Danziger, G. Jakubson, S. Schwartz, and E. Smolensky, "Work and Welfare as Determinants of Female Poverty and Household Headship," *Quarterly Journal of Economics* 97 (1982): 519–34; P. Cutwright and P. Madras, "AFDC and the Marital and Family Status of Ever Married Women Age 15–44: United States, 1950–1970," *Sociology and Social Research* 60 (1976): 314–27.

6. K. A. Moore and L. J. Waite, "Marital Dissolution, Early Motherhood and Early Marriage," *Social Forces* 60 (September 1976): 20–40; A. J. Cherlin, "Social and Economic Determinants of Marital Separation" (Ph.D. diss., Department of Sociology, University of California, Los Angeles, 1976); S. Hoffman and J. Holmes, "Husbands, Wives and Divorce," in *Five Thousand American Families*, ed. G. J. Duncan and J. Morgan, vol. 4 (Ann Arbor, Mich.: Institute for Social Research, 1976); R. M. Hutchens, "Welfare, Remarriage and Marital Search," *American Economic Review* 69 (1973): 303–22; D. Ellwood and M. J. Bane, "The Impact of AFDC on Family Structure and Living Arrangements" (Report to U.S. Department of Health and Human Services under grant no. 92A-82, John F. Kennedy School of Government, Harvard University, photocopy, 1984).

7. For a description of how these estimates were obtained, see I. Garfinkel and S. McLanahan, *Single Mothers and Their Children: A New American Dilemma* (Washington, D.C.: Urban Institute, 1986), 62. The much publicized results from the Seattle-Denver Income Maintenance Experiment have been interpreted to show that the effect of welfare benefits on divorce is much greater than the foregoing summary indicates. The SIME/DIME results, however, say nothing about the effects of raising or lowering the welfare benefits available to single mothers. The experiment was implemented in a world that already had a welfare system, and families in both the experimental and control groups retained whatever eligibility they would have had in the absence of the experiment. Many single mothers in the control group and some in the experimental group received welfare. Consequently, whatever effect the experiment had on behavior, it cannot be attributed to the availability of additional income to women

who became single heads of households. If divorce rates were higher in the experimental groups, this was due to something about the treatment other than an "independence" effect.

8. The divorce rates are from J. Sweet and L. Bumpass, *American Families and Households* (New York: Russell Sage, forthcoming).

9. In their reinterpretation of the Seattle-Denver Income Maintenance Experiment, Cain and Wissoker found that it was eligibility for a training program rather than eligibility for a cash negative income tax program that led to increases in divorce. Wives were more prone than husbands to enroll in training. See G. G. Cain and D. A. Wissoker, "Do Income Maintenance Programs Break Up Marriages? A Reevaluation of SIME-DIME" (Institute for Research on Poverty Discussion Paper no. 850–87, University of Wisconsin, Madison, 1987).

10. S. H. Preston and A. T. Richards, "The Influence of Women's Work Opportunities on Marriage Rates," *Demography* 2 (May 1975): 209–22.

11. Ross and Sawhill, *Time of Transition.*

12. Cherlin, "Social and Economic Determinants of Marital Separation."

13. E. W. Bakke, *Citizens without Work* (New Haven: Yale University Press, 1942); M. Komarovsky, *The Unemployed Man and His Family* (New York: Octagon Books, 1940).

14. E. Liebow, *Talley's Corner* (Boston: Little, Brown and Co., 1967).

15. R. Catalana and C. D. Dooley, "Economic Predictions of Depressed Mood and Stressful Life Events in a Metropolitan Community," *Journal of Health and Social Behavior* 18 (1977): 292–307; M. A. Straus, R. Gelles, and S. Steinmetz, *Behind Closed Doors* (New York: Anchor Books, 1981).

16. D. P. Moynihan, *The Negro Family: The Case for National Action* (Washington, D.C.: U.S. Department of Labor, Office of Policy Planning and Research, 1965). South reinforces these findings; see S. J. South, "Economic Conditions and the Divorce Rate: A Time Series Analysis of Postwar United States," *Journal of Marriage and the Family* 47 (1985): 31–34. While previous researchers concluded that divorce rates dropped during the Great Depression, Cherlin finds that the cohort that got married during or just before the Depression had higher divorce rates than cohorts marrying before and after the Depression. See A. J. Cherlin, *Marriage, Divorce, Remarriage* (Cambridge: Harvard University Press, 1981), 24.

17. W. J. Wilson and K. M. Neckerman, "Poverty and Family Structure: The Widening Gap between Evidence and Public Policy Issues," in *Fighting Poverty: What Works and What Doesn't*, ed. S. H. Danziger and D. H. Weinberg (Cambridge: Harvard University Press, 1986).

18. Garfinkel and McLanahan, *Single Mothers and Their Children*, 68–78.

19. Cherlin, *Marriage, Divorce, Remarriage.*

20. In 1985 45.4 percent of all families with a female householder, no husband present, and related children under 18 years of age were poor. See U.S. Bureau of the Census, "Money Income and Poverty Status of Families and Persons in the United States: 1985 (Advance Data from the March 1986 Current Population Survey)," *Current Population Reports*, P-60, no. 154 (Washington, D.C.: U.S. GPO, 1986). Twenty-six percent of divorced women with own children under 21 years of age present from absent fathers had income below the pov-

erty level in 1985. See U.S. Bureau of the Census, "Child Support and Alimony: 1985 (Advance Data from March–April 1986 Current Population Surveys)," *Current Population Reports*, P-23, no. 152 (Washington, D.C.: U.S. GPO, 1987).

21. The official government data on poverty understate the extent to which the increases in government benefits for mother-only families have reduced their economic insecurity. The two biggest sources of benefit increases in the 1965–1980 period—food stamps and Medicaid—are ignored in the official figures. According to the official data, the poverty rate for single mothers who head families remained about the same between 1967 and 1983 (around 50 percent), although it dropped during the Great Society years. If the cash value of food stamps and the cash insurance value of Medicaid benefits are added to cash income, the poverty rate for single women who head families declined from 50 percent in 1967 to between 29 and 41 percent in 1983, depending on how one estimates the values of in-kind benefits. These poverty rates are still well above those for other demographic groups.

22. G. J. Duncan and S. Hoffman, "Welfare Dynamics and Welfare Policy: Past Evidence and Future Research Directions" (paper presented at the annual meeting of the Association for Public Policy Analysis and Management, Washington, D.C.: October 1985).

23. S. McLanahan, "Family Structure and Stress: A Longitudinal Comparison of Two-Parent and Female-Headed Families," *Journal of Marriage and the Family* (May 1983): 347–57.

24. G. J. Duncan and S. D. Hoffman, "A Reconsideration of the Economic Consequences of Marital Dissolution," *Demography* 22 (November 1985): 485–97.

25. McLanahan, "Family Structure and Stress."

26. B. Dohrenwend and B. Dohrenwend, eds., *Stressful Life Events: Their Nature and Effects* (New York: Wiley, 1974).

27. M. Guttentag, S. Salassin, and D. Belle, *The Mental Health of Women* (New York: Academic Press, 1980).

28. S. McLanahan, "Single Mothers and Psychological Distress: A Test of the Stress and Vulnerability Hypotheses," in J. Greenley, ed., *Research in Community and Mental Health*, vol. 5 (Greenwich, Conn.: JAI Press, 1985).

29. D. T. Ellwood, "Targeting the Would-Be Long-Term Recipients of AFDC: Who Should Be Served?" (Unpublished preliminary report, Harvard University, 1985).

30. I. V. Sawhill, "Discrimination and Poverty among Women Who Head Families," *Signs* 2 (1976): 201–11.

31. U.S. Bureau of the Census, "Child Support and Alimony: 1985," *Current Population Reports*, Special Studies Series P-23, no. 152 (Washington, D.C.: U.S. GPO, 1987).

32. Ibid.

33. See also Garfinkel and McLanahan, *Single Mothers and Their Children*, 18–21.

34. L. J. Weitzman, *The Divorce Revolution: The Unexpected Social and Economic Consequences for Women and Children in America* (New York: Free Press, 1985).

35. J. A. Seltzer and I. Garfinkel, "Property Settlements and Child Support

Awards: Inequality in Divorce Settlements" (Institute for Research on Poverty Discussion Paper no. 867–88, University of Wisconsin, Madison, 1988).

36. Ibid.

37. H. Clark, *The Law of Domestic Relations* (St. Paul, Minn.: West Publishing Co., 1968), 450–51.

38. D. J. Freed and T. B. Walker, "Family Law in the Fifty States: An Overview," *Family Law Quarterly* 20 (1987): 486.

39. See, for example, Arkansas Stat. §34–1214 (A) (L); North Carolina Gen. Stats. § 50–20(c); Wisconsin Stat. § 767.255.

40. Weitzman, *The Divorce Revolution*, 74. Another study of property division before and after no-fault divorce was done in a separate property state, Connecticut. Although Connecticut has adopted no-fault, it retains fault as a factor in dividing property. The results of the Connecticut study are mixed, but the author feels that, in general, they indicate that women did better in the 1970s (under fault) than they are doing in the 1980s (under no-fault). However, he concludes that fault is not the explanation for the difference (J. B. McLindon, "Separate but Unequal: The Economic Disaster of Divorce for Women and Children," *Family Law Quarterly* 21 [1987]: 351–409).

41. We are grateful to M. S. Melli, University of Wisconsin Law School, for providing the material on the division of property.

42. See Duncan and Hoffman, "Welfare Dynamics and Welfare Policy," Table 14.A.13.

43. Ibid., Table 14.A.12.

44. See C. U. Chiswick and E. L. Lehrer, "The Determinants of Remarriage: An Economic Perspective" (Unpublished paper, University of Illinois at Chicago, August 1987).

45. This is an upper-bound estimate, since the denominator (families and subfamilies with a divorced female householder and no husband present) includes only groups with *own* children *less than 18* years of age, while the numerator (divorced mother-child subfamilies plus households with two unrelated adults and a divorced female householder) may include groups with children *over 18* or female householders *without own children*. In other words, the numerator would, for example, incorrectly include both of the following groups: (1) a single father and his 10-year-old child who are sharing quarters with an unrelated divorced female householder, and (2) a divorced female householder and a 20-year-old child who are sharing quarters with another unrelated adult.

Our sources for this crude estimate are the following: U.S. Bureau of the Census, "Household and Family Characteristics: March 1985" and "Marital Status and Living Arrangements: March 1985," *Current Population Reports*, P-20, nos. 411 and 410 (Washington, D.C.: U.S. GPO, 1986).

46. See Duncan and Hoffman, "Welfare Dynamics and Welfare Policy," Table 14.A.2.

47. Duncan and Hoffman's estimate is undoubtedly too low but their point is correct nevertheless.

48. Data collected as part of the Survey of Income and Program Participation (SIPP) for the period December 1984 through March 1985 is available on the child care arrangements for the three youngest children under 15 years old of

women who worked. The report distinguishes between primary and secondary child care arrangements. Primary care is the usual form of care or that in which the child spends the greatest number of hours. The discussion in the text refers to primary child care arrangements.

49. Here we are comparing the SIPP child care data from 1984–1985 to the Census Bureau Child Care Studies of 1977 and 1982. See U.S. Bureau of the Census, "Trends in Child Care Arrangements of Working Mothers, 1982," *Current Population Reports*, series P-23, no. 117.

50. S. L. Hofferth, Statement on Child Care in the U.S. before the House Select Committee on Children, Youth, and Families, July 1, 1987, Table 4A.

51. A. Kahn and S. Kamerman, *Child Care: Facing the Hard Choices* (Dover, Mass.: Auburn Publishing Co., 1987), 19.

52. P. K. Robins, "The Role of Child Care in Promoting Economic Self-Sufficiency among Low-Income Families" (Testimony before the House Select Committee on Children, Youth, and Families, March 1987).

53. D. Frye, "The Problem of Infant Day Care," and M. Rutter, "Social-Emotional Consequences of Day Care for Preschool Children," in *Day Care: Scientific and Social Policy Studies*, ed. E. F. Zigler and E. W. Gordon (Boston: Auburn House Publishing Co., 1982).

54. Quoted in *Fortune* magazine, February 16, 1987, p. 37.

55. H. O. Krause, *Child Support in America: The Legal Perspective* (Charlottesville, Va.: Michie, 1981).

56. U.S. Bureau of the Census, "Child Support and Alimony, 1985."

57. For more evidence on the inequity in award determination, see K. White and T. Stone, "A Study of Alimony and Child Support Rulings with Some Recommendations," *Family Law Quarterly* 11 (1976): 75–85; L. Yee, "What Happens in Child Support Cases," *Denver Law Journal* 57 (1979): 21–68.

58. A. Nichols-Casebolt, I. Garfinkel, and P. Wong, "Reforming Wisconsin's Child Support System" (Institute for Research on Poverty Discussion Paper no. 793-85, University of Wisconsin, Madison, 1985), Table 3.

59. I. Garfinkel, *Utilization and Effects of Immediate Income Withholding and the Percentage-of-Income Standard: An Interim Report on the Child Support Assurance Demonstration* (Institute for Research on Poverty Special Report No. 42, University of Wisconsin, Madison, 1986).

60. D. Chambers, *Making Fathers Pay: The Enforcement of Child Support* (Chicago: University of Chicago Press, 1979).

61. See Krause, *Child Support in America*; and Chambers, *Making Fathers Pay.*

62. I. Garfinkel and M. Melli, *Child Support: Weaknesses of the Old and Features of a Proposed New System*, vol. 1 (Institute for Research on Poverty, University of Wisconsin, Madison, 1982); Krause, *Child Support in America*; and Chambers, *Making Fathers Pay.*

63. U.S. Bureau of the Census, "Child Support and Alimony, 1985."

64. U.S. Department of Health and Human Services, Office of Child Support Enforcement, *Child Support Enforcement Statistics Fiscal Year 1985*, Vol. II, Table 1, and *Child Support Enforcement, Fifth Annual Report to the Congress for the Period Ending September 30, 1980*, Table 2 (Rockville, Md.: National Child Support Enforcement Reference Center, 1980 and 1985).

65. M. Melli, *Child Support: A Survey of the Statutes* (Institute for Research on Poverty Special Report no. 33, University of Wisconsin, Madison, 1984).

66. Current Population Survey, Child Support Supplement, 1979–1984.

67. A. J. Kahn and S. B. Kamerman, *Child Care, Family Benefits, and Working Parents: A Study in Comparative Policy* (New York: Columbia University Press, 1981).

68. Estimates of private child support are taken from U.S. Bureau of the Census, "Child Support and Alimony, 1985." Estimates of public child support transfers were derived from Garfinkel and McLanahan, *Single Mothers and Their Children*, Table 11. Though the estimates are not exactly comparable—private child support payments include those to remarried mothers whereas the public transfers are limited to female heads—the orders of magnitude are right.

69. The proportion of AFDC families receiving private support is obtained from U.S. Department of Health and Human Services, *Child Support Enforcement Statistics Fiscal Year 1985*, Vol. II, Tables 21 and 23. The 10 percent figure is likely to be an underestimate, however, because the government is unlikely to have collected any amount for families that go on welfare for only one or two months and then become self-sufficient.

70. I. Garfinkel and P. K. Robins, "Child Support, Work and Welfare Dependence," in *The Effect of Economic Status on the Family: The Effect of the Family on Economic Status* (Research proposal submitted to the Assistant Secretary for Planning and Evaluation, U.S. Department of Health and Human Services, by the Institute for Research on Poverty, University of Wisconsin, Madison, 1987).

71. The reductions in welfare caseloads are very crudely estimated. On the one hand they are too high because they assume an annual rather than a monthly accounting period. On the other hand, they are too low because they assume no increase in work among AFDC mothers in response to the prowork features of the child support assurance system.

6 INHERITANCE: THE TREATMENT OF WOMEN

Paul L. Menchik

In this chapter, we will discuss the treatment of women with regard to the inheritance of wealth in the United States. To understand it, we will examine both statutory provisions and prevailing practices. Since the ownership of wealth represents power, security, and independence in a market economy like the United States, social scientists have long shown an interest in investigating how wealth is inherited. Among social scientists, economists have been interested in studying the patterns of inheritance because inheritance exerts a powerful effect on the distribution of wealth and income in an economy. In recent years, they have shown an increasing interest in understanding how wealth holders use their wealth as a means to manipulate and influence the behavior of other members of family.[1]

This chapter is organized as follows: First, we will review the historical background of inheritance in the West. Second, we will discuss the quantitative importance of estate wealth. Third, we will examine the testamentary treatment of wives by their husbands, and vice versa. Fourth, we will examine the extent to which surviving spouses—and surviving wives in particular—consume their wealth during their widowhood. Fifth, we will look at the testamentary treatment of daughters, in comparison to sons, by their parents. Finally, we will cover the topic of a "negative bequest" from parent to child—that is, a transfer of resources, time, and effort, as well as money, from child to parent.

HISTORICAL BACKGROUND

Looking at inheritance practice as far back as the feudal times, we can observe that lineal succession from parent to child, as opposed to conjugal equity between husband and wife, was of primary importance. Having an heir, who was invariably a male child, was a great concern to wealthy men and noble men. To appreciate how important it was, one only needs to look at the behavior of King Henry VIII of England, who married several women to ensure the presence of an heir.

In premodern times, the bulk of wealth was real—that is, land and structures. The inheritance rule in those days was primogeniture, bequeathing of the entire estate to one child, generally the firstborn male. (An estate is the value of person's wealth at death.) Some argue that the type of wealth and primogeniture inheritance were closely related. They explain that, because of economies of scale involved in agriculture, the partitioning of land through a more equal division of real wealth would create inefficient, small farms. This is why the land was not divided among children but was bequeathed to only one heir.

There are some problems with their argument, however. For instance, one can offer a counterargument, such as the following. If economies of scale in agriculture indeed existed in those days and if each child received a portion of the land, then it would be in the interest of a child—e.g., the most able farmer—to attempt to purchase the land of his or her siblings. In such a case, each child would be endowed with either land or a payment. The payment might take the form of either lump-sum money payment or an income stream of money or crops. Thus, there would be no reason to favor in one's will any one child over others either by birth order or gender.

In any case, inheritance was practiced with the sole purpose of preserving the family wealth across generations. As a result, the eldest son was favored over later-born sons, and all daughters, regardless of their birth order, were excluded from consideration as heirs. One could argue, on the other hand, that the institution of the dowry constituted a partial compensation for the less favorable treatment daughters received in inheritance.

With economic development and industrialization, wealth in forms other than real, such as financial, increased in importance. As a result, the practice of unequal bequeathing for the sake of "efficient" utilization of wealth became less meaningful. In those rapidly changing days, different European countries followed different inheritance customs. France, after the French Revolution in 1789, put into effect a legal system of equal estate division. This new law was consistent with the principle of equality enunciated by the French at that time. England, however, made no such break with the past. In England, testators (meaning persons who write the will that governs the distribution of property among heirs upon their death) had the freedom to bequeath as they wished. This testamentary freedom resulted in the continuance of unequal treatment of heirs, although probably less harsh than under strict primogeniture. Writing in the 1920s, Josiah Wedgewood detailed inheritance patterns that differed between the sexes and by birth order. He stated:

There is little doubt that, among the very wealthy, equal division of the spoils among the family irrespective of place and sex, is not the general rule. It appeared to be usual, among wealthier predecessors in my sample, for the sons to receive a larger share than the daughters. In the case of the smaller estates, equal division is much more common.[2]

He also said:

I found that, in many cases, the richer predecessors bequeathed the lion's share of their property to one particular son—usually, but not always, the eldest. This was not only the custom of primogeniture among the landed aristocracy. For the desire to leave a large property intact in the hands of a single descendant caused a number of wealthy testators, who did not strictly belong to the landed classes, to reject the principle of *legitime*.[3]

The United States in the twentieth century is neither like France nor like England in terms of inheritance institution and practice. Unlike the French, Americans have a great deal of testamentary freedom. To Americans, the will is an expression of the testator's final wishes on the disposition of his or her property. Within certain limits, Americans can indeed distribute wealth according to their wishes expressed in a will. Furthermore, unlike the English, Americans do not normally choose to bequeath unequally by sex, by birth order, or by any other demographic characteristics of children.

To be also noted is that the current American practice, compared with the past practice, emphasizes conjugal bequests instead of lineal bequests.[4] That is, if a testator is married at death and leaves a will, this person will almost always bequeath the entire estate to the surviving spouse.

Indeed, this practice represents a major change in the United States from past centuries, or even from past decades. In the 1930s and 1940s, a decedent husband often would bequeath a "life interest" in an asset to his wife, making a third party control the asset. The asset so controlled by a third party would then be passed on to the decedent's children or grandchildren upon the death of the wife.[5] This meant that the wife would never own the wealth but rather would be entitled to the income accruing from it, e.g., the interest income from a bond or dividends from a stock. Now husbands are less likely to engage in this type of practice and are more likely to bequeath the asset itself to their wives.

THE QUANTITATIVE IMPORTANCE OF
ESTATE WEALTH

How much is being bequeathed by testators? As mentioned earlier, the value of a person's wealth at death is referred to as an estate. Menchik and David studied the size of estate in relation to the lifetime earnings of a sample of Wisconsin men. It was found that estates averaged about 5 percent of lifetime earnings, or about two years' worth of earnings. However, estates of men who were in the highest decile of earnings were as large as 10 percent of lifetime earnings, or four years' worth of earnings.[6] Of course, these are average figures. Thus, in reality, some high-income earners may indeed leave a negligible estate while some low-income earners may leave a proportionately large estate.

For widows, estate wealth could be a very important part of their financial resources, since widows face a serious risk of becoming poor if they do not inherit an estate. Additionally, of course, widows could receive social security payments, life insurance benefits, and private pensions.

Since women are five times as likely as men to become widowed, wives are more likely to survive their husbands than vice versa. Accordingly, Nuckols writes a scenario that applies to most cases in the United States.[7] Wealth is accumulated during marriage. At the time of death of the husband, his entire estate, through a will, goes to the wife. Then, when the wife dies, the remaining wealth devolves to the children. We will discuss interspousal and intergenerational bequests in more detail.

INTERSPOUSAL BEQUESTS

Inheritance in the United States today is characterized by substantial, but not complete, testamentary freedom. The most important departure from complete testamentary freedom occurs in the area of interspousal bequests. Some states, such as Texas and California, are community property states. In such states, any property accumulated by a spouse is deemed to be community property, and hence its ownership is legally, and equally, shared by husband and wife. Shared ownership differs fundamentally from the concept of gift or inheritance. Thus, in such states, a husband is prohibited from bequeathing the entire amount of wealth he accumulated during marriage to someone other than his spouse. He only has freedom, through writing a will, to distribute one-half of the accumulated wealth as he wishes. That is, in community property states, only one-half of accumulated wealth is bequeathable by the husband. Thus, if the husband dies intestate—that is, dies with no will—only one-half of wealth can be distributed among heirs by the rules of intestate succession.

The rules of intestate succession vary from state to state. Here we will discuss rules that are typical. If a spouse with no will dies in a non-community property state, the estate would go to the surviving spouse in its entirety if there are no children or their descendants. If children or grandchildren are alive, the estate would be divided between them and the spouse. However, the grandchildren only share in the estate if their parents are not alive. Suppose, for example, a husband dies intestate and leaves a widow, one child, and two grandchildren, who are the daughters of a deceased second child. In this case, the wife would receive one-third of the estate, the child would receive one-third, and each grandchild would receive one-sixth. This allocation procedure, under which estate is allocated equally by family line, is called *per stirpes*. This procedure differs from another procedure called *per capita*, under which the estate is divided equally among existing lineal descendants. When there are two or more children (or their issue if a child is deceased), the standard proportion received by the surviving spouse is one-third. If only one child (or issue) is living, the spouse would receive one-half of the estate.

When a spouse dies in a community property state, the picture changes drastically. If a spouse dies intestate in such a state, the surviving spouse would receive three-quarters of the estate. This is because in a community property state the surviving spouse is entitled to one-half of wealth as an equal owner of wealth accumulated during marriage plus one-quarter as a surviving spouse. If there are two children, then the surviving spouse would receive two-thirds. In this case, one-half represents ownership under the community property principle and an additional one-sixth (that is, one-third of the remaining one-half) represents the spouse portion of inheritance.

Some states, such as Ohio, have special provision for spouse's allowances. The purpose of providing such allowances is to prevent the surviving spouse from becoming destitute immediately after the death of one's husband or wife. Under inheritance law, these allowances are first deducted from estates. The remainder, then, is distributed to legal heirs. In Ohio, the amount of allowances is decided at the discretion of probate courts—a legal institution whose purpose is to ensure an orderly distribution of the property of the deceased. Since the surviving spouse receives spouse's allowances, it often happens, when there is no will, that the combined amount of spouse's allowances and the spouse share of estate exceeds the amount of the entire estate. This occurs especially when the estate is small. In my study of Ohio estates in the mid-1960s, there was a case in which a husband died with no will and left an estate of $6,000. Survivors were his wife and multiple children. Because the estate was so small, little or no estate remained to distribute to children after the probate court provided the widow with spouse's allowances plus her share of the remaining estate. In cases of large estates, however, such an anomaly would not occur. This is because, in these cases, spouse's allowances would not appreciably increase the spouse share above the intestate amount.

How often is intestacy observed? When a will is written how is the spouse treated?

Most decedents—about two-thirds, according to a number of recent studies—leave a will. The probability of a person having a will varies depending on the person's age. An old person is more likely to have a will than is a young person. Further, the probability of a person having a will depends on the level of earnings, while alive, and the size of estate. High-income earners are more likely to leave a will than are low-income earners; the wealthy more likely than the less wealthy. Of course, in rare occasions, some very wealthy persons leave no will. In such cases involving wealthy decedents, the spouse may be treated unfairly. That is, in the absence of a will, there is no way that the surviving spouse can receive an extra payment for services rendered to the decedent during a lifetime of marriage; all the surviving spouse would receive is the spouse share of the estate.

When a married decedent has no children and leaves a will, the surviving spouse is nearly always bequeathed the entire estate. There are rare anomalous cases, of course. In my Ohio study, I found a case in which a wife wrote a will stating that she wished to leave to her husband "only what the law requires, and no more," with the remaining estate to be given to her brother and sister. The probate court in this case distributed one-third to the husband and two-thirds to the siblings. I considered the disposition of the case by the court rather unusual. Even if there were more than one child, the husband would have been entitled to one-third. This case involved two siblings—not children. Thus it would seem that the husband should have been granted more than one-third of the estate, which is totally warranted by the Ohio inheritance law.

More interesting is the situation where a decedent has a will and is survived by the spouse and children. To study this type of situation, I drew from the Ohio records a random sample of 215 such cases filed between 1964 and 1965. There were 149 male and 66 female decedents. Of all the 149 males, 108 (or 72 percent) were testate, that is, died with a will. Of all the 66 females, 50 (or 78 percent) were testate. Among the 108 testate males, 100 (or 93 percent) bequeathed the entire estate to their wives. Similarly, among the 50 testate females, 44 (or 88 percent) bequeathed the entire estate to their husbands. The "spouse all" bequest rule appears to be the preponderant practice among testate decedents of both sexes, whether or not they have children.

In that study, there were eight cases in which husbands did not practice the spouse-all bequest rule. In these cases, the husbands gave 90, 90, 75, 50, 42, 25, 33, and 33 percent, respectively, of the estate to their wives. In the last case, the husband attempted to completely disinherit the wife. But the probate court disregarded the will and gave the wife a forced share of one-third, which is the minimum that the wife was entitled to under the intestacy statute.

In the same study, there were six cases in which wives did not practice the spouse-all bequest rule. In these cases, the wives gave 90, 75, 50, 33, 33, and 10 percent, respectively, of the estate to their husbands. In the last case, the decedent wife had a husband and nine children. She bequeathed 10 percent of the estate to each of the ten. The probate court did not change the wishes of the decedent wife. Thus, the surviving husband received just 10 percent of the estate.

We can summarize the foregoing discussion as follows. When either a husband or a wife dies with a will, the estate is nearly always bequeathed to the surviving spouse. The probability of leaving a will varies according to one's age and the estate size. An old person is more likely to leave a will than is a young person; the wealthy more than the less wealthy. In the absence of a will, a surviving spouse with children can expect to receive only one-third or one-half of the estate, with the rest going to the surviving children. In the states with the provision of spouse's allowances, the surviving spouse can expect to receive such allowances before the estate is divided according to the inheritance law. Because the wife is more likely to survive the husband than the other way around, women face a greater risk of facing intestacy.

CONSUMPTION OF INHERITED WEALTH BY THE SURVIVING SPOUSE

Economic historians specializing in the distribution of wealth have long been interested in studying the degree to which the surviving spouse consumes the inherited wealth. Stanley Lebergott has developed a model for studying the behavior of wealthy families and hypothesizes the course of events as follows: Wealthy men accumulate a fortune. At the time of their death, they bequeath their estates to their wives. These surviving widows live, on average, an additional twelve years. He argues that, during these twelve years, these widows dissipate relentlessly the family wealth. He further argues that if widows did not dissipate inherited wealth, the concentration of wealth would be greater than what it is today.[8] Writing about the period of widowhood, he claims:

During this decade one would expect wealthy widows to consume the inheritances rather than add to them. A substantial share of the estates that millionaires fiercely accumulate is destined to be slowly consumed away during twelve years of widowhood. Should the widow marry a fortune hunter, the estate can be consumed more gaily and faster.[9]

As a way of providing evidence that widows deplete estates of their families, Lebergott cites a number of anecdotes in which the wealthy widow dissipates her husband's fortune among feckless fortune hunters. For example:

Millionaires have left large portions of their estates to their wives with no legal hindrance nor social impediment. In so doing, some millionaires have guaranteed the prompt dissolution of the great fortunes they have accumulated. Margaret Sage, for example, inherited the vast estate put together by her husband. Apart from a tiny fraction for her living expenses, she converted the entire estate to one or another charitable enterprise. And when George Lorillard's widow (tobacco) married Count Di Agreda, or Mrs. Hamersley (real estate) became the Duchess of Marlborough, or Mrs. Isaac Singer became the Duchess de Camposelice, decumulation surely succeeded upon accumulation.[10]

In a recent paper, I tested Lebergott's hypothesis using a matched sample of ninety-nine husbands and wives drawn from Connecticut probate record data.[11] Starting with a sample of wealthy male testators who died in the 1930s and 1940s, I located the estates of their wives. On average, the widows lived an additional thirteen years. In each case, I compared the estate size of the wife with both the estate size of her husband and the amount he bequeathed to her. In general, I found that the widows did not dissipate the estates but left estates that, on average, were 75 percent as large, in real terms, as the estates of their husbands and twice as large as the amount their husbands bequeathed to them in their wills. Although it certainly is possible for the widows to have acquired wealth in ways other than through interspousal bequests, it is simply not the case that the widows of wealthy men leave small estates. Statistical analysis showed that a longer period of widowhood did not correspond to a smaller estate, other things being equal. Thus, the findings from this study tell us that affluent widows tend not to dissipate but to preserve and, in some cases, increase the family wealth during their widowhood.

INTERGENERATIONAL BEQUESTS

When wealth is bequeathed intergenerationally, how is the wealth divided among children and between sexes? In the United States, bequests made to children generally are not primogeniture—quite different from the British tradition. In a study of bequests made to children (N=82), I discovered that daughters received as large bequests as those received by sons.[12] More specifically, in families with two children involving a son and a daughter, I found that daughters, on average, received 51.7 percent, and sons 48.3 percent, of the net amount of estate bequeathed to children. If I include the amounts bequeathed to the grandchildren of the testator, the share for the female and male lines would be 50.7 and 49.3 percent, respectively. Furthermore, if I include gifts made to the children from the parents before death, that is, *inter vivos* transfers, the share for females was 50.5 percent in comparison to 49.5 percent for males, as another study of mine indicated.[13] These findings clearly show that parents divide their estates equally between male and female children.

In the same study mentioned above, I looked into the situation of families with three children.[14] Again, research findings were similar. Among forty-eight families with three children, who included two sons and one daughter, the average share going to the two sons under three different circumstances as described above was as follows: When I considered the net estate bequeathed to children only, the share for the two male children was 66.5 percent; when I included the amounts bequeathed to the grandchildren, the share for the two sons was 66.1 percent; and when I included *inter vivos* transfers, the share for the two sons was 65.4 percent.

In the same study, there were thirty-nine families with three children, who included one son and two daughters. Under the three different circumstances described above, the share going to the son was found to be 34.3, 34.5, and 34.9 percent, respectively. I also found that parents generally distributed estates equally among children, regardless of their birth order. All these findings indicate that parents indeed follow a rule very close to the rule of equal division *pro rata*.

There are always exceptions. One example of unequal treatment across sexes is found in cases involving a family farm or a family business. I found the amount bequeathed to sons and daughters to be equal; however, the type of assets bequeathed to them was quite different. For example, when a small, less-partible business was involved, such an asset normally was bequeathed to the male child. The assumption is that the male child would be a more effective owner-operator than the female child. This bequeathing behavior on the part of parents implies that parents prefer unequal inheritance of occupation but adhere to the principle of equal distribution of wealth in value, between the sexes. Equality in the value of inheritance is achieved by bequeathing the daughter financial assets that are equal in value to the business assets received by her brother.

DEVIATIONS FROM EQUAL DIVISION

Although I have found that dividing an estate equally among children is the rule in both the Connecticut and Ohio samples, it is instructive to examine cases in which equal division is not practiced. Investigating these cases will help us understand the motivation of testators. When parents bequeath estates unequally to their children, they state their reasons for doing so. (They seldom do when they bequeath equally.)

In one case, the parent bequeathed the most to a child who, according to the will, supported him. In another case, the favored beneficiary was a daughter who lived with the decedent. In a third case, a daughter was favored for the reason of "kindness and care she extended to me during my stay at her home." In two other cases, particular children were favored "in consideration of the care and companionship shown to me and my deceased wife" and because they "furnished me a home and were close in time of stress."

In these cases, it appears that the bequest took on, in part, the appearance of payment for past services rendered by the child. In such a case, it would seem to me that equity would require unequal bequests to compensate for past unequal efforts and devotion to parents. The relevant question here is this: Who cares for aged parents? In the United States, the overwhelming majority of children caring for parents are daughters.[15] Consequently, one can argue that the equal treatment of children widely practiced in the United States results in unfair treatment of daughters who normally provide a disproportionate amount of services to their frail parents.

CONCLUSIONS

Inheritance patterns of spouses are symmetric in the United States. Generally, husbands bequeath the bulk of their estates to their wives, and wives bequeath to their husbands. Although most people die testate, a minority fail to do so. Dying intestate subjects heirs to the legal statutes on intestate succession. These statutes provide the surviving spouse with one-third or one-half of the estate if the decedent has living children. More will go to the surviving spouse if the decedent was living in a community property state. Since women normally live longer than men, female spouses are more likely to experience intestate succession of wealth than male spouses.

It has been hypothesized by some researchers that widows tend to dissipate the large estates that their husbands accumulated and later bequeathed to them. However, empirical evidence taken from probate records does not support such a hypothesis.

Parents tend to bequeath estates equally to sons and daughters. This finding seems consistent with our notion of equity and fairness. However, since daughters exert more effort in caring for aged parents than do sons, one can argue that daughters are receiving unequal inheritance. The equity principle seems to dictate that daughters should inherit more than their proportionate share.

NOTES

1. B. D. Bernheim, A. Shleifer, and L. Summers, "The Strategic Bequest Motive," *Journal of Political Economy* 93 (1985): 1045–76.

2. J. Wedgewood, "The Influence of Inheritance on the Distribution of Wealth," *Economic Journal* 38 (1928): 48.

3. Ibid., 47.

4. J. N. Cates and M. B. Sussman, "Family Systems and Inheritance," *Marriage and Family Review* 5, 3 (1982): 1–24.

5. P. L. Menchik, "A Study of Inheritance and Death Taxation: A Microeconometric Approach" (Ph.D. diss., University of Pennsylvania, 1976).

6. P. L. Menchik and M. David, "The Incidence of a Lifetime Consumption Tax," *National Tax Journal* 35 (1982): 189–204; P. L. Menchik and M. David, "Income Distribution, Lifetime Savings, and Bequests," *American Economic Review* 73 (1983): 672–90.

7. R. C. Nuckols, "Widowhood, Income Maintenance, and Economic Well-Being," *Marriage and Family Review* 5 (1982): 39–60.

8. S. Lebergott, *Income, Wealth, and Want* (Princeton: Princeton University Press, 1976).

9. Ibid.

10. Ibid.

11. P. L. Menchik, "Is the Family Wealth Squandered? A Test of the Merry-Widow Model," *Journal of Economic History* 44 (1984): 835–38.

12. P. L. Menchik, "Primogeniture, Equal Sharing, and the U.S. Distribution of Wealth," *Quarterly Journal of Economics* 94 (1980): 299–316.

13. Menchik, "Is the Family Wealth Squandered? A Test of the Merry-Widow Model," 835–38.

14. Menchik, "Primogeniture, Equal Sharing, and the U.S. Distribution of Wealth," 299–316.

15. T. M. Chang, *Support for National Caregiving*, Report #3, Bureau of Human Resources, Division of Community Services, Wisconsin Department of Health and Social Services, 1984; K. G. Manton and K. Liu, "The 1982 and 1984 National Long Term Care Surveys: Their Structure and Analytic Uses" (Paper prepared for National Conference on Long-Term Care Data Bases, May 21–22, Washington, D.C., 1987).

7 WOMEN'S ECONOMIC STATUS IN OLD AGE AND WIDOWHOOD

Karen C. Holden

Widowhood is a state whose probability, duration, and economic effect may be seriously underestimated by married women and their husbands. For many women the death of a husband not only denies them companionship—it is also associated with a sudden decline in economic well-being. Because they lose so much when their husbands die, many women find their widowhood to be a time of relative economic deprivation. This chapter presents data on the incomes and assets of women before and after the deaths of their husbands and describes the type of economic resources that continue to the widow after her husband's death.

One-third of women in the United States are widowed by the time they reach age sixty-five. At age seventy-five well over half are widowed, and by eighty-five over 80 percent are. This is, of course, a reflection of the greater longevity of women, but simple differences in the life expectancy of women and men underestimate the probable duration of the wife's widowhood if the husband should die. For example, at age sixty-five a man can expect on average to live another 14.9 years but his wife at that same age can anticipate another 18.8 years of life—a 3.9–year difference.[1] The expectation of *widowed* life, however, is far greater since widowhood is not a phenomenon among the very old alone. Over time, increases in life expectancy among both women and men have lengthened the joint-survival period of married couples and postponed the average age at which women are widowed from about age sixty-two for the cohort born in 1893 to sixty-six for those born in 1945. But the greater gains in life expectancy among older women than men has meant, according to Schoen, only a small decline in the number of years women can expect to spend widowed—from 14.96 to 14.32 years for the female cohorts born in 1893 and 1945, respectively.[2]

Mortality rates among both women and men are expected to continue to decline in the future. By the year 2010, life expectancy at age sixty-five is projected to rise to 21.3 years for women and to 16.1 for men.[3] Taking into account the age difference between husbands and wives and using more recent life table values than did Schoen, it is projected that women now in their thirties and forties will spend an average fifteen years as widows.[4] Thus, for married women the years added to life will be a mixed blessing, if they mean a greater emphasis by couples on economic well-being during their joint-retired lifetime, to the neglect of the well-being of the probable widow.

Surprisingly little is known about the extent to which couples recognize either the high probability of a wife's ever becoming a widow or the number of years she can expect to live after her husband's death. Perhaps even more surprising is the scarcity of information on whether husbands and wives consider the future economic well-being of the wife as a widow in allocating income over the different periods of their expected lifetimes, including the period when only the wife survives. The higher incidence of poverty among widows than married couples that is observed in cross-sectional data implies that in the financial planning of couples insufficient weight has been given to the financial risks associated with widowhood and, thus, that fewer resources are protected against the husband's death than would be necessary if a wife is to be assured an equivalent level of consumption after her husband's death.

This chapter describes how widowhood alters the incomes of elderly women in the United States and the way in which public policy mitigates its consequences. It is organized as follows. First, income differences between married and widowed women are described. The next section looks at ways in which women may be protected against the income consequences of widowhood: first, through the federal Old-Age and Survivors Insurance program; second, through the choice by husbands of a pension that continues to be paid to their surviving spouse; and third, through the share of the couple's nonpension assets that is inherited by the widow. The final section discusses expected changes in the future economic status of elderly women and alternative public and private pension approaches that have been proposed to mitigate gender differences in old-age income security.

INCOME OF WOMEN AS WIVES AND WIDOWS

A major accomplishment of federal policy over the last two decades has been a dramatic fall in poverty among the aged. In 1960 over one-third of all individuals sixty-five years of age or older were counted as poor; by the mid-1980s that percentage had fallen to 12.4, a rate which has remained fairly constant since then. Although in 1960 poverty was

Table 7.1
Poverty Rates and Mean Incomes of Noninstitutionalized Women Aged 60
and Older, by Household Type, 1980[a]

Household type	Percentage in group (1)	Mean Income		Percent in Poverty (4)
		Household (2)	Personal (3)	
All ages		$21,553		13.0
Nonaged individuals		23,638		10.4
All women age 60+:	100.0	14,309	5,345	16.3
With husband	44.3	18,060	4,034	6.9
In relative's house	10.0	24,165	4,144	7.2
Head, with relative	8.1	15,640	6,528	12.9
Alone	35.1	7,013	7,013	29.7
With nonrelative	2.5	6,192	6,192	43.8

[a] Data are from the 1980 U.S. Population Census. Household composition is that at the time of the census, and income refers to the 1979 calendar year.

Sources: U.S. Department of Health and Human Services, Social Security Bulletin: Annual Statistical Supplement, 1986 (Washington, D.C.: U.S. Government Printing Office, 1986); and K. C. Holden, "Poverty and Living Arrangements among Older Women: Are Changes in the Well-Being of Elderly Women Understated?" Journal of Gerontology 43 (January 1988) : S22-S27.

far more prevalent among the elderly than for the general population (35.2 versus 22.4 percent, respectively, were poor), the percentage of the elderly who are poor is now less than that in the population (12.4 versus 13.6 percent, respectively).[5]

Despite overall improvements in the incomes of the elderly, pockets of poverty still exist, most notably among older widows. In 1986 women living alone or only with individuals unrelated to them—most of whom are widows—accounted for one-quarter of all elderly individuals, but because over 27 percent of these were poor, the poor among them accounted for over 54 percent of all aged poor.[6]

There is no doubt that married women are (and always have been) more economically secure than unmarried women despite the fact that the former typically live in a larger household with consequent higher consumption needs. The economic advantage to a woman of shared living is demonstrated in Table 7.1, which presents data on the mean income and poverty status of elderly women in 1979 and shows how these varied across women living in different types of households.[7] Two measures of income are given—the mean total income of the household and the mean personal income received by the woman herself. The economic consequences of being married are most evident when household mean income and poverty rates of the women who lived alone—again, these are primarily widows—are compared to those for women who lived with their husbands. While married women had lower personal income than did unmarried women ($7,013 versus $4,034—col. 2), the additional income their husbands brought to the consumption unit reduced their poverty rate to only 7 percent (col. 4), versus the almost 30 percent of women living alone who were impoverished. The higher personal incomes of women without husbands were far less than is necessary to achieve a level of economic well-being equivalent to that enjoyed by women whose husbands were alive.

These cross-sectional differences between the incomes of women with and without husbands, however, do not describe what happens to the incomes of wives when they *become* widows. These differences may be due, in part, to the fact that in any single year widows are on average somewhat older than are married women, and that older couples and widows are more likely to be poor than are younger elderly units. This is because younger cohorts, because of real increases in wages over time, are recipients of higher social security benefits based on their more favorable earnings history and are more likely to be eligible for and receive higher benefits from employer pensions. Thus, differences between one-person and family households in Table 7.1 may reflect age and cohort effects rather than those of marital status alone.

Second, it may also be that widowed women are selective of couples who, when both spouses were still alive, had lower household incomes and were more likely to be poor compared to couples of the same age in which the husband had not died. That is, husbands with relatively low incomes may die first, while higher-income couples remain intact. There is little doubt that persons of lower socioeconomic status experience greater mortality risks at all ages, but most studies have looked only at differences among individuals rather than at the mortality hazard faced by couples of different socioeconomic statuses.[8] If it is poorer couples in which widowhood is more likely to occur, then cross-sectional differences in the average income of married and widowed women will for this reason as well exaggerate the actual influence of widowhood on income.

To observe the true effect of widowhood on economic status, it is necessary to use data that follow the same group of women over time and measure their incomes when married and after their husbands die. The longest series of data for which this is possible comes from the 1950 through 1980 decennial U.S. Censuses. Ross, Danziger and Smolensky used these data to track individual birth cohorts of women— that is, women born during the same five-year calendar period—as they aged and an increasing proportion were widowed.[9] They found that older women were far more likely to be poor than were either younger women or older men in any given census year (i.e., in each cross section) and that the relative risk of an older woman's being poor compared to other groups had increased over the 1950–1980 period (although for all groups the absolute risk had fallen). Following birth cohorts over time and comparing the incomes of married women in one census year to the incomes of widowed women in the next year, they conclude that the transition from wife to widow led to a sharp and permanent decline in economic well-being. Widowhood was associated for each birth cohort with a fall in the average income-to-needs ratio that ranged between 30 and 50 percent.[10] In years after widowhood no further decline in the income-to-needs ratio was observed for any cohort, and, in fact, real incomes grew slightly.

Even these time-series comparisons of cohort data, however, will exaggerate the effect on economic well-being of widowhood, if there is selective attrition of low-income couples into widowhood. Longitudinal panel surveys overcome this problem, since the same individuals are followed over time and their changes in income observed. Data from two such studies—the Retirement History Study (RHS) and the Survey of Income and Program Participation (SIPP)—allow us to follow women through the transition from wife to widow.

The RHS is a sample of single women and men and husbands of couples who were aged fifty-eight to sixty-three in 1969. They were interviewed in 1969 and at two-year intervals through 1979. In the case of couples, if a respondent died the widow was interviewed in subsequent periods. The 1984 panel of SIPP is a nationally representative sample of households whose members were interviewed at four-month intervals between October 1983 and August 1986. At each interview (or "wave"), data were collected on the incomes of each household member over the four preceding months. Because all members of originally sampled households are followed (except when they become institutionalized), it is possible to look at that group of women who were married in the initial interview but whose husbands died prior to the end of the survey.[11]

Table 7.2 looks at the sample of "eventual widows" in the RHS and SIPP defined as women who were interviewed in the initial survey and whose husbands died during the survey periods.[12] To capture the effect of widowhood itself on the risk of poverty, the poverty rate of the couples just prior to the husbands' deaths is compared to the poverty rates for the first full income-reference period the women were widows.[13]

Three points stand out in Table 7.2. Even in the initial interview, couples in which the husbands later died were worse off than were all couples. For example, in 1968 12 percent of the RHS eventual widows

Table 7.2
Poverty Rates as Marital Status Changes[a]

Income Period	RHS	SIPP	
		Below Poverty	*1 to 1.5 X Poverty*
Initial Interview			
All couples[b]	8.8%	8.2%	8.1%
Eventual widows	11.8	10.9	11.9
Before widowhood	14.2	18.1	14.0
After widowhood	26.1	17.3	24.5

[a] Poverty rates are based on incomes of couples or widows alone. Income reference period is one year in RHS, four months in SIPP.
[b] Includes eventual widows.

Sources: D. A. Myers, R. V. Burkhauser, and K. C. Holden, "The Transition from Wife to Widow," *Journal of Risk and Insurance* 54 (December 1988): 752-59; and K. C. Holden, "The Income Shock of Widowhood: Findings from the Survey of Income and Program Participation," Final report to the American Association of Retired Persons, December 1986.

were poor compared to only 8.8 percent of all couples. Almost two decates later the same difference is observed in SIPP. Based on a four-month income-reference period, 11 percent of the SIPP eventual widows were poor compared to 8 percent of all couples at the initial survey.[14] Second, poverty rates appear to rise as women approach widowhood, for in both surveys poverty rates were higher in the last interview the husband was alive (that is, 14.2 percent for the RHS sample) than when they had first been interviewed. But, third, in the first full period spent as a widow, poverty rates for the RHS sample were much higher than in the prewidowhood years. For the SIPP sample, the percentage below poverty does not rise, but the percentage near poor does.

Both the samples, from the 1970s and from the early 1980s, confirm a potential exaggeration of the widowhood effect in cross-sectional data from the greater risk of death among relatively low-income men. But it remains the case that the death of a husband leads to a sharp decline in the income of the surviving widow. Since the 1970s, when the RHS sample were widowed, the risk of entering poverty as a new widow seems to have fallen, but the percentage of women who hover just above the poverty threshold is increased at widowhood. Selective mortality is only a partial and less important explanation than is the effect of the husband's death for the higher cross-sectional rates of poverty among widows than couples.

A third possible explanation for higher poverty rates among widows than married couples is the long-term economic influence of being a widow. That is, once husbands have died and as widows age, it may be more difficult to adjust to income shortfalls through the labor force mechanisms available to married women. As described earlier, Ross, Danziger, and Smolensky report that mean incomes of women as widows did not fall after the initial shock of the husbands' deaths. Holden, Burkhauser, and Feaster look more closely at time spent as widows for the RHS eventual widows and report that after this group had weathered initial widowhood the probability of becoming poor was no greater than it had been during the prewidowhood period.[15] While the SIPP survey period is too short to investigate the influence of a long widowhood on income, Holden does find that over the periods of widowhood (data for up to seven four-month reference periods are possible), neither the poverty rate, the near-poor rate, nor mean or median income-to-needs ratios change.

Both cross-sectional and longitudinal data indicate a higher risk of being poor as a widow compared to that risk when married. Most important, from longitudinal panel data it is evident that the relatively high single-year poverty rates of widows are not due solely to selective mortality and age effects, but that at the time the husband dies the decline in income for a widowed household is greater than the reduction in consumption needs owing to the loss of one household member. Poverty rates capture this change for women whose incomes as widows cross that threshold, but studies that look at changes in income-to-needs ratios and thus at income changes over all income groups tell the same story—widowhood is an economically risky transition.[16] It appears that throughout the past few decades, for widows who had not been poor when married, poverty has been more closely linked to the death of their husbands. It is the death of their husbands that deals a substantial and immediate blow to their income status.

The reasons why widowhood should present so severe an economic risk are not completely understood. For a widow of a relatively young, working husband, the loss in his earnings may be of overwhelming importance because he had fewer years than expected to accumulate retirement assets. But the effect of widowhood on the risk of entering poverty is large even among widows whose husbands had retired prior to death. For some widows the receipt of survivor benefits from social security and employer pensions, and the inheritance from husbands of bequeathable income-producing assets, can cushion the impact of their husbands' deaths. The curiosity is that they do not do so for more women.

Table 7.3
Income of Couples and Unmarried Women 65 and Older, 1984

Income Source[a]	Percentage with Income		Proportion of Total Income	
	Couples	*Unmarried Women*	*Couples*	*Unmarried Women*
Earnings	37	12	24	9
Asset Income	77	60	22	24
Pension	51	24	17	11
Social Security	91	100	34	49
Median annual income			$12,830	$6,520

[a]Residual "other" income not included. For this reason, columns 3 and 4 will not add to 100.

Source: S. Grad, *Income of the Population 55 and Over, 1980,* Social Security Administration Publication No. 13-11871 (Washington, D.C.: U.S. Government Printing Office, 1983).

MEANS ENSURING THE ECONOMIC STATUS OF WIDOWS

In this section the safety net provided by social security, employer pensions, and the inheritance of assets is examined. Again, descriptive, cross-sectional data are presented first and then what can be learned from the RHS and SIPP data is discussed. Some data on asset changes with widowhood are presented, but a more in-depth discussion of the inheritance of assets is left to chapter 6.

Table 7.3 shows the percentage of income received from each of four major sources by elderly couples and unmarried women.[17] The potential importance of the social security and pension safety net, which accounts for over half of the income of couples, in protecting widows against the loss of their husbands' earnings and retirement income is apparent. Unmarried women are far more dependent on income from social security (and the excluded "other income" category that includes all means-tested income) than is the case for couples, suggesting that widows are not compensated fully through the inheritance of income-producing assets and pensions for their husbands' deaths. Income from assets maintains its relative importance in the total income of all widows, but the percentage of widows who receive this income falls.

These cross-sectional data, of course, are subject to the same biases due to selective mortality and aging that were discussed above. But, it is also clear from the above discussion that the far lower incomes of unmarried women than of couples are not due primarily to these effects. Thus, these data on income by source for couples and widowed women imply that in the past many couples failed to provide for the continuation of even a share of pension wealth and income-producing assets as a means of insuring the relative well-being of the eventual widow. For older widows, survivors benefits from social security are assured and it may be that this certainty reduced the incentive to provide other forms of insurance against the husbands' deaths. Note that except for life insurance and private annuities, asset values are not tied directly to age or family composition, and hence the smaller income from assets for widows suggests a failure by couples to preserve a proportionate share of income-producing assets to wives after their husbands die.

Social Security

Old-Age and Survivors Insurance (OASI), commonly known as "social security," is the cornerstone of old-age insurance in the United States.[18] During 1985 $167.4 billion was paid to 33.2 million beneficiaries or to 92 percent of all persons aged sixty-five or older. Benefits from OASI alone provided 38 percent of the income of new social security beneficiaries.[19] To understand how this program mitigates income falls as women are widowed, it is helpful to briefly review how benefits are calculated for wives and widows, both for those who are eligible based on their own work records and those who are not.

Table 7.4 illustrates the types of age-related risks against which OASI provides protection by listing in the top panel the number of beneficiaries by type of benefit and, in the bottom panel, average monthly benefit amounts paid to each beneficiary group. Excluded from this table are children of deceased or retired workers and spouses and survivors who receive benefits only because an eligible child is in their care.[20]

OASI pays retired-worker benefits (Table 7.4, row 2) to individuals who have worked a sufficient length of time in covered employment to meet eligibility requirements. Although ultimately individuals must have forty quarters of covered work to be eligible for retired-worker benefits, transitional rules that allow eligibility with far fewer quarters have resulted in almost universal receipt of social security benefits by individuals sixty-five years and older. Retired-worker benefits are payable to fully insured workers upon their reaching age sixty-two, but benefits will be reduced because of early receipt.

The benefit amount paid to retired workers and to their dependent spouses, survivors, or children is based on OASI covered earnings averaged over the required numbers of quarters of coverage. The spouse of a retired-worker beneficiary is eligible for a benefit that is equal to approximately one-half of the retired worker's if the spouse is sixty-five or older, but that benefit is reduced if the spouse is between age

Table 7.4
Number and Average OASI Monthly Benefit Amount by Beneficiary Category (end of 1985)

Beneficiary Group	Both Sexes	Women	Men
	Beneficiaries (in 1,000s)		
All beneficiaries[a]	30,256	18,372	11,884
Retired workers	22,432	10,615	11,817
Spouse of retired workers[b]	2,962	2,962	36
Surviving spouse[b]			
Nondisabled	4,755	4,725	30
Disabled	107	106	1
	Average Monthly Amount		
Retired workers		$412.10	$538.40
Spouse of retired workers[b]		250.30	169.50
Surviving spouse[b]			
Nondisabled		433.90	317.80
Disabled		316.60	191.70

[a] Excludes child beneficiaries and persons eligible only because a child of a retired or deceased spouse is in their care.
[b] Divorced surviving wives and husbands and divorced spouses of retirees are included in the spouse categories.

Source: U.S. Department of Health and Human Services, *Social Security Bulletin: Annual Statistical Supplement, 1987* (Washington, D.C.: U.S. Government Printing Office, 1987), Table 70.

sixty-two (the earliest age of possible receipt) and age sixty-five. A widow (or widower) is eligible for a survivor's benefit as early as age sixty, or age fifty if she (or he) is deemed disabled. While the full amount of that benefit is equal to the benefit that would have been paid to the deceased spouse, the survivor's benefit will be reduced for months it was paid between age sixty and sixty-five. (No reduction is made for the months before age sixty for disabled surviving spouses.)

For some married women (and a handful of men) who are eligible for a retired-worker benefit based on their own covered work record, the spouse or survivor's benefit may be larger. These "dually entitled" women are included in Table 7.4 only as retired-worker beneficiaries (row 2); women counted as spouse or survivor beneficiaries are eligible only for this benefit (i.e., they are not also eligible for and receiving

Table 7.5
Benefit Amounts Paid to Dually Entitled Women (end of 1985)

Benefit Type for Dually Entitled	Number (in 1,000s)[a]	Benefit Amount[b]
As spouse	1,594	$293.90
Retired-worker benefit		195.10
Reduced secondary benefit		98.80
As widow	2,112	515.90
Retired-worker benefit		296.20
Reduced secondary benefit		219.60
As parent	2	455.70
Retired-worker benefit		247.00
Reduced secondary benefit		208.60

[a] Includes 27,700 beneficiaries for whom monthly benefit data are not available.

[b] Averages of individual benefit amounts may not add to average total because of rules applied to each benefit that round fractions of cents to the nearest $0.10.

Source: U.S. Department of Health and Human Services, *Social Security Bulletin: Annual Statistical Supplement, 1987* (Washington, D.C.: U.S. Government Printing Office, 1987), Tables 118 and 119.

their own retired-worker benefit). The benefits paid to dually entitled women, however, are disaggregated in Table 7.5 into that amount paid as a retired-worker benefit and the supplemental benefit that is equal to the difference between what they receive as a retired worker and their spouse or survivor benefit.

Consider, for example, a dually entitled wife who is eligible for her own retired-worker benefit of $200 but is also eligible for a higher benefit equal to one-half of her husband's $600 per month benefit. Ignoring any reduction due to early benefit receipt, her total monthly OASI benefit would be equal to her own $200 retired-worker benefit plus an additional $100 as a spouse (i.e., 1/2[600] − 200). While her husband theoretically is also eligible for a $100 spouse benefit based on his wife's work record, his own far larger $600 retired-worker benefit means that he is counted in administrative records as receiving only his retired-worker benefit. Note that the social security benefits of a couple are increased by the wife's covered earnings only if her retired-worker benefit is larger than her spouse benefit. Married women whose spouse benefits are larger than their retired-worker benefit have no retirement-income advantage over wives with no work history.[21]

While the majority (74 percent) of all age-eligible OASI beneficiaries (col. 1, Table 7.4) receive benefits as retired workers (row 2), the rest receive benefits based solely on the eligibility and earnings record of a retired or deceased family member (rows 3 and 4). But there are important differences between women and men both in the reason for their eligibility and in the average size of their social security benefits. Virtually all male beneficiaries are eligible for social security benefits as retired workers (col. 3), but female beneficiaries (col. 2) are equally divided into those eligible for benefits based on their own covered work records (58 percent) and those whose entitlement is based solely on the earnings records of their husbands.[22]

Over one-third of all female retired-worker beneficiaries (that is, the 3.7 million in Table 7.5 among the 10.6 million female retired workers in Table 7.4) receive higher benefits as a spouse or widow. The high percentage of the dually entitled among women, but not among men, reflects well-substantiated gender differences in lifetime work and earnings patterns, since to receive a retired-worker benefit that is equal to or greater than her spouse benefit, a woman must have average earnings over her lifetime equal to at least one-half of her husband's average lifetime earnings, if he is still alive, and equal to that of her husband if he is deceased.[23] It may surprise some to discover that the changing labor force commitment by women over the past decades has not diminished the percentage whose total income from social security remains tied to the work records of their retired or deceased husbands. In 1985 as in 1960, only 38 percent of female beneficiaries were receiving benefits solely as retired workers. The decline in total dependency—only 42.2 percent of female beneficiaries in 1985 were entitled solely as wives and widows compared to 56.4 percent in 1960—was offset entirely by an increase in dual entitlement from 4.6 percent of all female beneficiaries in 1960 to 20.2 percent in 1985.

The second panel of Table 7.4, which gives average benefit amounts for each beneficiary group, and the second column of Table 7.5, which shows average amounts for each portion of the benefit paid to dually entitled female retired-worker beneficiaries, demonstrate the importance of dual entitlement in raising social security benefits paid to wives and widows.[24] On average, benefits paid to female retired-worker beneficiaries were equal to 77 percent of those paid to male retired-worker beneficiaries. But this is an average for three groups—women receiving benefits solely as retired workers, dually entitled wives, and dually entitled widows—and the reduced secondary benefits paid to the last two groups are included in Table 7.4 benefit totals. By definition, dually entitled women are recipients of relatively low retired-worker benefits, but their total benefit is raised substantially by the payment of spouse or survivor benefits (Table 7.5). Widows, of course, received a greater absolute and relative supplementation since a widow's benefit is equal to 100 percent of her deceased husband's. But even when retired-worker benefits paid to women entitled solely on the basis of their own covered work record are distinguished from those of the dually entitled, these benefits are on average only 76 percent of the average paid to men.

What do data on benefit amounts imply about the role of social security in the maintenance of income as women are widowed? Consider the annual benefit amount that, based on benefit data in Table 7.4, would be paid to the average male retired-worker and his wife and to his widow, should he die. When these benefits are compared to a standard equivalency ratio—the poverty threshold—the peril of widowhood to the maintenance of the wife's economic position is apparent from the following illustration.

Status	Annual Benefit	Income-to-Needs Ratio
As a Couple	$9,691.20	1.49
As a Widow	6,460.80	1.25

The average couple would receive a benefit equal to at least 150 percent of the highest earner's (here and in most cases the husband's) benefit. Upon widowhood the benefit paid falls by one-third to an amount equal to 100 percent of the deceased husband's. But this fall is considerably more than the 20 percent prescribed by the poverty level as compatible with no change in economic well-being. Thus, despite assurance that social security payments will continue to be paid to widows of retired-worker beneficiaries, this program alone fails to eliminate entirely the economic peril arising from a husband's death.

Employer Pensions

Social security is only one way to protect women against the economic consequences of widowhood. Pensions from employers provide another insurance alternative, whose role in income maintenance as individuals retire and are widowed is expected to increase in the future. Protection through an employer pension can accrue to a widow either from her own pension coverage while working or from the continuation of her husband's pension income after his death. In the first instance—her receipt of pension income based on her own preretirement work—her husband's death will not threaten her income from this source. Because the purpose of this chapter is to discover how widowhood influences income, the focus in this section will be on how a wife can be protected against the loss upon his death of her husband's pension income. As was the case in the discussion of social security, it is helpful first to review the institutional and legal rules governing survivor benefits.

Sixty percent of men currently entering retirement receive benefits from an employer pension.[25] This is far greater than the 34 percent receipt rate among women retirees, who are less likely to have worked in jobs covered by a pension and, because of shorter job tenure, are less likely to meet vesting requirements if covered. The share of a couple's pension income derived from the husband's pension coverage is difficult to ascertain from available data since in most surveys couples are asked to report an amount received from all pensions combined. In addition, widows are asked for their total pension income without distinguishing those benefits they receive based on their own pension-covered work from any pension benefit inherited from their deceased husbands. It is likely, however, that the pension income of married couples is overwhelmingly that from the husbands' pensions. Among the SIPP eventual widows only half of the couples reporting pension income prior to the husbands' deaths received some of that income through the wives' own employment.

Pension plans are primarily of two types: defined-benefit plans and defined-contribution plans. In a defined-benefit plan, benefits paid to an individual are determined by a fixed formula; in a defined-contribution plan, an individual's benefit will be equal to that from an annuity purchasable with his or her accumulated pension contributions. Under both types of plans, it is possible for a pensioner to choose a joint-and-survivor pension, which continues benefits to a survivor, rather than a single-life pension that ceases when the pensioner dies. In fact, the Employee Retirement Income Security Act of 1974 (ERISA) requires pensions in the private sector to offer a joint-and-survivor benefit as the default form. Further, the default joint-and-survivor option must be at least a joint-and-one-half, or one which after the pensioner's death continues to pay no less than one-half of the married retiree's benefit amount to a surviving spouse. However, pension plans may and typically do offer more generous joint-and-survivor options either as the default or electable form. Under the 1984 Retirement Equity Act (REA), the spouse must agree in writing when a married worker chooses against the default option. Although pension plans covering workers in federal, state, and local government are not subject to the provisions of ERISA and the REA, even in these plans joint-and-survivor options that pay as much as 100% of the retiree's benefit to a widow are typically available.

The joint-and-survivor option is not chosen by all married retirees. It is estimated from data in the early 1980s that about 42 percent of male pensioners chose against a single-life annuity.[26] This population includes men whose pensions, taken many years earlier, were not subject to the joint-and-survivor provisions of ERISA and the REA. More recent estimates are that almost 60 percent of married male pensioners now choose that option.

While data on couples who choose this option indicate a substantial gain in income protection through pensions to wives, the protection pensions in fact provide to widows may be less. This is due both to the selective mortality of widows from among lower-income husbands and, for women of men who survive a long retirement period, to the provisions of typical joint-and-survivor options that reduce the real value of the option over time.

Selective mortality increases the risk of being widowed for women married to men who either have no pension or whose pensions are too low to provide much protection against poverty either before or after widowhood. Thus, the population of women who become widowed over any period of time is likely to be overrepresentative of this group. That this is the case is indicated again from RHS and SIPP data on eventual widows. Although the pension-option choice was not explicitly identified in the RHS, it is possible to infer that choice for men who died (that is, for eventual widows in Table 7.2) based on the pension questions asked of widows of respondents.[27] In SIPP, respondents who were already pension recipients in wave 4 of that survey were asked if they had taken a "reduced benefit in order to elect a survivor option." In neither survey is it possible to distinguish between a joint-and-survivor option and a period certain, both of which would appear as pension income to women widowed during the certain period in the RHS and both of which typically result in a reduced pension to the retiree (in SIPP).

In the RHS sample of eventual widows—those in which the husbands died between 1969 and 1979 and had received a pension prior to death—40 percent chose some form of survivor benefit. This is comparable to the percentage of all male pensioners that is estimated to have chosen such an option. This is unexpectedly low. First, the data for all pensioners does not distinguish by marital status, and one would expect data for married men only to indicate a higher percentage with some form of survivor option. Second, the data for all pensioners includes those retired not only during the 1970s, but in earlier decades as well when ERISA was not in effect. Hence the RHS results should be more heavily influenced than would general U.S. data by the effects of ERISA on the pension-option choice of the younger cohorts. Third, the RHS eventual widow sample includes only husbands who died relatively young—that is, respondents' deaths are only observed if they took place between fifty-eight and seventy-three years of age. If these men had anticipated their early death one would expect a higher percentage than among all retirees to choose a survivor option.

Similarly, the SIPP data does not coincide with the more optimistic view of pension protection to widows provided by recent evidence that a majority of men choose some form of survivor option. Among the SIPP eventual widows sample in which husbands received a pension and were alive in wave 4 (that is, the group that would answer the pension choice question), only 40 percent responded that some form of survivor benefit had been chosen.

It appears then that women who entered widowhood during the 1970s and more recently between 1984 and 1986 were less protected against income falls by the pension choice of their husbands than is indicated by data from other sources on all male pensioners. This suggests that the selective mortality of nonpensioned husbands or of those in which the choice of a survivor pension is less probable—those with low pension benefits—reduces the actual economic impact of ERISA and the REA.

Ironically, while men who are most likely to die earlier than average—and whose widows can anticipate a longer widowhood—may be less likely to have a pension or to take the survivor option, men who anticipate a longer than average survival may also choose against that option since the real value of the benefit paid to the survivor may be small by the time the worker dies. A pensioner must choose between the pension paid during his own lifetime with no survivor benefit and a reduced benefit while he lives in return for an assured income to his widow. While the loss in income to the husband begins immediately upon benefit receipt, inflation over his lifetime will erode the real value of the survivor's benefit for which current income was forgone.[28] For this reason, couples who anticipate a fairly long joint-survival period may opt for a single-life benefit and choose to insure the wife against the economic effects of widowhood in other ways.

The actual effect of the joint-and-survivor choice on the well-being of widows can be observed by comparing the pre- and post-widowhood incomes of women whose husbands chose a joint-and-survivor pension with those whose husbands' pensions ceased at their deaths. A comparison of RHS and SIPP data suggests the effect of ERISA on the economic well-being of widows of pensioners. Any conclusions, however, must be viewed with caution since the number of men who received a pension in SIPP and consequently died and whose widows continued in the survey is small. Table 7.6 shows mean incomes of couples in the two periods just prior to the husbands' deaths and of the widows in the first period after widowhood. All values are expressed in 1985 dollars. The income of widows is for the first income-reporting year after the husbands' deaths. This avoids the possibility of seriously underestimating the incomes of widows whose husbands died during the income reference year. Differences in the sample of pensioners—relatively young retirees in the RHS, men of all ages in

Table 7.6
The Mean Incomes of Couples and Widows by Pension-Option Choice
(in 1985 dollars)

Marital State and Pension Options	Pension Options	
	Single Life	*Joint-and-Survivor*
	Retirement History Survey	
Income of:		
Couple	$21,998	$28,786
Widow	10,012	17,083
Widow/couple	.46	.59
	Survey of Income and Program Participation	
Income of:		
Couple	$16,353	$16,016
Widow	6,344	8,429
Widow/couple	.39	.53

Source: Calculated by author from the RHS and SIPP.

SIPP—probably accounts for the lower income of couples in SIPP than the RHS. It is not the level that matters, however, but changes in income as women were widowed.

As expected, women whose husbands had chosen a single-life benefit had significantly lower income as widows than did women whose husbands had chosen the joint-and-survivor benefit ($10,012 versus $17,083 in the RHS). But women in both groups experienced a surprisingly large decline in average total income when they were widowed, with the RHS widows' mean incomes equal to 46 and 59 percent of their prewidowhood incomes for single-life and joint-and-survivor couples, respectively. The change was somewhat greater in the SIPP sample, though this could be accounted for by the difference in age composition of the two samples. Nevertheless, in both cases this change is well below the 20 percent judged by the poverty threshold as necessary to maintain the relative consumption levels of these one-person versus the former two-person households. Myers, Burkhauser, and Holden have investigated for the RHS sample how important the choice of a joint-and-survivor option was to the income of widows of joint-and-survivor beneficiaries. If the husbands of these women had elected a single-life benefit, their widows would have had only 40 percent of the couples' incomes and an annual income not much higher than that of widows who in fact inherited no pension benefits from their husbands. Whether this still remains true for more recent cohorts of widows remains to be investigated.[29]

The reason why joint-and-survivor benefits were so important to women in the second group and one reason why their incomes when married were greater is that pension benefits accounted for a far higher fraction of their prewidowhood income even though couples in which the husband had chosen a joint-and-survivor benefit already had pension benefits reduced by that election (data not shown). Because pension benefits were more important to the prewidowhood income of couples who did choose joint-and-survivor benefits, the loss of this pension income by the surviving widows would have resulted in a far greater decline in income for them than did in fact occur for widows of single-life pensioners. Nevertheless, for them and for women whose husbands did not choose a survivor's benefit, the pension safety net was not sufficient to ensure the same relative level of well-being into widowhood as they had enjoyed when married.

Inheritance of Assets

Data on income alone underestimate the resources available to couples and widows; such data alone may also overestimate the decline in economic resources as wives are widowed. Widows may inherit assets that do not earn income but contribute substantially to their economic security. For example, the economic value of home ownership is not reflected in income measures of well-being. Yet widows who are left with a house will be economically better off than those with no property since they do not pay rent and, at some later date, may convert the equity value in their home into an income-producing asset. Thus, it may be that the inclusion of inherited assets in a measure of well-being will show smaller changes in the economic status of women as they are widowed. Further, if the inheritance of assets is an important means of ensuring the economic well-being of widows, it may also be that men who elect a single-life pension do not, in fact, leave their wives with fewer resources than do men who elect a joint-and-survivor pension. The consideration of all assets held by couples both before and after the deaths of the husbands may indicate that those with less pension wealth compensate by holding assets in other forms when married and widowed.

Once again, data from the RHS provide information with which to explore this issue. The number of eventual widows in SIPP and the lack of information with which to estimate social security wealth make a similar analysis difficult. Table 7.7 considers the mean value of all bequeathable assets held by the two groups of pensioner couples just prior to the husbands' deaths. Different measures of assets are compared; the most comprehensive measure is the last, which includes the net value of financial wealth, property other than the home, equity in

Table 7.7
Mean Assets of Couples and Widows by Pension-Option Choice
(in 1986 dollars)

Financial and Property Assets and Marital State	Single-Life Couples	Joint-and-Survivor Couples
Excluding house and pensions		
As couple	$36,784	$62,278[a]
As widow	27,291	36,613
Including house		
As couple	84,941	122,203[a]
As widow	36,078	43,344
Including social security[d]		
As couple	156,359	191,255[a]
As widow	77,841	87,083
Including employer pension[e]		
As couple	190,230	243,828[b]
As widow	77,841	107,126[c]

[a] Difference between pensioner groups significant at the .10 level.
[b] Difference between pensioner groups significant at the .05 level.
[c] Difference between pensioner groups significant at the .01 level.
[d] Social security wealth is calculated using a 2% discount rate.
[e] Pension wealth is calculated using a 5% discount rate.

Source: Calculated by author from the Retirement History Study.

the home, social security wealth, and the wealth value of the employer pension. Wealth of the widow is all financial and property wealth she reports after her husband's death, plus the wealth value of estimated survivor social security and pension benefits. Pension and social security wealth values are calculated over their probable joint-survival period for couples and for widows, over their probable years of survival after their husbands' deaths.[30] Comparisons across wealth definitions indicate the importance of pensions in the asset portfolios of couples and widows.

As was the case for income alone, the wives of joint-and-survivor pensioners were economically better off both before and after their husbands' deaths. Single-life pensioner husbands did not on average accumulate more assets in other forms to offset their failure to provide for their widows through a survivor's pension. On the other hand, these men bequeathed to their widows a somewhat greater share of the nonpension, non-social security wealth they did hold (43 percent versus 35 percent for joint-and-survivor pensioners). The better-off position of joint-and-survivor widows was more closely tied to their inherited pension wealth. The lower share of prewidowhood nonpension assets that they inherited would alone have left them with no more wealth than single-life widows. As a result of their receipt of a joint-and-survivor pension, the decline in their wealth (including social security wealth) was approximately the same as that experienced by the widows of single-life pensioners (to 44 versus 41 percent of prewidowhood wealth).[31]

When all sources of wealth are considered, it is still the case that the economic resources of women declined upon widowhood. Using the approximately 20 percent reduction in resources allowable under income equivalency scales to judge the economic well-being of one- (versus two-) person households, income and wealth data tell the same story about relative status of these RHS couples before and after the husbands' deaths. The receipt of pensions by husbands and the choice of a joint-and-survivor option by those with the greatest pension wealth were the means by which these couples maintained the relative economic position (compared to the other couple group) of the wives as they were widowed. Nevertheless, total wealth bequeathed to the widows was less than that necessary to maintain prewidowhood levels of economic well-being during their expected years of widowhood. But whether the resources accruing to widows were unexpectedly small or couples had planned to consume the greater share of resources while both were alive requires further research before it can be concluded that the present sharing of resources over the couples' years of retirement and the wives' widowhood represents a less than optimal distribution of resources.

THE ECONOMIC WELL-BEING OF WIDOWS IN THE FUTURE

Despite dramatic gains in the economic status of elderly individuals, the transition from wife to widow remains an economically risky event for some women. The relatively low economic status of elderly widows remains a major policy concern in the United States. It is not surprising that this concern has led to changes in income transfer policies targeted on older widows. These include the increase in 1972 in social security survivor benefits from 82½ percent of the deceased spouse's benefit to 100 percent and the limit placed on the maximum reduction in widows' benefits due to early receipt. In addition, pension laws passed in 1974 and 1984 are expected to increase the percentage of husbands choosing pensions that continue to pay benefits to their widows.

These changes probably improved the well-being of wives in widowhood, since they increased the share of the couples' income that continued after the husbands' deaths. Women whose husbands' high retirement income enabled them to benefit most from these changes in social security and pension rules were the most secure as they entered widowhood. Yet the average fall in income upon widowhood remains above the amount that is estimated by the most widely used equivalency scale—the poverty threshold—as necessary to preserve the lifetime consumption stream of the smaller widowed household. That this fall is no smaller is in part conditioned by the joint-and-two-thirds offered by the social security system and the default joint-and-one-half pension option.

It may be that women will over time depend less on their husbands' social security earnings behavior and bequests of other assets and more on their own insurance as their labor force participation and pension coverage grow. But this is not certain. The discussion of Table 7.5 pointed out that despite greater percentages of women eligible for retired-worker benefits under social security, the percentage whose total benefit amount is tied to their husbands' earnings records has not changed. On the other hand, more liberal pension vesting and participation standards mandated by both ERISA and the REA will increase the likelihood of women meeting eligibility requirements for pension receipt. But, to the extent that women continue to work in small, low-wage, and nonunion firms without pension coverage, this expansion in eligibility will be slowed. In addition, it may be that some husbands will respond to the greater social security and pension income of their wives by reducing the share of their own pension and assets that they allocate to their wives as widows. This is likely, for example, if the current allocation of resources across the remaining lifetime of the household represents the preferences of husbands and wives for greater consumption when they both are alive.[32]

If widowhood itself continues to be an economic threat facing women as they age, greater attention is likely to be paid to the role of public policy in easing that transition in marital status. Expected increases in men and women's years of life will lengthen both their years of marriage and widowhood. It is likely, nevertheless, that widowhood will be a greater risk and occur at relatively young ages among the most vulnerable women—those whose low-wage husbands have lower pension wealth and higher health and personal-care needs, and who therefore may be less able to sustain long work careers.

For better-off couples, wives widowed at a later age may be unable to supplement inadequate income with market earnings and, perhaps, less likely to receive economic and physical assistance from children who themselves are approaching retirement. In this case, even a currently optimal allocation of resources over the lifetime of the couple and widow may prove inadequate to maintain the well-being of women during their longer widowhood. Public policy efforts may be necessary to encourage couples to give greater attention to the well-being of the wife as a widow. Unless public policy requires resource allocation to ensure adequate economic security in widowhood, facing longer joint-survival years in the future, couples may give even greater weight in their retirement income planning to their joint retirement period.

Several options are possible to encourage greater effort on the part of couples to insure the eventual widow against the income consequences of the husbands' deaths. Because a joint-and-one-half pension option allocates an income amount that appears insufficient to sustain real levels of consumption into widowhood, it may be necessary to mandate a more generous default form, such as a joint-and-two-thirds or a 100-percent survivor option in private plans. Studies using RHS data indicate that the choice of a more generous joint-and-survivor pension would make only a small difference in the income of couples, but could have a large impact on that of pensioners' widows.[33]

On the other hand, a longer survival period by husbands and wives will increase the threat to the real value of the widows' pensions from price increases both prior to and following the husbands' deaths. Some form of inflation protection may have to be devised to protect the value of the joint-and-survivor options before workers can be expected in greater number to choose the pension with a longer payout period.

In the RHS and SIPP samples, however, the risk of widowhood was greatest among women whose husbands had no or small pensions. These wives would not benefit from changes in laws governing the precise form of the joint-and-survivor option, although they may from any expansion in their own or their husbands' pension coverage and vesting.

For the wives of the men who chose a joint-and-survivor pension, their husbands' pension choice was a major factor in the relative level of their economic well-being as widows. These couples possessed greater assets in all forms but the husbands' pensions accounted for a larger share of total assets (22 percent versus 18 percent for single-life pensioners) and income. If their husbands had not chosen a joint-and-survivor pension, the absolute incomes and assets of these widows would have been equal to that of widows whose husbands did not bequeath them a pension, and the mean percentage reduction would have been far greater. But these data also suggest that husbands offset their bequests of a greater share of their pension wealth to their widows by reducing the share of other assets that remain to the widow. Thus, caution may be in order about attempts to improve the well-being of widows by mandating an increased sharing of pension wealth by husbands and wives.

The data presented in this chapter on the importance of social security to the well-being of all widows should cause serious concern over proposals to change the current social security program in ways that would reduce the certainty of benefits paid to widows of workers.[34] Social security has played a primary role in economic gains among the elderly; for the average widow these benefits represent the most important source of income and wealth. This is especially the case for wives of workers without pensions and wives of single-life beneficiaries. These benefits provide perhaps the most effective means by which the public sector can maintain and further influence the economic well-being of widows. The joint-and-two-thirds survivors' benefits, universal coverage, portability, and full indexing for inflation are not duplicated in any employer pension plan. Virtually no employer pension plan grants, as does OASI, survivor benefits to both divorced and current spouses. As long as the transition to widowhood requires a safety net that is not now voluntarily and universally provided by husbands, proposals for increasing the relative role of the private sector in the provision of income to retirees and their families should be examined closely for the certainty of the protection they provide to surviving widows.

NOTES

1. A. Wade, *Social Security Area Population Projections: 1988*. Actuarial Study No. 102 (Washington, D.C.: Office of the Actuary, Social Security Administration, 1988).

2. R. Schoen, "United States Marital Status Life Tables for Periods 1910–1975 and Cohorts Born 1888–1945" (Unpublished manuscript, Department of Sociology, University of Illinois, Urbana, 1983).

3. This projection is based on the intermediate demographic assumptions of the Social Security Administration. See U.S. Department of Health and Human Services, *Life Tables for the United States: 1900–2050*, Actuarial Study No. 87 (Washington, D.C.: U.S. Government Printing Office, 1982).

4. J. S. Siegel and C. M. Taeuber, "Demographic Dimensions of an Aging Population," in *Our Aging Society: Paradox and Promise*, ed. A. Pifer and L. Bronte (New York: W. W. Norton and Company, 1986), 79–110.

5. U.S. Department of Health and Human Services, *Social Security Bulletin: Annual Statistical Supplement, 1987* (Washington, D.C.: U.S. Government Printing Office, 1987), 75.

6. U.S. Department of Health and Human Services, *Social Security Bulletin: Annual Statistical Supplement, 1987*.

7. In this table women are classified into five different household catego-

ries—those who lived with their husbands in their own household, those who lived in the household of a relative (or in-law), those who were themselves the household head and had other relatives living with them (but not a husband), women living alone, and, finally, those who lived with nonrelatives only. In U.S. Census data, women living with nonrelatives only are treated as separate households, hence only their own income is considered in determining household poverty status. The vast majority of women living alone or with nonrelatives only are widows. This is also the case for female household heads who may have their children, siblings, or other relatives sharing their household.

8. E. M. Kitagawa and P. M. Hauser, *Differential Mortality in the United States* (Cambridge: Harvard University Press, 1973).

9. C. M. Ross, S. Danziger, and E. Smolensky, "Interpreting Changes in the Economic Status of the Elderly, 1949–1979," *Contemporary Policy Issues* 5 (April 1987): 98–112.

10. The income-to-needs ratio compares the income of a household to an equivalency scale—here the poverty threshold—that adjusts for differences in size and age composition across households. A decline in this ratio indicates that income has declined by more than the decline in consumption needs assumed to result from the husband's death.

11. For a description of the RHS, see L. M. Irelan, "Retirement History Study: Introduction," *Social Security Bulletin* 35 (November 1972): 3–8. For a description of the SIPP, see U.S. Bureau of the Census, *Survey of Income and Program Participation Users' Guide* (Washington, D.C.: U.S. Department of Commerce, 1987).

12. See K. C. Holden, R. V. Burkhauser, and D. A. Myers, "Income Transitions at Older Stages of Life: The Dynamics of Poverty," *The Gerontologist* 26 (June 1986): 292–97, for a fuller discussion of the RHS sample of "eventual" widows. This sample does not include all women at risk of widowhood since many of the husbands die eventually but their deaths after the surveys ended are not recorded. The RHS sample is more precisely defined as those couples in which the retirement-age husband died at a relatively early age (but after age 58) while the SIPP sample, which includes husbands of all ages, is more representative of the age of women at risk.

13. The period after first reported widowhood is used since poverty rates in the first survey a woman reports becoming a widow may be exaggerated due to the way in which income data are gathered. See R. V. Burkhauser, K. C. Holden, and D. A. Myers, "Widowhood and Poverty: The Role of Survey Procedures in Artificially Creating Poverty," *Demography* 23 (November 1986): 621–31. In both the RHS and SIPP, widows are asked about the income they received during the survey income-reference period. If the husband died during that period, his income will not be reported for those months he was alive. This underestimates the resources available in that year to the wife. The RHS fails to make any adjustment for this problem. In SIPP, widows are not asked about their husband's income, but the Census Bureau imputes the data. Holden discusses why these imputations give misleading results if used to measure income transitions upon widowhood. See K. C. Holden, "The Income Shock of Widowhood: Findings from the Survey of Income and Program Participation." Final Report to the American Association of Retired Persons, De-

cember 1988. Thus, for both surveys it is more accurate to use data reported in the next period of widowhood to measure income changes associated with widowhood and this is done in Table 2.

14. Only the income of the widow or of the couple is considered in measuring income and poverty in this chapter. Consequently, the poverty threshold reflects only the consumption needs of a single or two-person household, and in the case of SIPP is adjusted to a four-month accounting period. In 1985 the poverty thresholds for one- and two-person households headed by individuals 65 years of age or older were $5,156 and $6,503, respectively.

15. K. C. Holden, R. V. Burkhauser, and D. J. Feaster, "The Timing of Falls into Poverty after Retirement and Widowhood," *Demography* 25 (August 1988): 405–14.

16. The increase in poverty is sensitive to the particular equivalency scale adopted, that is, the estimated income required to finance the consumption of households of different sizes. The official poverty threshold implies that income can fall by approximately 30 percent when one member of the two-person household dies in order to leave the survivor equally well off. But Lazear and Michael estimate greater returns to scale in household consumption than is implied by the poverty thresholds for elderly one- and two-person households. This means that their equivalency scales indicate a smaller difference in the minimum income needs of two- and one-person households, thus that a larger percentage of single elderly individuals should in fact be described as poor. See E. P. Lazear and R. T. Michael, "Family Size and the Distribution of Real Per Capita Income," *American Economic Review* 70 (March 1980): 91–107.

17. A difficulty in gathering data on widows is that published data typically group the never-married, widowed, divorced, and separated into one "unmarried" category. Widowed women are over 80 percent of this group, however, and it is their characteristics that predominate.

18. The Health Insurance and Disability Insurance programs are excluded from the OASI benefit and cost data presented in this chapter.

19. V. Reno and S. Grad, "Special Anniversary Feature: Economic Security, 1935–85," *Social Security Bulletin* 48 (December 1985): 5–20.

20. These benefits of course represent valuable protection provided to the families of workers against their retirement or death. But because the focus of this chapter is on the economic well-being of elderly women, younger beneficiaries are not considered here.

21. Women who are eligible for their own retired-worker benefit, however, are protected during their working years by the disability insurance program, and their survivors may be eligible to receive benefits upon their death. In addition, a woman may receive social security benefits independent of the work and retirement behavior of her husband while women eligible only for a spouse benefit may do so only if their husbands are also social security beneficiaries. But the dual entitlement provisions make it likely that when retired, a two-earner couple will receive lower combined social security benefits than will a single-earner couple with the identical lifetime total earnings but with all earnings reported by the husband. For a discussion of the impact of dual entitlement on the total benefits of one- and two-earner couples see R. V. Burkhauser

and K. C. Holden, eds., *A Challenge to Social Security* (New York: Academic Press, 1982): chapters 1, 3, and 4.

22. Since eligibility for retired-worker status requires being at least 62 years of age, younger widows included in Table 4 are likely to become eligible for retired-worker benefits. About 5 percent of these widows were under 62 (4 percent of nondisabled widows and 65 percent of disabled widows). The higher percentage in the last group is due to their being eligible for benefits at age 50 and the automatic conversion to nondisabled widow status at age 65.

23. For spouse benefits this is only approximately the case because of the progressive benefit formula that provides a higher replacement rate to workers with low average earnings than for those with high average earnings.

24. Differences by sex are not due to the different treatment of women and men under this program—benefits are computed in precisely the same manner for female and male retired workers as must also be the case when benefits are computed for dependents and survivors of beneficiaries. This equal treatment by earnings-related benefit programs, of course, does not mean equal benefit amounts. Lower benefits paid to husbands and widowers than to wives and widows reflect gender difference in labor market earnings.

25. D. C. Snyder, "Pension Status of Recently Retired Workers on Their Longest Job: Findings from the New Beneficiary Survey," *Social Security Bulletin* 49 (August 1986): 5–21.

26. L. J. Kotlikoff and D. E. Smith, *Pensions in the American Economy* (Chicago: University of Chicago Press, 1983), 99. This includes men who chose a period-certain annuity, that is one that continues for a guaranteed number of years even if the recipient should die sooner. In the RHS and SIPP data discussed below it is impossible to distinguish between a period-certain and joint-and-survivor annuity.

27. Beginning in 1975 recent widows were asked questions about receipt of income from their husbands' pensions and all women in 1979 were asked the source of their pension income, the number of pensions for which they were eligible, and whether their primary pension was from their own work or that of their husband. For most women we know whether they were eligible for a pension from their own covered employment and, therefore, whether their 1979 pension was based on their own or their husband's. For a description of how the pension-option choice was determined see K. C. Holden and R. V. Burkhauser, "Pensioners' Annuity Choice: Is the Well-Being of Widows Considered?" Institute for Research on Poverty Discussion Paper no. 802–86 (Madison: Institute for Research on Poverty, University of Wisconsin, 1986).

28. Private and public pensions rarely adjust fully for inflation although some plans provide partial indexing. See R. L. Clark and D. A. Sumner, "Inflation and the Real Income of the Elderly: Recent Evidence and Expectations for the Future," *The Gerontologist* 25 (April 1985): 146–52. If pensions are not fully indexed for inflation during the husband's lifetime, the widow will receive a benefit whose real value is well below the percentage specified in the original pension option chosen at the husband's retirement.

29. D. A. Myers, R. V. Burkhauser, and K. C. Holden, "The Transition from Wife to Widow," *Journal of Risk and Insurance* 54 (December 1987): 752–59.

30. To calculate the wealth value of the pension, an assumption had to be

made about the exact form of the pension elected, the actuarial adjustment imposed by the pension plan, and an appropriate discount rate. For a discussion of these assumptions, see Myers, Burkhauser, and Holden, "Transition from Wife to Widow." The calculation of social security wealth is more straightforward, since we know the benefits for which husbands and wives are eligible and that the survivor benefit offered is a joint-and-two-thirds option. Because social security benefits are adjusted by changes in prices, a 2 percent discount rate was used in calculating its asset value, and a 5 percent discount rate in the case of pension wealth. Benefit provisions in force at the time the husband first received pension benefits were used to calculate the future stream of social security benefits.

31. Because the distribution of assets is skewed toward high asset holders, a comparison of medians shows a somewhat greater decline in assets held by widows compared to those of couples.

32. For example, in making the pension-option choice couples may choose an absolute level of consumption for the wives as widows, devoting any additional resources to their own joint enjoyment. Higher pension income of the wife will reduce the incentive for husbands to allocate a share of their own pension income to their widows. Widows who have their own pensions will be no better off than they would otherwise have been. In this case the income decline with widowhood will be greater, since the difference between the couples' incomes (which now includes the husbands' higher single-life pension) and the widows' incomes will be larger.

33. For the impact of these different options see Myers, Burkhauser, and Holden, "Transition from Wife to Widow."

34. Several plans have been proposed for substituting a private insurance type pension for all or part of the current social security system. See articles and discussant comments in *Cato Journal* 3 (Fall 1983).

8 LONG-TERM CARE FOR THE ELDERLY

Dorothy P. Rice

The population of the United States is aging and, among the old, becoming increasingly feminine. Life expectancy of females born in 1985 was 78.2 years, or seven years longer than that of men. The disparity between survival of men and women in the United States has widened significantly since the turn of the century. The current seven-year gap contrasts with the two- to three-year gap in the first three decades of the century (1900–1930). Although the gender gap in life expectancy appears to be decreasing slightly, a substantial difference is projected for the future.

Living longer has its blessings and benefits, but also may mean illness, disability, and dependence. Aging is a process that continues over the entire life span. Old age is shaped by many forces throughout the life cycle, including educational, economic, health, occupational, and environmental factors. A major question facing our aging society is, what effect longevity has on health status and quality of life.

Although many elderly people lead productive lives and are economically secure, there are substantial numbers, especially among older women, who struggle with severe health problems, economic hardships, and loneliness. As women move through their life cycle, what economic and other problems do they face when they take on the burden of providing long-term care for their relatives or when they become ill and disabled and recipients of long-term care?

This chapter focuses on long-term care for the elderly with special emphasis on older women. It describes the changing demographic structure of the population and the socioeconomic and health characteristics of the elderly as background for understandinig the scope of the long-term care problem. The provision of long-term care is examined from the perspectives of society and of women as caregivers and recipients of long-term care. The emerging policy issues and challenges for long-term care will then be addressed.

DEMOGRAPHIC SHIFTS

The population of the United States has shifted in recent years in the number and the proportion of the total that are age 65 and over. At the turn of the century, the nation's 3.1 million elderly people comprised 4.0 percent of the total population (Table 8.1). Forty years later, the number of elderly tripled to 9 million and constituted 6.8 percent of the nation's total. By 1980, the elderly population almost tripled again, to 25.7 million persons, representing 11.3 percent of the total population. By the year 2030, it is likely that one out of five Americans will be sixty-five years old or older, and the total number of elderly is projected to be 64.6 million.

Within the age group 65 years old and over, the number and proportion of the very old also have increased rapidly. In 1900, less than 125,000 persons were eighty-five years old and over, comprising 4 percent of the elderly; by 1980, there were 2.3 million persons in this age group, or 9 percent of the elderly. In the period from 1980 to 2030, the very old population is projected to almost quadruple to 8.6 million and will comprise 13 percent of the elderly at the end of the period.

There also has been a significant shift in the sex composition of the population, especially among the aged. In 1900, men outnumbered women. By 1940, there were slightly more women than men. In 1980, 51 percent of the 228 million people in the United States were women. Among the elderly, women comprised 49 percent of the total in 1900. By 1980, 60 percent of aged elderly people were women; this proportion is projected to decline slightly to 58% by 2030.

The very old population, age 85 and over, has been and will continue to be predominantly female. In 1940, 57 percent of the 370,000 very old population were women. In 1980, 70 percent of the 2.3 million persons in this age group were women; by 2030 this proportion will rise slightly to 71 percent.

LIFE EXPECTANCY

The demographic shifts in the population are due in part to improvements in mortality rates and increasing longevity. Since the turn of the century, twenty-five years have been added to life expectancy at birth for men and thirty years for women (Table 8.2). Based on mortality experience in 1900, a man born in that year could expect to live an average of 46.3 years, women 48.3 years. By 1985, life expectancy at birth rose to 71.2 years for men and 78.2 years for women, a differential of seven years. In 1900, a man age 65 would expect to live 11.5 additional years to reach age 76.5 years and a woman age 65 would

Table 8.1

Population of the United States by Age and Sex, Selected Years, 1900–2040 (in thousands)

Year	All Ages	Age 65 and Over			
		Total	65-74	75-84	85 and Over
All Individuals					
1900	76,094	3,099	2,200	772	123
1940	131,122	9,031	6,367	2,294	370
1950	152,271	12,397	8,493	3,314	590
1960	180,671	16,675	11,053	4,681	940
1970	204,879	20,085	12,486	6,166	1,432
1980	227,658	25,708	15,648	7,787	2,274
Projections[a]					
1990	249,657	31,697	18,035	10,349	3,313
2000	267,955	34,921	17,677	12,318	4,926
2010	283,238	39,196	20,318	12,326	6,551
2020	296,597	51,422	29,855	14,486	7,081
2030	304,807	64,580	34,535	21,434	8,611
2040	308,559	66,988	29,272	24,882	12,834
Males					
1900	38,867	1,565	1,124	441[b]	(NA)
1940	66,352	4,410	3,162	1,089	159
1950	75,849	5,857	4,091	1,523	243
1960	89,320	7,542	5,133	2,043	366
1970	100,266	8,405	5,458	2,450	497
1980	110,834	10,363	6,787	2,886	691
Projections[a]					
1990	121,518	12,638	7,863	3,856	919
2000	130,491	13,763	7,773	4,640	1,350
2010	138,029	15,609	9,112	4,706	1,791
2020	144,457	21,211	13,574	5,695	1,942
2030	147,905	26,934	15,890	8,573	2,471
2040	149,118	27,430	13,533	10,093	3,804
Females					
1900	37,227	1,534	1,076	458[b]	(NA)
1930	65,770	4,621	3,205	1,205	211
1950	76,422	6,541	4,402	1,792	347
1960	91,352	9,133	5,921	2,639	574
1970	104,613	11,680	7,028	3,717	935
1980	116,824	15,345	8,861	4,901	1,583

Table 8.1 (continued)

Year	All Ages	Age 65 and Over			
		Total	*65-74*	*75-84*	*85 and Over*
		Females			
Projections[a]					
1990	128,139	19,059	10,172	6,494	2,393
2000	137,464	21,159	9,905	7,678	3,576
2010	145,209	23,588	11,206	7,621	4,761
2020	152,140	30,211	16,280	8,792	5,139
2030	156,902	37,645	18,644	12,861	6,140
2040	159,442	39,559	15,739	14,790	9,030

[a] Based on middle series.
[b] Includes ages 85 and over.

Sources: United States Bureau of the Census, *Current Population Reports,* Series P-25, Nos. 311, 511, 917, and 952.

live 12.2 additional years to 77.2 years; by 1985, life expectancy at age 65 increased to 14.6 years for men and 18.6 years for women.

Projections for the future assume an increasing life expectancy for both men and women, with a continuation of the gender differential. Life expectancy at birth for men is projected to increase to 75 years by 2040, for women to 83.1 years, a differential of 8.1 years. At age 65, life expectancy is projected to increase to 17.1 years for men and 22.6 years for women. These are the "middle series" projections of the U.S. Bureau of the Census.[1]

SOCIOECONOMIC CHARACTERISTICS OF THE ELDERLY POPULATION

The demographic shifts described above indicate clearly that the population of the United States, as in most industrialized societies, is aging and the aged are predominantly female. Not only do women live longer than men, they tend to marry men older than themselves, so they are often widowed, and they are unlikely to remarry once widowed. In 1985, two-fifths of the noninstitutionalized women age 65 to 74 and two-thirds of those age 75 and over were widowed. In contrast, less than one-tenth of the men age 65 to 74 and a fourth of those age 75 and over were widowed.[2] An increasing number of older persons live alone rather than in family settings. In 1950, 14 percent of all elderly persons lived alone; by 1985 this proportion increased to 30 percent. The disparity in the marital status of older men and women re-

Table 8.2
Life Expectancy at Specified Ages by Sex, Selected Years, 1900-2040

| | At Birth | | At Age 65 | |
Year	Males	Females	Males	Females
1900	46.3	48.3	11.5	12.2
1940	60.8	65.2	12.1	13.6
1950	65.6	71.1	12.8	15.0
1960	66.6	73.1	12.8	15.8
1970	67.1	74.8	13.1	17.0
1980	70.0	77.5	14.1	18.3
1985	71.2	78.2	14.6	18.6
Projections[a]				
1990	71.6	79.2	15.0	19.5
2000	72.9	80.5	15.7	20.5
2010	73.8	81.5	16.1	21.2
2020	74.2	82.0	16.5	21.7
2030	74.6	82.5	16.8	22.1
2040	75.0	83.1	17.1	22.6

[a] Based on middle series.

Sources: National Center for Health Statistics, *Health, United States, 1986*, DHHS Pub. No. 87-1232, Table 12, p. 84; and Bureau of the Census, "Projections of the Population of the United States, by Age, Sex, and Race 1983 to 2080," *Current Population Reports*, Series P-25, No. 952.

sults in significant differences in their living arrangements. In 1985, three out of four elderly men were married and living with their wives, but only two-fifths of the elderly women were married and living with their husbands.

Almost 9 million elderly people live alone and 2 million of these persons are old, alone, and poor. About two-thirds of the elderly poor living alone are widows who often lack the essential economic, physical, and emotional support that are essential to maintain their independence and the quality of their lives.[3]

As persons age, they tend to leave the labor force or to work fewer hours. When they retire, their pensions are generally lower than their prior earnings. Thus there is a pattern of declining income for older persons. The lower incomes of the elderly are associated with factors over which they have little control: their sex and race, the health and survival of their spouses, their health, their ability to work, their educational attainment (which is strongly associated with lifetime earnings), their investments, and their assets.[4] For men, income tends to increase with age until about age 55, when significant numbers retire and income levels begin to decline steadily. Median income levels for women begin at lower levels than for men and start to decline at age 50. In 1985, the median income of men 65 years and older was $10,900, about 73 percent higher than that for elderly women ($6,313).[5]

Labor-force participation decreases rapidly with increasing age. In October 1987, 68 percent of the 55- to 64-year-old men and 44 percent of the women in the same age group were in the labor force. For persons age 65 and over, however, these figures dropped to 17 percent for men and 8 percent for women.[6]

Social Security benefits are the largest source of income for the elderly; 91 percent of the elderly population receive benefits. More than half of the population age 65 and over depend on Social Security for over half their income, and a fifth receive 90 percent or more of their income from this source.[7]

In 1985, 3.5 million persons, or 12.6 percent of elderly persons, lived in poverty.[8] (This rate represents a significant improvement from 1967 when the poverty rate was 29.5 percent.) Poverty among the elderly is accounted for partly by the substantial reduction in income occurring at retirement and by the likelihood of major expenditures for health care. Poverty is disproportionately high among elderly women (17 percent) and blacks (36 percent). The current government definition of poverty does not include the value of in-kind transfers under income. If the value of in-kind food, housing, and medical care transfers received by the low-income elderly population were regarded as income, the poverty rate would be reduced.[9] There is serious disagreement, however, over the inclusion of medical care, especially institutional care, in determining poverty status.

The demographic and socioeconomic characteristics of the elderly are associated with their health status and use of health care services. Therefore, these statistics serve as a basis for understanding the magnitude of the problem of providing medical and long-term services to the increasing number of persons who live to an age at which they are vulnerable to chronic illnesses that can cause limited or total disability.

HEALTH STATUS OF THE ELDERLY

A variety of measures apply to the health of the elderly: their own perception of their health, limitation in their usual activities, and restricted and bed-disability days. Table 8.3 summarizes these health status measures by age and sex. In 1986, 30 percent of the noninstitutionalized elderly reported that their health was fair or poor compared with other people their age. Approximately 33 million persons, 14 percent of the noninstitutionalized population, reported limitations of activity

Table 8.3
Health Status and Utilization Measures by Sex and Age, 1986

Measure	All Ages	Under 18	18-44	45-64	65 and Over
Percent feeling fair or poor, total	10.0	2.7	5.7	18.1	29.9
Males	9.1	2.5	5.1	17.4	29.2
Females	11.0	2.8	6.3	18.9	30.4
Percent limited in activity, total	14.0	5.0	8.7	23.2	38.8
Males	13.4	5.8	9.2	22.0	37.2
Females	14.5	4.2	8.1	24.2	40.0
Percent unable to carry on major activity, total	3.9	0.4	2.2	8.6	10.7
Males	4.4	0.4	2.7	10.6	11.3
Females	3.5	0.4	1.8	6.8	10.2
Restricted activity days per person, total	15.2	9.9	11.6	20.6	32.1
Males	13.1	9.3	10.1	18.1	27.6
Females	17.2	10.4	13.1	22.9	35.2
Bed disability days per person, total	6.5	4.6	4.7	8.3	14.9
Males	5.4	4.2	4.1	6.9	11.6
Females	7.7	5.1	5.3	9.6	17.2
Physician contacts per person, total	5.4	4.2	4.6	4.7	9.1
Males	4.5	4.2	3.4	5.4	8.4
Female	6.2	4.2	5.7	7.6	9.5
Short-stay hospital discharges per 100 persons, total	11.8	4.8	10.8	14.2	27.5
Males	10.1	4.8	6.5	16.1	29.8
Females	13.4	4.8	15.0	12.5	25.9
Average length of hospital stay, total	6.6	5.7	6.3	6.8	8.5
Males	7.2	4.8	7.0	7.2	8.5
Females	6.1	6.7	4.6	6.3	8.6

Source: National Center for Health Statistics, "Current Estimates from the National Health Interview Survey: United States, 1986," *Vital and Health Statistics,* Series 10, No. 164, DHHS Pub. No. (PHS) 87-1592 (Washington, D.C.: Government Printing Office, October 1987).

due to chronic diseases. Not surprisingly, the number suffering limitation of activity increases with age: 5 percent of the total under 18 years, 9 percent at ages 18–44 years, 23 percent at ages 45–64 years, and 39 percent at age 65 and over.[10]

Men tend to report slightly better health than women. The exception is the percent reporting inability to carry out their major activity due to chronic conditions. At each age group 18 years and over, a higher proportion of men than women report that they are unable to carry on their major activity.

The incidence of chronic illness increases with age and becomes a major cause of disability requiring medical care. The prevalence of specific chronic conditions causing limitations of activity among the noninstitutionalized elderly population is high. In 1986, 48 percent had arthritis, 39 percent had hypertensive disease, and 28 percent had heart disease. Many elderly persons suffered from impairments: 30 percent had hearing impairments, 10 percent had visual impairments, and 17 percent had orthopedic impairments. Among women 75 years and over, the prevalence of these chronic conditions is significantly higher: arthritis—63 percent, hypertensive disease—48 percent, heart disease—33 percent, hearing impairments—34 percent, visual impairments—13 percent, orthopedic impairments—13 percent.[11]

USE OF MEDICAL CARE SERVICES

Use of health-care services increases with age. For example, elderly people make more frequent visits to physicians than younger people. In 1986, noninstitutionalized elderly people had a physician contact (other than visits to hospital inpatients) an average of 9.1 times a year, in contrast to an average 4.7 times for persons 45–64 (Table 8.3). About 81 percent of elderly men and 86 percent of elderly women had a physician contact within the preceding year. Only about 5 percent had not seen a physician for five or more years.

Elderly people are hospitalized more frequently and stay in the hospital longer than younger persons. There were 7.6 million elderly discharges from nonfederal short-stay hospitals in 1986 with a total of 65 million days of care. More than one-quarter (27.2 percent) of all people discharged were elderly and two-thirds (35.3 percent) of all days spent in hospitals were by elderly people. Less than 5 percent of the civilian noninstitutionalized people were 75 years of age or older in 1986, yet they accounted for 13 percent of the discharges and 16 percent of all the days of care. Elderly men have a higher rate of hospital discharges, but the average length of stay for women is slightly higher.

For elderly patients discharged from short-stay hospitals in 1985, the ranking of conditions and surgical procedures differed from the prevalence rates reported by the elderly in household interviews. The five highest discharge rates per 1,000 aged persons by first-listed major diagnostic category were: diseases of the circulatory system (including heart disease, hypertension, and cerebrovascular disease)—113, diseases of the digestive system (including cholelithiasis, ulcers, and hernia)—44, neoplasms—42, diseases of the respiratory system—39, and injuries and poisoning (including fractures)—28. A total of 36.8 million procedures were performed in short-stay hospitals in 1984. Of this total, 11 million, or 30 percent, were for persons age 65 and over. About 650,000 C.A.T. Scans were performed on the elderly, the most frequently listed procedure. There were 157,000 extractions of lens and 139,000 insertions of prosthetic lens. Other frequent procedures among the elderly included endoscopy of large intestine (269,000) and prostatectomy (284,000).[12]

The prevalence of chronic conditions in nursing homes presents still a different picture. The 1977 National Nursing Home Survey reported almost all residents had one or more chronic conditions or impairments (99 percent), with an average of 3.9 chronic conditions per resident. The most prevalent condition suffered by residents was arteriosclerosis (48 percent), followed by heart trouble (34 percent), senility (32 percent), chronic brain syndrome (25 percent), and arthritis and rheumatism (25 percent).[13]

Not surprisingly, older persons who suffer from chronic and disabling conditions are high utilizers of medical resources. The elderly with chronic activity limitation had 8.7 visits to physicians per year, in contrast with 4.3 visits for persons with no activity limitation. They had 41.2 hospitalizations per 100 elderly persons per year, in contrast with 14.8 for those with no limitation of activity. The 46 percent of elderly people who were limited in activity because of a chronic condition accounted for 63 percent of physician contacts, 71 percent of hospitalizations, and 82 percent of all the days that older people spent in bed because of health conditions.[14]

According to the 1985 National Nursing Home Survey 1.3 million elderly persons, about 5 percent of the total age 65 and over, resided in nursing homes, but the rates of institutionalization increase significantly with age: 1.2 percent of the 65–74-year-olds, 5.8 percent of those 75–84 years, and 22 percent of those 85 years and over. Nursing home residents are also predominantly female, comprising 75 percent of the total.[15] Females age 85 and over consitute 46 percent of total elderly residents. Median length of stay for all men in nursing homes was 488 days compared witht 643 days for women.[16]

PROVISION OF LONG-TERM CARE

In addition to medical care, many elderly persons who have lost some capacity for self-care require a wide range of social, personal, and sup-

portive services. Long-term care is defined as physical care over a prolonged period for those persons incapable of sustaining themselves
without this care.[17] Long-term care is viewed as a spectrum of services
responding to different needs along a trajectory of chronic illness and
disability. To address the multiple and varied long-term care needs of
the aged population, services must cross the boundaries between income maintenance and health, social, and housing programs.[18]

The federal and state governments provide funds for long-term care,
mainly under the Medicare and Medicaid programs. Medicare benefits,
however, are designed to cover acute care services for the elderly and
disabled, and only a very small portion of their long-term care needs
are met by this program. Total Medicare spending for long-term care
is estimated at $2 billion (4 percent of total expenditures) in fiscal year
1983, of which three-quarters are for home health benefits and the remaining quarter for skilled nursing home care.

Medicaid spending for long-term care is considerably higher, estimated at $15.4 billion in fiscal year 1983, almost half of total Medicaid
expenditures in that year. Medicaid long-term care services are mainly
for institutional care—skilled nursing facilities, intermediate care facilities, and intermediate care facilities for the mentally retarded. Only
$600 million was spent for home health services under Medicaid in
fiscal year 1983, accounting for less than 4 percent of the total long-
term care spending in that year under the program.[19]

Other government programs fund some long-term care services, but
their expenditures are small relative to Medicare and Medicaid. Included are the Veterans Administration, social services block grant funds,
Older Americans Act, Supplemental Security Income payments, the
Developmental Disabilities Assistance and Bill of Rights Act, and the
alcohol, drug abuse, and mental health block grant funds.

Nursing home care is by far the most expensive part of long-term
care. Nursing home care expenditures in 1987 amounted to $41.6 bil-
lion. About 1 percent was paid by Medicare, 1 percent by private insurance, 5 percent by the Veterans Administration, 42 percent by Medicaid, and the remaining 51 percent was paid by the patient or his or
her relatives.[20]

Even though nursing home care is the largest health-related financial
burden most elderly people will face, many think they are already protected against its high cost. A national survey conducted in 1985 by
AARP revealed that 79 percent of the population at large and 70 percent of the elderly believed that Medicare would cover a long nursing
home stay. Half of those with Medicare and supplemental insurance
policies believed that they were covered, which is not the case.[21]

For elderly people with out-of-pocket expenses of over $2,000 in 1980,
nursing home costs were responsible for over 80 percent of these costs,
indicating that nursing home care is a very large burden for about 1

million elderly persons subject to very high financial liabilities.[22] Since the average annual cost of a nursing home stay in 1987 is $22,000, many elderly people find themselves in a financial bind. Many enter nursing homes as private pay patients and "spend down" rapidly, leaving them few assets. They then become eligible for Medicaid.

With the growing numbers of chronically ill elderly and disabled adults, increasing consideration is being given to alternatives in providing long-term care services and to preventing the need for institutionalization. A variety of recently developed community-based services, such as day care, home health, Meals-on-Wheels, and respite care, are aimed at maintaining the independence of the aged or disabled person at home, in order to avoid institutional placement, which is often viewed as a measure of last resort.

A successful local model for maintaining the frail elderly in their own community, preferably in their homes, is On Lok, which serves the severely impaired elderly in San Francisco's Chinatown-North Beach-Polk Gulch community. It is one of the nation's most successful and well established prepaid, capitated programs for delivering long-term care to the elderly. On Lok provides an integrated package of medical and social services, including transportation to a day care center, up to three meals a day, therapy, and hospitalization. The program also provides accommodations for the community's low-income elderly. The program is supported by Medicare, Medicaid, and the individual. With support from the Robert Wood Johnson Foundation, On Lok is exploring the feasibility of extending its risk-based, consolidated model of long-term care services to the frail elderly persons in other parts of the country.[23]

Despite the availability of a variety of health and social services, families, friends, and neighbors still provide the bulk of long-term care to the aged and disabled in the United States. As much as 60 to 80 percent of the care presently received by the disabled and aged comes from these sources.[24] For every elderly person residing in a nursing home, it is estimated that there are twice as many persons living in the community requiring similar levels of care. The ability to maintain independent living is a function of the complex interrelationships among many factors, including the extent of disability and functional impairment; sociodemographic characteristics of the individual, such as age, sex, and living arrangement; availability of another person to provide needed assistance; and the availability of community services and their accessibility to people who need them.

ROLE OF WOMEN IN LONG-TERM CARE

The growth in the number of persons who survive into their eighties and nineties makes it increasingly likely that many elderly persons, especially women, will have a surviving aged parent who requires long-term care. As a woman ages, she may take on the role of provider or caregiver for her parents or her spouse. She may also have a chronic condition and be a recipient of long-term care. Both of these situations have their problems and significant monetary and personal costs.

Midlife and older women perform an essential caregiving function in American society which has a significant impact upon both the labor force participation of women and the rate of poverty among them. Of the approximately 2.2 million caregivers providing unpaid assistance to 1.2 million frail elderly at home, 72 percent are women. The average age of all caregivers is 57 years.[25] The most common relationship of caregiver to the recipient of care is that of daughter or wife. Almost 29 percent of all caregivers are daughters and 23 percent are wives of the recipient. Another 20 percent of the carergivers are more distant female relatives or nonrelatives. More wives than husbands provide care to disabled elderly spouses, reflecting the fact that women outlive men by an average of seven years.

The caregiving role significantly affects labor force participation of women. More than 8 percent of all female caregivers quit work to become a caregiver. Of those who continue to work, more than 20 percent worked fewer hours, rearranged schedules, or took time off without pay to fulfill their caregiving responsibilities. Of the 1.6 million women who are caregivers, 37 percent are poor or near poor and 44 percent are in fair or poor health.

For working women who assume the responsibility of caregiving, acute conflicts may arise between their own lives and their elderly parents' lives. Some quit their jobs, but many struggle to maintain their jobs while functioning in their caregiving role. A Philadelphia team of investigators identified these as "women in the middle."[26] Employers are beginning to recognize the stress placed on many of their female employees whose productivity may be affected, especially when an emergency situation arises. An employee benefit, known as "elder-care," is emerging to assist employees. It may take various forms, including information and referral services, flexible hours, and company-sponsored day care centers for both children and elderly parents. Some companies have flexible spending plans whereby employees can set aside a certain amount of funds that is not taxed to help pay for care of their parents while they are at work. Insurance coverage for long-term care allows employees to buy nursing home insurance for themselves, their spouses, or their parents at group rates.[27]

Women who need and receive long-term care services at home face vastly different problems from those who are caregivers. For those with chronic illnesses or other impairments, inability to perform the activities of daily living (such as walking, bathing, dressing, eating, using the toilet) or the instrumental activities of daily living (such as meal preparation, shopping, managing money, using the telephone, and doing housework) may be an indicator of high risk for in-home assistance or long-term care in an institution. The Supplement on Aging of the 1984 National Health Interview Survey reported that the most frequent limitation on the group of activities of daily living among the elderly was difficulty in walking, ranging from 13 percent for the 65–74-year-old men to 32 percent for men age 85 and over; for women, 15 percent of the 65–74-year-olds had difficulty in walking and the percentage increased to 43 percent for those age 85 and over. Fourteen percent of men age 85 and over 18 percent of the women of the same age had difficulty dressing. Elderly women at all ages had more difficulty using the toilet and controlling urination. For all the instrumental activities of daily living, except talking on the telephone, women were more likely than men to have difficulty with these groups of activities.[28] This differential could be partly due to the somewhat older age distribution of women than men.

Elderly people who have difficulties described above often require assistance of another person to enable them to function at home. Information is available from the 1982 National Long-Term Care Survey that showed that of the 4.4 million disabled elderly persons in the community, almost three-fourths (3.2 million persons) relied exclusively on nonpaid sources. Almost 1 million (21 percent) received both paid and nonpaid care, and only 240,000 (5.5 percent) used paid care only.[29] The survey also showed that a large proportion (two-thirds) of total private expenditures for home-based care went for nonmedical assistance ranging from payments for care that might otherwise be provided by informal caregivers to payments for supplementation of care that was provided by family and friends. The amount of payment was directly related to family income. It is clear that prolonged, high out-of-pocket expenditures for home-based care may result in a severe financial burden and ultimately become a risk factor for institutionalization.

A 1986 National Survey of Problems Facing Elderly People Living Alone reported that three out of ten elderly persons say they face at least one serious problem in their lives, citing too many medical bills and not having enough money on which to live. Those in poor health and below the poverty line are most likely to face these problems. The consequences of such problems create major difficulties in their lives, including feeling depressed, fear of letting people into their homes, and going without medical help when they think they need it. Many elderly people also have profound fears about the future, including fear of being in poor health, not having enough money to live on, and having to depend on others. Those in poor health, those below the poverty line, women, and those not living with a spouse are most vulnerable to these fears about the future.[30]

FUTURE NEEDS FOR LONG-TERM CARE

Fears about the future concern the individual aged person and society at large. The implications of the aging of the population on the demand for long-term care and on public policy are significant. The number of the very old is increasing rapidly, the average period of diminished vigor will probably rise, chronic diseases will probably occupy a larger proportion of our life span, and the needs for medical and long-term care in later life are likely to increase substantially.[31] Another theory holds that improvements in life-styles will delay the onset of disability and chronic disease and morbidity at the older ages.[32] There is considerable controversy, however, regarding the latter theory of "compression of morbidity".[33]

Whatever else happens in the future, the projected changes in the size and age distribution of the population alone would have a significant impact on the use and cost of medical and long-term care services. The projections shown in Table 8.4 are based on age-sex-specific rates of health status, utilization, and costs in 1980 and applied to population projections for the sixty-year period 1980–2040.[34] The total population is projected to increase 41 percent, while the elderly will increase 160 percent. The total number of persons limited in activities of daily living is projected to more than double; the elderly with limitations will more than triple. The impact of the aging of the population on physician visits and hospitalization will be high. In 2040, 40 percent of the days of hospital care are projected to be used by those age 75 and over, compared with 20 percent in 1980. The effect on nursing home residents, however, will be greatest: the number is projected to more than triple, increasing from 1.5 million in 1980 to 5.2 million in 2040 to meet the needs of the aging population. Finally, 11 percent of the population age 65 and over consumed 29 percent of total health expenditures; by 2040 the elderly are projected to comprise 21 percent of the population and almost all of the expenditures will be made in their behalf.

Another set of projections show that, in 1985, 5.2 million elderly noninstitutionalized persons were mildly to severely disabled with need for assistance and special aids to maintain independence. This figure is projected to reach 7.2 million by the turn of the century, 10.1 million by 2020, and 14.4 million by 2050.[35]

Although changes in the levels of morbidity, the availability of therapies and technologies, the cost of care, and social and economic conditions will undoubtedly occur, the above projections can serve as parameters of health status, and medical and long-term care use for planning future needs for these services.

Table 8.4
**Current and Projected Population, Limitations in ADL, Medical Care
Utilization and Expenditures, by Age, 1980–2040**

| | | | 65 and Over | | |
Characteristic and Year	All Ages	Under 65	*Total*	*65-74*	*75 and Over*
Population (thousands)					
1980	232,669	206,777	25,892	15,627	10,265
2000	273,949	237,697	36,252	18,334	17,918
2020	306,931	254,278	52,653	30,093	22,560
2040	328,503	261,247	67,256	29,425	37,831
Persons with limitation in activities of daily living (thousands)					
1980	3,142	1,362	1,780	648	1,132
2000	4,509	1,734	2,775	784	1,991
2020	5,952	1,998	3,954	1,309	2,645
2040	7,922	2,002	5,920	1,288	4,632
Physician visits (millions)					
1980	1,102	936	166	100	66
2000	1,314	1,083	231	116	115
2020	1,499	1,164	335	191	144
2040	1,621	1,193	428	187	241
Days of hospital care (millions)					
1980	274	169	105	49	56
2000	371	211	160	58	102
2020	459	234	225	95	130
2040	549	236	312	93	219
Nursing home residents (thousands)					
1980	1,511	196	1,315	227	1,088
2000	2,542	226	2,316	265	2,051
2020	3,371	242	3,129	434	2,695
2040	5,227	248	4,979	425	4,554
Personal health expenditures (in constant 1980 billions of dollars)					
1980	$219.4	$154.9	$64.5	(NA)	(NA)
2000	273.4	183.1	90.3	(NA)	(NA)
2020	328.3	197.1	131.2	(NA)	(NA)
2040	369.0	201.5	167.5	(NA)	(NA)

Source: D. P. Rice and J. J. Feldman, "Living Longer in the United States: Demographic Changes and Health Needs of the Elderly," *Milbank Memorial Fund Quarterly* 61 (Summer 1983): 362-96.

LONG-TERM CARE POLICY ISSUES

The aging of the population, the high costs of institutional care, and budgetary pressures and deficits have focused attention and stimulated debate on pressing long-term policy issues. Although the debate surrounding what to do about long-term care has intensified in recent years, there is little if any consensus regarding how the disparate elements of the organization, delivery, and cost and financing of long-term care should be brought together to develop a coherent set of national policies.

Organizational Issues

The elderly person who is functionally impaired and in need of long-term care services is faced with a vast array of services that are confusing and difficult to access. A major problem emphasized by many experts is the fragmentation of long-term care services and the need for linking and integrating health and social services. The division of authority between health and social services agencies at all levels of government is recognized as a major obstacle to an effective and efficient strategy to meet the long-term care needs of the elderly. Coordinating the vast system of medical, social, and welfare services available to the functionally impaired elderly person is currently receiving attention through various research and demonstration programs.[36]

Delivery of Long-Term Care Services

A major obstacle to meeting the long-term care needs of the elderly in the future is the current health system's focus on management and treatment of acute illness instead of chronic illness. Those with chronic illnesses and disabilities not only need long-term care services, but also may need hospital, ambulatory medical care, drugs, eyeglasses, nursing, podiatric, and dental care as well as an array of social support and homemaker services. They require access to a full range of services within one comprehensive system and the availability of appropriate levels of care, both institutional and community-based services.[37] Several studies indicate that some nursing home patients do not need the level of care provided in an institution and could remain in their homes if community-based services were available. At the same time, a significant number of the noninstitutionalized population need but do not receive long-term care.[38] If long-term care services continue to be delivered and financed separately from acute care, then patients and their families will continue to have difficulty obtaining needed services from one system or the other.

Quality of long-term care services, both institutional and home-based services, is of grave concern. Monitoring quality of care is very difficult, but the promulgation of federal nursing home regulations following an Institute of Medicine study undoubtedly will improve the quality of institutionalized care.[39]

Another important issue in the delivery of long-term care services is the training and availability of appropriate manpower. At all stages of the long-term care process, the involvement of physicians, dentists, optometrists, pharmacists, nurses and nurse's aides, therapists, nutritionists, social workers, and others is needed. Matching the supply of health practitioners with the requirements and needs of the elderly is a challenge for the future. The supply of health practitioners has increased substantially in the past two decades and continued growth is projected in the future, indicating an excess of supply over requirements for some health professions, but it is clear that there will be a shortage in the number trained in geriatrics and gerontology to meet the needs of an aging population.[40]

Cost and Financing of Long-Term Care Services

Medicaid and Medicare are the primary payers of long-term care services that are oriented toward institutional care. The limitations of the Medicare program, particularly in the care of the chronically ill and disabled, resulted in Medicaid becoming the primary vehicle for the payment of long-term services in the form of nursing home services. Part of the rationale for emphasizing alternatives to institutionalization for long-term care is based on the belief that community- and home-based services could reduce the use and costs of nursing homes and hospitals.

The economic perspectives of the 1980s focused attention on the rising costs of health care and the limited resources available for such care. With significant political pressure facing states to control their rising expenditures, the Medicaid program has been a primary target of cost containment efforts. Program changes include service coverage reductions, more stringent program eligibility, and a variety of efforts to reduce the volume and cost of services that will have a serious impact on the growing number of elderly who are high utilizers of these services.[41]

As noted earlier, many elderly people are mistaken about the extent to which they are covered for long-term care services under Medicare combined with their Medigap insurance policies. A prolonged nursing home stay can quickly deplete resources, result in poverty, and lead to Medicaid taking over payment responsibilities. A variety of solutions to the problem of preventing financial catastrophe among the growing number of elderly requiring long-term care have been proposed and will be discussed briefly below.

POLICY OPTIONS FOR LONG-TERM CARE

Long-term care is currently a major issue facing policymakers. A wide range of options have been discussed and some have been initiated to promote a continuum of care, eliminate the fragmentation of services, and deliver appropriate and high-quality care in a cost-effective manner. Both the private and public sectors are involved in the development of long-term care strategies to meet the needs of the growing number of elderly at risk.

One approach to financing long-term care is to develop private long-term care insurance. Prototype policies covering nursing home care and home health services have been developed. By the end of 1986, an estimated forty companies marketed long-term care products, most of which are indemnity policies and experimental. Three states have introduced legislation mandating long-term benefits and more than ten states have commissioned special committees to examine how they can foster the development of these policies.[42]

There are multiple barriers to private long-term care insurance: the insurance industry's fear of open-ended liability, absence of reliable data for making estimates of utilization and costs, insurance regulation and tax laws, lack of consumer interest and demand by the elderly who do not understand that Medicare and Medigap policies do not include long-term care, and limited incomes of the elderly to purchase additional policies.

The market for long-term care is in its infancy. Employers are becoming aware that the current delivery and financing of long-term care affects both their workers and their retirees and there are efforts under way to structure viable employer-sponsored long-term care group insurance.[43]

Another obvious approach to financing long-term care would be to establish public plans at either the federal or state level, financed with a variety of funds including tax dollars, premiums by employees and employers, and/or private premiums. Another option would be to develop prepaid long-term care plans and social health maintenance organizations (S/HMOs) which allow individuals to purchase a comprehensive benefit package that includes long-term care. It is clear that a program to finance adequate and good-quality long-term services requires broad risk pooling through insurance, taxation, and reasonable cost-sharing.[44]

The Harvard Center for Health Policy and Management recently proposed a restructuring of the Medicare program to pay for long-term care services.[45] Medicare should cover the cost of extended nursing home care financed in the same way as the entire Medicare program, i.e., a combination of Social Security taxes, premium payments, and general revenues. The unique feature of financing long-term care in this proposal is that Medicare beneficiaries in nursing homes would cover nonmedical costs by making "residential copayments" that are equal to 80 percent of their Social Security benefits. The proposal calls for simplifying the way Medicare is administered and expanding the types of care covered.

The recent interest in providing the nation's elderly with increased protection against the economic consequences of catastrophic illness should not be interpreted as covering long-term care services. The Medicare Catastrophic Coverage Act of 1988 extends the current Medicare program to cover catastrophic expenses and drug costs. It places an overall cap on out-of-pocket expenditures for health care services covered by Medicare. In addition, the act extends Medicare coverage eventually to 80 percent of the cost of prescription drug expenses incurred after a stipulated amount of deductible. However, only a small portion of the expenses of long-term care in nursing homes, averaging $22,000 a year per patient, is covered. It is often the ongoing cost of long-term care in nursing homes that reduces families, especially spouses, to poverty.

While Congress is seeking ways to cover the cost of nursing home care, home health care, and other long-term care services, nearly forty states have taken steps so that some form of private long-term care insurance is available to the elderly.[46] Included are incentives for the purchase of long-term policies by reducing the premium tax that insurers pay for such coverage, setting standards for private policies, or mandating coverage under health insurance policies. Private insurance is not a viable option for everyone and does not preclude the need for a much larger public sector role. Whether Medicare is expanded or a new long-term care program is created, a comprehensive solution will be expensive. A public commitment is needed to a broad-based revenue source to adequately cover long-term care services.

In defining the parameters of long-term care, Rice and Estes outline four basic principles:

First, it must be comprehensive, including a full range of health and social services covering the long-term care continuum from community-based care to institutional care. It must also include preventive and restorative services as well as treatment and illness management. Long-term care services must be linked with other health and social services as well as with hospital and physician services. Second, it must provide incentives for providers to keep costs at a reasonable level, to prevent overutilization, and to promote the use of appropriate services. Third, it must have a financing system that provides protection from impoverishment to individuals who need long-term care, and that allows for combining private and public resources to assure protection for individuals before they become ill. Fourth, it must ensure access to those who need the services regardless of financial ability to pay or other characteristics.[47]

Implementation of these principles will require action at the community, state, and national levels to develop a long-term care policy that meets the multiple needs of the increasing number of elderly persons and encourages healthy aging and independence in our age.

CONCLUSION

The nation is experiencing a demographic revolution that presents major challenges for the medical and long-term care delivery systems. Greater demands to respond to these challenges are likely to be felt in various ways:

- Increases in the number of elderly persons. The number of persons age 65 and over will continue to grow in the remainder of this century and will rise more rapidly beginning in the decade 2010 to 2020.
- The high rate of growth of the very old population. Persons age 85 and over are projected to be the fastest-growing segment of the population.
- Rise in life expectancy. Life expectancy at age 65 is projected to continue to increase for both males and females with a continuation of a wide gender gap.
- Changes in morbidity patterns. The prevalence of chronic illness and attendant functional impairments among the elderly, especially older women, will rise as the number and proportion of those in the oldest age groups will increase and diseases, whose incidence rates rise with age, will become more prevalent.
- Increasing need for long-term care services. The growing numbers of chronically ill disabled elderly will mean an increasing need for a variety of long-term care services to maintain their independence at home and to avoid institutional placement.
- Rising expenditures for medical and long-term care. Since the aged are sicker than younger people and use more medical and long-term care services, expenditures for their care will increase.
- Budgetary pressures. The rising costs of long-term care provided under Medicaid and other government programs are forcing governmental cutbacks in these programs and the search for alternatives to high-cost institutional services.
- Rising out-of-pocket payments for long-term care. As the burden of long-term care is shifted to the older individual and his or her family, policymak-

ers are seeking more equitable and cost-effective methods of financing long-term care in which the public and private sectors will assume their fair share of responsibilities.

• Stress on caregivers. As more working women assume the responsibilities of caregiving, employers are recognizing that caregiving is a work-force issue that needs to be addressed with innovative approaches to providing and financing long-term care.

The vulnerability of elderly persons, especially women at advanced ages, to deteriorating health, impaired functional mobility, diminishing resources, and the fears and stresses of being alone requires concerted action of policymakers and activists to meet the challenges and opportunities within the public and private sectors to improve the quality of the remaining years of their lives.

NOTES

1. United States Bureau of the Census, "Projections of the Population of the United States, 1983 to 2080," *Current Population Reports*, Series P-25, No. 952 (Washington, D.C.: U.S. Government Printing Office, May 1984).

2. United States Bureau of the Census, "Marital Status and Living Arrangements: March 1985," *Current Population Reports*, Series P-20, No. 410 (Washington, D.C.: U.S. Government Printing Office, November 1986).

3. The Commonwealth Fund Commission on Elderly People Living Alone, *Old, Alone, and Poor* (Baltimore, Md., April 16, 1987).

4. United States Bureau of the Census, "America in Transition: An Aging Society," *Current Population Reports*, Series P-23, No. 128 (Washington, D.C.: U.S. Government Printing Office, 1983).

5. United States Bureau of the Census, "Money Income and Poverty Status of Families and Persons in the United States: 1985," *Current Population Reports*, Series P-60, No. 154 (Washington, D.C.: U.S. Government Printing Office, August 1986).

6. United States Bureau of Labor Statistics, *Employment and Earnings*, 34, No. 11, November 1987.

7. United States Senate Special Committee on Aging and the American Association of Retired Persons, *Aging America: Trends and Projections*, PL 3377 (584) (Washington, D.C.: U.S. Senate Special Committee on Aging, 1984).

8. United States Bureau of the Census, "Money Income and Poverty Status."

9. United States Bureau of the Census, "Estimates of Poverty Including the Value of Noncash Benefits: 1979 to 1982," Technical Paper 51 (Washington, D.C.: U.S. Government Printing Office, 1984).

10. National Center for Health Statistics, "Current Estimates from the National Health Interview Survey: United States, 1986," *Vital and Health Statistics*, Series 10, No. 164. DHHS Pub. No. (PHS) 87–1592 (Washington, D.C.: U.S. Government Printing Office, October 1987).

11. Ibid., 85–88.

12. National Center for Health Statistics, "Utilization of Short-Stay Hospitals, United States, 1985 Annual Summary," *Vital and Health Statistics*, Series 13, No. 91, DHHS Pub. No. (PHS) 87–1752 (Washington, D.C.: U.S. Government Printing Office, May 1978).

13. National Center for Health Statistics, "Characteristics of Nursing Home Residents, Health Status, and Care Received: National Nursing Home Survey, United States, May-December 1977," *Vital and Health Statistics*, Series 13, No. 51, DHHS Pub. No. (PHS) 81–1712 (Washington, D.C.: U.S. Government Printing Office, 1981).

14. National Center for Health Statistics, "Health Characteristics of Persons with Chronic Activity Limitations: United States, 1979," *Vital Health Statistics*, Series 10, No. 137, DHHS Pub. No. (PHS) 82–1565 (Washington, D.C.: U.S. Government Printing Office, 1982).

15. National Center for Health Statistics, "Use of Nursing Homes by the Elderly: Preliminary Data from the 1985 National Nursing Home Survey," *Advance Data from Vital and Health Statistics*, No. 135, DHHS Pub. No. (PHS) 87–1250 (Hyattsville, Md.: Public Health Service, May 14, 1987).

16. National Center for Health Statistics, "Health Statistics on Older Persons, United States, 1986," *Vital and Health Statistics*, Series 3, No. 25, DHHS Pub. No. (PHS) 87–1409 (Washington, D.C.: U.S. Government Printing Office, June 1987), 71–75.

17. Robert L. Kane and Rosalie A. Kane, "Long-Term Care: Can Our Society Meet the Needs of Its Elderly?" *Annual Review of Public Health* 1 (1980): 227–53.

18. Charlene Harrington, Robert J. Newcomer, Carroll L. Estes and Associates, *Long-Term Care of the Elderly* (Beverly Hills: Sage Publications, 1985).

19. Pamela Doty, Kobrin Liu, and Joshua Weiner, "An Overview of Long-Term Care," *Health Care Financing Review* 6, 3 (Spring 1985): 69–78.

20. Division of National Cost Estimates, "National Health Expenditures, 1986–2000," *Health Care Financing Review* 8, 4 (Summer 1987): 1–36.

21. American Association of Retired Persons, *Income Security and Long-Term Care for Women in Midlife and Beyond: U.S. and Canadian Perspectives*, WI3976 (887), D12890 (Washington, D.C.: American Association of Retired Persons, 1987), 9.

22. Thomas Rice and Jon Gabel, "Protecting the Elderly against High Health Care Costs," *Health Affairs* 5, 3 (Fall 1986): 6–21.

23. "Profile: On Lok Senior Health Services" and "The Risk-Based Long-Term Care Initiative" (San Francisco: On Lok, 1987).

24. United States Department of Health and Human Services, *Long Term Care: Background and Future Directions*, HCFA 81–20047 (Washington, D.C.: Health Care Financing Administration, 1981).

25. Robyn Stone, Gail L. Cafferata, and Judith Sangl, "Caregivers of the Frail Elderly: A National Profile," *The Gerontologist* 27, 5 (1987): 616–26.

26. Ruth Campbell and Elain M. Brody, "Women's Changing Roles and Help to the Elderly: Attitudes of Women in the United States and Japan," *The Gerontologist* 25, 6 (1985): 584–92.

27. Georgina I. Lucas, "Caregiving: A Growing Workforce Issue," *The Aging Connection* 8, 6 (December 1987/January 1988): 7.

28. National Center for Health Statistics, "Health Statistics on Older Persons, United States, 1986," *Vital and Health Statistics*, Series 3, No. 25, pp. 41–55.

29. Korbin Liu, Kenneth G. Manton, and Barbara M. Liu, "Home Care Expenses for the Disabled Elderly," *Health Care Financing Review* 2 (1985): 51–58.

30. Louis Harris and Associates, Inc., *Problems Facing Elderly Americans Living Alone: A National Survey*, Study No. 854010 (New York, 1986).

31. Edward L. Schneider and Jacob A. Brody, "Aging, Natural Death, and the Compression of Morbidity: Another View," *New England Journal of Medicine* 309 (October 6, 1983): 854–56.

32. James F. Fries, "Aging, Natural Death, and the Compression of Morbidity," *New England Journal of Medicine* 303 (July 17, 1980): 130–35.

33. Kenneth C. Manton, "Changing Concepts of Morbidity and Mortality in the Elderly Population," *Milbank Memorial Fund Quarterly* 60 (1982): 183–244.

34. Dorothy P. Rice and Jacob J. Feldman, "Living Longer in the United States: Demographic Changes and Health Needs of the Elderly," *Milbank Memorial Fund Quarterly* 61 (1983): 362–96.

35. Kenneth G. Manton and Korbin Liu, "The Future Growth of the Long-Term Care Population: Projections Based on the 1977 National Nursing Home Survey and the 1982 Long-Term Care Survey" (Paper presented at the Hillhaven Foundation's Third National Leadership Conference on Long-Term Care Issues: The Future World of Long-Term Care, Washington, D.C., March 7–9, 1984).

36. Dorothy P. Rice, "Long-Term Care of the Elderly and Disabled," *International Social Security Review* 3 (1983): 299–326.

37. Dorothy P. Rice and Carroll L. Estes, "Health of the Elderly: Policy Issues and Challenges," *Health Affairs* 3 (Winter 1984): 25–49.

38. Congressional Budget Office, "Long-Term Care for the Elderly and Disabled" (Washington, D.C.: CBO, 1977).

39. National Research Council, *Improving the Quality of Nursing Homes*, Committee on Nursing Home Regulation, Institute of Medicine (Washington, D.C.: National Academy Press, 1986).

40. Dorothy P. Rice, "Demographic Realities and Projections of an Aging Population," in *Health Care for an Aging Society*, ed. Spiros Andreopoulos and John R. Hogness (New York: Churchill Livingstone, 1989).

41. Carroll L. Estes, Robert J. Newcomer, and Associates, *Fiscal Austerity and Aging* (Beverly Hills: Sage, 1983).

42. Rice and Gabel, "Protecting the Elderly against High Health Care Costs," pp. 6–21.

43. Robert Friedland, "Is Business Playing a Role in Providing Long-Term Care?" *The Aging Connection* 8, 6 (American Society on Aging, San Francisco: December 1987/January 1988): 7.

44. Anne R. Somers, "Insurance for Long-Term Care," *New England Journal of Medicine* 317 (July 2, 1987): 23–29.

45. David Blumenthal, Mark Schlesinger, P. B. Drumheller, and the Harvard

Medical Project, "Special Report—The Future of Medicare," *New England Journal of Medicine* 314 (March 13, 1986): 722–28.

46. American Association of Retired Persons, *News Bulletin* (June 1987).

47. Rice and Estes, "Health of the Elderly," p. 45.

9 CONCLUSIONS: WOMEN AND SOCIETY

Martha N. Ozawa

Preceding chapters pointed out that the economic fate of women is largely determined by three critical events in the life cycle: divorce, widowhood, and teenage pregnancy and childbearing. When women share their husbands' economic well-being by living with them, their economic standing is secure. But when their marital status changes, women's economic standing deteriorates overnight. Once the marital relationship is severed by divorce or widowhood, women simply do not have the same earning capability as men to sustain the level of economic standing beyond these events in the life cycle. Women's relative inability to earn is, to a great degree, a product of their earlier socialization and education at home and at school and of the social roles of mother and wife they are asked to play. Teenage pregnancy and childbearing is a problem relatively unique to the United States and adds another dimension to women's economic insecurity.

The underlying theme of the foregoing chapters is that the current problem of economic insecurity and poverty is largely demographically determined. In particular, economic insecurity increasingly occurs when a certain event strikes a person in relation to another person. In the case of divorce, a mutual economic compact is broken as a result of the spouses' decision to terminate their marital relationship. In the case of widowhood, a mutual economic compact is undermined as a result of a spouse's death. In the case of childbearing among unmarried teenagers, one establishes an economic responsibility for a person (the baby) by deciding to bear that child without establishing a firm mutual economic compact with another person (the other sex partner). In each of these events, women seem to be locked into an economically compromised position.

Such life-cycle events are quite different from the causes of economic insecurity we used to know. In the past, we were inclined to look at income insecurity and concomitant poverty as economic phenomena.

That is, we sought causes of poverty in the economic fluctuations of a given time. Such a perspective was appropriate when income insecurity was indeed caused directly by economic forces. For example, during the Great Depression, poverty was caused by massive unemployment; many families, regardless of their demographic backgrounds, suffered economically. At other times, the economic insecurity of many families may be caused by an extremely skewed distribution of income and wealth. For example, in many of the Third World countries, income distribution is so unequal that the income of people in the bottom half is not adequate enough ever to sustain them from day to day. In both these cases, income insecurity is economically induced and creates a class issue: the struggle between the rich and the poor.

Class struggle between the rich and the poor certainly exists in the United States. However, this book has shown another, emerging dimension of income insecurity. That dimension involves the economic battle between men and women. The economic struggle between the sexes is unique in the sense that it is a struggle between demographic groups; thus, it creates a *horizontal* economic issue, in contrast to the class struggle, which creates a *vertical* economic issue. The economic struggle between men and women is also unique because it involves events in their *private* lives; divorce, widowhood, and teenage pregnancy and childbearing. In other words, economic insecurity involving divorce and widowhood is produced by the breakup of the private relationship between two individuals. Likewise, economic insecurity involving teenage pregnancy and childbearing is caused by an event of two privately related individuals—an adolescent girl and an adolescent boy.[1] In contrast, economic insecurity associated with the class struggle does not involve privately related individuals, but economically defined *groupings*.

Because of the unique aspects of demographically induced economic insecurity, its causes and consequences are different from and often more complex than those of economically induced economic insecurity. So are the solutions. At the least, traditional approaches to income maintenance that have been applied in the United States seem inadequate to deal effectively with demographically induced economic insecurity. Such economic insecurity requires a new scheme of thinking for establishing new objectives, new structures, and new strategies.

Furthermore, in a broader context, women's economic insecurity needs to be understood from women's biological role as childbearers. Women's inability to earn as much as men do stems largely from the fact that women spend some crucial years in childbearing and child rearing, as the chapter by Smith has shown. Put another way, women's economic insecurity, per se, can be resolved to a great extent if women decide not to bear children. Such a decision would solve the economic predicament of individual women. But what would be the impact of such a choice on the macro level—on the long-term economic growth of a nation, on the nation's ability to care for the elderly, and, ultimately, on national survival?

The foregoing discussion indicates that the United States needs to deal with demographically induced economic insecurity in both short- and long-term perspectives. For now, it needs to ameliorate the economic plight facing many women and their children. For the future, it needs to develop social policy that addresses these broader, long-term macro policy issues. In a nutshell, the question confronting this nation is this: How can women be empowered economically through developing their earning capability and, at the same time, how can the United States be assured of birthrates high enough to maintain a viable population?

These questions are almost overwhelming for any one book to deal with. However, this chapter attempts to shed light on a future direction that policymakers may consider as a starting point for future debate. Before I delineate my thinking on future directions, however, I will review briefly the current situation of American women.

CHANGING ENVIRONMENT AND INSTITUTIONAL INERTIA

Economic and Social Change

The United States is undergoing profound changes in its economy, demography, and family structure. It has entered the stage of postindustrial revolution, with the majority of the labor force working in the service sector of the economy. The rate of women's participation in the labor force has been rising steadily. On the demographic front, the U.S. population is aging. The proportion of the elderly is increasing rapidly, while the proportion of children and youths is declining. The median age is rising as well. The family structure has changed so that the nuclear family no longer is the dominant form of family.

The depth and breadth of the social problems associated with these changes are enormous, as evidenced by higher rates of divorce and teenage pregnancy. Furthermore, the incidence of never-married mothers is rapidly increasing, especially among black women. All this indicates that the United States is entering a new stage of social change: the denuclearization of the family to create individual-based families. As a result, the proportion of female-headed families with children is high: one in every five families with children.[2] In many cases, female headship originates in childbearing by adolescent girls.[3] The birthrate among unmarried teenagers is 28.9 live births per 1,000 unmarried mothers.[4]

Increasingly, American women are being thrust into the center of dynamic economic and social changes that are taking place in the United States. On the one hand, women are becoming a vital part of the labor force. To some women, work is a challenge and an opportunity to further their career goals. To others, work is a necessity, either to sustain their middle-class life-style because their husbands' earnings are not sufficient to do so or to manage their own households. At any rate, women's greater participation in the labor force is helping the United States sustain its viable economic growth. On the other hand, women are increasingly burdened by the destruction of social relationships that have been fundamental to their economic security. Thus, women are caught in the crosscurrents of economic and social changes. The net result of women's greater capacity to earn and the economic loss they sustain because of these changing social relationships is hard to measure precisely. But, it is safe to say that the level of women's economic well-being at critical junctures in the life cycle—the aftermath of teenage childbearing and the period of divorce and widowhood—is precarious and plunges many women into poverty.

Institutional Adaptation and Inertia

How is American society coping with these dynamic economic and social changes? In particular, what adaptations is it making to deal with the economic insecurity that an increasing number of women are facing?

Institutional change always lags behind economic and social changes. Thus, laws and governmental provisions that were developed to meet the needs of earlier times are applied to meet the emerging needs, which creates gaps in the philosophical rationale for the provision of income and services, the types of programs, and the level of benefits. Likewise, schools are slow to change to prepare women for well-paying jobs later on. Similarly, employment practices—the way women are recruited, promoted, and considered for tenure—are slow to change. A few examples follow.

Income Maintenance Policy. A clear institutional inertia is seen in the way the United States provides income support to female-headed families with children, whose economic dependence stems from divorce, desertion, or nonmarriage. As Garfinkel, McLanahan, and Watson discussed, Aid to Families with Dependent Children (AFDC) is the only public program through which the income maintenance needs of such female-headed families are met. Although this program was developed originally with the noble intent of helping mainly widows stay at home and raise children, it has become, over the years, an antipoverty program for divorced mothers and never-married mothers with children. More recently, the expectations for mothers who receive AFDC have changed; these mothers are now expected to go out to work or to obtain further education and training so they become employable. Meanwhile, the public has become increasingly hostile to the recipients of AFDC. The message coming from the public is this: having children and becoming a public charge is contrary to the national interest.

The negative attitudes toward AFDC strongly reflect the inertia of the U.S. ideology of individualism, which tends to attribute the causes of economic dependence to the failings of individuals. In the meantime, American women, including the poor and adolescents, are adapting to these economic forces and the often-painful social forces by choosing to have fewer children (the increasing illegitimacy rates notwithstanding). Thus, here we see a blind alley of public policy in the United States. Stuck with the old ideology of individualism, which justifies a program like AFDC, society is sending women a signal that is counter to the long-term national interest: the preservation of a viable population. Unfortunately, few policymakers are linking the current public policy stance to women's reproductive behavior.

In valuing individualism instead of collectivism, the United States seems unable to meet the needs of children more effectively. Because it is so concerned with work incentives of parents, the United States has not been able to develop income support programs that directly address the needs of children, as other industrialized societies have done.[5] Japan, for example, has developed several layers of income support programs for children, all taking the universal approach or its derivatives. First, under its social security system, all children, regardless of their parents' earnings, receive flat-amount benefits, and there is no rule of a maximum family benefit as there is in the United States. Second, it has a program of children's allowances that provides cash payments to second and subsequent children. Finally, it has a program to provide child support payments for children who are being raised only by their mothers. This program has a "level-income testing"; that is, when the income level of the mother exceeds a certain level, the payments are simply reduced by a flat amount.[6] Only after all these programs are allowed to operate to ensure an adequate level of income for children does the noncategorical public assistance program come into play.[7] Thus, it is no accident that only 1.1 percent of the Japanese population is on public assistance, compared to 6.4 percent in the United States.[8] This fact is all the more significant because the Japanese public assistance program provides poverty-line income, but no state public assistance program in the United States does so.

The American public's adherence to individualism is also reflected in the way social security benefits are calculated. First, the social security program uses a basically earnings-related benefit formula instead of a double-decker benefit formula as other industrialized countries do. Second, benefits for auxiliary beneficiaries (spouses, children, widows, and the like) are a straight proportion of the benefits for the worker. In contrast, many other countries provide flat-amount benefits for such beneficiaries. Third, the U.S. system has a provision of maximum family benefits, which is intended to tie family benefits to previous earnings levels of workers. But other countries, such as Japan and Canada, do not have a maximum family benefit rule. These provisions underscore that the U.S. social security system emphasizes the principle of individual equity over the principle of social adequacy. The individual equity principle is an activation of individualism and the social adequacy principle, of collectivism.

The foregoing discussion regarding the public policy on income maintenance in the United States indicates that the country is dealing with income maintenance for children less adequately and with more social controversy than do other countries. The United States is not doing well because income support for children is tied closely to the parents' earnings experience. The inadequate provision for children is the price the U.S. social security system is paying for its adherence to the ideology of individualism.

Because the economic fate of women is tied to the economic well-being of children, the U.S. system is faring poorly in meeting the nationally defined minimum level of income for women and children. Yet, it does fairly well in meeting the *relative* economic well-being of aged widows because widows, in essence, are allowed to "inherit" their husbands' benefits. However, widows also are not guaranteed a certain level of minimum income from social security. Furthermore, the way pension programs are administered tends not to improve the widows' financial condition, as discussed by Holden. The Supplemental Security Income (SSI) program does not provide poverty-free income either. In sum, the U.S. income maintenance system is not an effective antipoverty instrument for women.

Education and Employment. Smith paints an optimistic picture of the earnings prospects of both American and Japanese women. He does so on the basis of two types of empirical data: the rising participation of women in the labor force of both countries and the rising level of earnings of young female workers who are entering the labor force.

Smith's analysis may be only half the story, however. For example, Nakajima, a labor economist, paints a pessimistic picture of the Japanese situation, arguing that women's economic position has not changed much.[9] She develops her argument by explaining employment practices in Japan, by showing empirical data on the patterns of earnings by men and women in various industries, and by analyzing differential earnings by sex, controlling for the level of education and for the terms of hiring (such as part-time versus permanent jobs). Nakajima further shows that Japanese women's participation in the labor force over their life cycle still follows the "M" shape—an increase in the rate of participation before marriage or childbearing, a drop during the years of child rearing, a rise later on, and finally a sharp decrease—but that American women no longer follow such a pattern; rather, they have a continuous high rate of labor force participation.

The most compelling basis for Nakajima's argument is the tracking mechanism that Japanese employers use to channel men and women to divergent career paths. One path is developed through the terms of employment called "comprehensive employment" (or *Sougoshoku*) and the other path, through "general employment" (or *Ippanshoku*). The former is generally applied to men; the latter, to women. Workers in comprehensive employment can expect to receive age-determined salaries (*Nenkou Chingin*); workers in general employment cannot. Thus, the earnings levels of male and female workers tend to diverge as they get older. According to Nakajima, employers continue to track employees, despite governmental efforts to encourage equal employment opportunities for men and women, as evidenced by the enactment of the Law of Equal Employment of Men and Women (*Danjyo Koyo Byodou Ho*), which was put into effect in 1986. Finally, the tracking of workers in different career paths in Japan is closely related to Japanese educational tracking, which originates as early as the end of ninth grade.[10]

The peripheral nature of the female labor force further contributes to our understanding of why Japanese women earn less than men. Specifically, Japanese women who reenter the labor market after childbirth and several years of child rearing can do so only as "part-time" workers or as workers in low-paying jobs, regardless of their earlier work experience or educational background. In Japan, "part-time work" means two things: employment involving less than full-time work and less-than-equal treatment in fringe benefits and promotional and tenure practices, although the workers involved work full time. In both cases, "part-time work" is a dead-end job with inferior fringe benefits and fewer prospects for promotion. Thus, part-time employment is another way that jobs are segmented within the same company.

This discussion of the economic situation of Japanese women has been lengthy to balance the argument advanced by Smith. That is, increasing earnings of women entering the labor force and the greater labor force participation by women do not tell the whole story about the economic condition of Japanese women. To obtain a fuller picture, one needs to analyze the institutional inertia under which the terms of employment are carried out.

Although the labor market situation of Japanese women sounds rather horrible, the economic condition of American women may not be so different. In spite of the Equal Pay Act of 1963, Title VII of the Civil Rights Act of 1964, and the Pregnancy Discrimination Act (a 1978 amendment to the 1964 act), episodes of subtle discrimination abound. More important, as Clark discussed, a clear educational tracking system seems to exist in the United States as well, which tends to lead to differential employment paths later on.

In sum, American women, like Japanese women, have come a long way toward economic self-sufficiency, but still have a long way to go to develop earning capabilities that are equal to those of men with the same educational background and employment experience. Even Smith's optimistic prognosis about the U.S. situation indicates that only one-half the current wage differential between men and women will be eliminated by the year 2000.

Legal Treatment. How American women are treated under the inheritance law reflects the cultural traditions of this country. American people leave most of their assets to their spouses; most often, they bequeath everything to their spouses by following a "spouse-all" rule. With few exceptions, such wills are respected. This is not the case in other countries. In Japan, for example, children have a legal right to force the court to provide them with their legal share, no matter what the will says.

In American intestate cases, the widow's share depends on the number of children. When one child is involved, the widow's share is one-half, but when more than one child is involved, the widow's share normally is one-third. In states with community property laws, the proportion of assets that the widow ends up owning after the death of her husband is clearly larger than in non–community property states. Reflecting the growing sense that a husband and a wife constitute a partnership in accumulating assets, many states are following the practice initiated by the state of Wisconsin. In 1986, Wisconsin enacted a law to enforce a version of what is called the "Uniform Marital Property Act," which was drafted by the National Conference of Commissioners on Uniform Law in 1983.[11] This act basically follows practices of community property states. Under the act, women and men would share equally the ownership of property.[12] In sum, because of the prevailing ethos of egalitarianism in the United States, American people have long embraced the practice of conjugal bequests with great ease.

The United States has come a long way toward establishing a uniform public child-support-assurance system. Many states are attempting to follow the lead of the state of Wisconsin in transforming the legal procedure into an administrative one by passing specific legislation for establishing such a system. However, empirical data presented by Garfinkel, McLanahan, and Watson indicate that divorced wives and their children are placed in an economically precarious position. The chances of actually receiving child support payments from absent fathers, as well as the level of payments, are low. Thus, it seems that most states have a long way to go to make adequate, continuous child support payments a reality.

SUMMARY OF RECOMMENDATIONS

To mitigate the economic plight of women at critical junctures of the life cycle, contributing authors proposed various ways to improve women's situation. To minimize the adverse impact of divorce, Garfinkel, McLanahan, and Watson recommended a more certain and more equitable system of child support. Such a system would involve a better collection of such payments from absent fathers and the public guarantee of a specific minimum level of child support payments. To help widows maintain a standard of living that is comparable to what they had before their husbands died, Holden suggested an internal redistribution of pension funds between spouses through a joint-and-two-thirds option—or a better option. The protection of private pension benefits against inflation was another of her proposals. Furthermore, Rice advocated, and Menchik implied the need for, the diffusion of financial and social responsibility for caring for the frail elderly. Financial diffusion may take the form of social or private insurance to pay the costs of nursing home care. Social diffusion may involve spreading the burden of caring for frail elderly people among their children, relatives, and community volunteers and strengthening the delivery of home-based services.

While these solutions address the need for both financial and physical maintenance, other recommendations focus on the empowerment of women by enabling them to develop greater human capital through education and by eliminating institutional barriers to women's promotion on the job, as Clark discussed. The pursuit of equal educational opportunity, both in words and in deed, by eliminating the tracking system would greatly improve women's future earnings prospects. The role of the guidance counselor will be crucial in implementing equal opportunity in education.

With regard to teenage pregnancy and childbearing, Furstenberg and Brooks-Gunn recommended that three approaches be taken simultaneously. These approaches are (1) the creation of greater educational and life opportunities for teenagers, (2) the dissemination of information about contraception, and (3) the provision of medical and social services to teenage mothers and their children.

Menchik and Rice noted the need to compensate for the time and energy that women devote to caring for their frail elderly relatives. Such concentrated efforts need to be recognized in the distribution of the estates of these relatives after they die.

These recommendations and new ideas are worthy of serious consideration by policymakers in the United States. They are all relevant to improving the economic well-being of American women.

TOWARD ESTABLISHING ECONOMIC AND SOCIAL PARITY BETWEEN THE SEXES

Looking to the future, it seems important to place women's income insecurity in the broader context of the economic and social changes that are taking place in the United States. By so doing, it will be possible for us to develop a new framework and a new rationale for public policy on income support for women and children.

As was already alluded to, women are increasingly thrust into the center stage of dynamic economic and social changes. This fact can best be understood if one thinks about why more and more women are participating in the labor force and bearing fewer children and delineates the probable long-term consequences of such a movement on the nation.

There are multiple forces behind women's increasing rates of labor force participation; some are purely economic and some represent social validation. As the United States becomes a service-dominated economy, its economy will be increasingly capable of deploying men and women equally because gender will no longer be a handicap in the execution of jobs. Put differently, employers will lose if they discriminate against women in hiring and promoting because discrimination causes an inefficient use of economic resources.[13] Thus, although many institutional obstacles still must be dealt with, the economic forces stemming from the service-dominated industry are already pulling more women into the labor force and compelling employers to engage in fair employment practices.

It is interesting to observe that industrialization at different stages has different effects on women. At an earlier stage of industrialization, women were pulled into their homes and were enabled to play the role of "housewife," thanks to the accumulation of surplus wealth in industrialized countries. Now that the United States is in the stage of postindustrialization characterized by service-dominated industries, women are pulled out of their homes and into the labor market to compete with other workers of both genders.

From an economic policy perspective, women's work outside the home is increasingly encouraged—or even enforced in some situations like in the AFDC program. U.S. policymakers understand that the United States can no longer maintain its economic power in isolation because its economy is increasingly subjected to world economic competition. To preserve its economic competitive edge in the world, policymakers believe, the U.S. economy must rely increasingly on the female labor force. In the context of domestic policy as well, the government welcomes the greater participation of women in the labor force so it can meet the challenge of financing social security programs for an increasing number of retired people.

Social validation of women's work is creating a force in the same direction. Because of their growing awareness that the worth of individuals is measured by their performance in paid work, more and more women are acquiring their identity and their worth not at home but in the workplace. Associated with out-of-home work are the excitement and social benefits. Work gives women opportunities to test their marketable skills, to measure the economic value of what they can offer, to develop social relationships at the workplace, and to establish economic independence.[14] It is not surprising that an increasing number of women prefer life in the workplace to life at home, which includes playing a role subservient to their husbands.

Furthermore, the decision to have and raise children is becoming harder and harder—a personal, private struggle—for many women and even for men. First, it costs an enormous amount of money to raise a child to adulthood; a 1980 study indicated that $100,000 to $140,000 are needed.[15] Second, since social security taxes are imposed on every worker and the eventual benefits received in old age do not depend on whether the worker has brought children into this world, women (as well as men) with children would have to lower their current standard of living and gain nothing later in old age. Indeed, a study by Fuchs proved indirectly that the per capita income of those in families with children (adjusted for economy of scale) is significantly lower than the per capita income of those in childless families.[16] Governmental data also indicate that the median income of families with children (expressed as a ratio of the poverty threshold) has declined over the years in relation to that of families without children.[17] Third, the federal government has not recognized the value of children in its income tax law and, therefore, has neglected to increase the value of the personal exemption per child to keep up with inflation. In nominal terms, this exemption was $600 in 1955; $1,080 in 1986. In real terms, the 1986 figure was only one-half the 1955 figure. As a result, the effective tax rates of families with children increased 43 percent, while the rates of other families did not.[18] Even under the new tax law, which was put into effect in 1987, the 1989 personal exemption per child of $2,000 will barely reach the 1955 level in real terms. Fourth, because of the lack of systematic provisions for day care, women individually have to hassle to arrange for the care of their children. Finally, if women go through a divorce and if, as a result, they ever have to resort to public assistance to escape from poverty, they are subjected to social disgrace as if it were a crime to have brought children into this world.

Thus, the United States has established powerful incentives for women to have fewer children or to have none at all. The momentum seems to have already started. The U.S. total fertility rate has reached the record low of 1.8, which is only half the rate recorded in 1957, the peak year of the baby-boom era. The current rate is to low to sustain a stable population. A rate of 2.1 children is needed to ensure a stable population beyond the year 2030.[19] The fertility rates among highly educated women are even lower than the average.[20]

The short-term impact of all this may well be greater economic growth in the United States. But the long-term effect will be sociological and more profound than just economic. That is, we will see a nation of individuals, women and men, striving for their own economic security and progress and forgoing their opportunity to have children. And, when they decide not to have children, they will see no need to marry.

Such a trend also seems to have started. In their study, Bloom and Bennett indicated that the proportion of women who will never marry will be three times as high for the younger generation (aged 26 to 30 years in 1982) as for the older generation (aged 46 to 50 years in that year). Furthermore, they reported, highly educated women are less likely ever to marry than are women with less schooling.[21] Their findings on the marital behavior and persistently low fertility rates among American women are important for policymakers to bear in mind, notwithstanding the high incidence of nonmarriage and childbearing among black women—a controversial phenomenon.

If the United States becomes such a nation—a nation of individuals striving for their own economic security without forming families with children—then its culture, demography, and economy will be greatly transformed. The United States probably will depend on a perpetual infusion of immigrants. But an excessive reliance on immigration may create other kinds of social problems. Recognizing such a possibility, in 1983–1984, the Federal Republic of Germany, for example, paid immigrants DM10,500 each to leave the country and an extra DM1,500 for every child, even though it is suffering from a labor shortage. The Japanese government is severely restricting the entry of foreign workers, although many Japanese companies want to employ them.[22] From an economic viewpoint as well, an infusion of immigrants does not necessarily translate into economic growth in the United States. It may instead heighten the rate of structural unemployment because most of these immigrants are unskilled and the U.S. economy increasingly will demand skilled workers.

There is not enough space here to elaborate on the future of the United States with a shrinking population, but it seems certain that, at the least, such a nation will suffer from slower economic growth or even decay.[23] Thus, we can anticipate a 180-degree turnabout from the current situation—from economic growth to economic decline.

Such a chain of events will take place, starting from the economic and social system we have created in which the society does not deal effectively with the demographically determined income insecurity of women. If this line of thought holds true, what direction should the United States take? What should be its objective and the strategy for dealing with the problem?

The foregoing discussion leads us to the conclusion that the objective of income maintenance in the future will transcend just "help" or "support" for women to maintain a certain level of economic well-being. In the past, income maintenance programs distributed income from the economically powerful to the economically less powerful because the latter needed "help" from the former. When the demographically determined income insecurity of women is placed in the broader context described earlier, however, it is reasonable to argue that the objective of future income maintenance programs should be to "invest in women", because society needs to accomplish national objectives that are broader than just "helping women have an adequate income," whatever stage of the life cycle they are in. And, these national objectives are (1) to maximize women's contribution to the economy and (2) to ensure that women can have and raise children without undue hardship. For the first time in the history of social welfare, policymakers need to establish policies in which the economic interests and social interests of the nation are interwoven.

How can a nation accomplish these two apparently divergent objectives? I recommend that the United States establish (1) the principle of economic and social parity between the sexes and (2) the principle of sharing the economic costs of raising children between families with children and those without children. A strategy that should be explored is the horizontal redistribution of income in two dimensions: one from men to women and the other from childless families to families with children.

The redistribution of income from men to women could be done internally, that is, with no additional costs to the public. Specifically, social security programs could be reformed to provide widows with benefits that would allow their standard of living to stay the same after the death of their husbands. Pension programs could be reformed in the same way; a scheme of doing so was extensively discussed by Holden. Formulas for alimony payments and private child support payments could be developed so that the living standards of divorced husbands and divorced wives would stay the same.

Social parity between the sexes means that married men and women share not only the joys but also the responsibilities of having a family. Thus, husbands and wives would share the responsibility for raising children and caring for ailing parents. Such a social norm needs to emerge, although it is difficult to legislate.

The horizontal redistribution of income from childless families to families with children could take various forms: children's allowances, refundable tax credits for children, flat-amount payments for children under social security without the maximum family benefit rule, and the payment of college tuitions. The public guarantee of minimum child support payments (suggested by Garfinkel, McLanahan, and Watson) would meet the objective, in part. In nonfinancial areas, day care services, medical services, and after-school educational and recreational services could be explored.

Some of these specific programs are already in place in the United States. The important point that should be emphasized here, however, is that the public and the government need to acknowledge the new objectives of such provisions and to embrace the horizontal redistribution of income as a viable strategy.

How does such a strategy of horizontal redistribution accomplish the twin objectives mentioned earlier? First, if the principle of economic and social parity between the sexes were established and implemented, women would be relieved of the undue burden they currently carry as workers, mothers, and wives. Thus, they could contribute to the economy to their full potential. They could also feel economically secure enough to marry and have children. In addition, they would not be economically threatened when they divorce or become widows. In short, men and women would be on an equal footing, both economically and socially, once they formed relationships through marriage.

Similarly, the horizontal redistribution of income from childless families to families with children would neutralize the economic pressure placed on families with children. As a result, families with children would not feel unduly disadvantaged for having children. Women who were willing to bear children still would have to spend a few crucial years in child rearing, but income transfers they received on behalf of their children would ameliorate the adverse economic effect of bearing children.

A clear public message would come from such a system of income redistribution: The public has a vested interest in women's work, and the public wants to make sure that women can have children without undue hardship. In the society that would emerge, neither women nor men would need to pay a price for their gender. Such an image of society may not be too farfetched. The economy is already heavily reliant on the deployment of personnel, whatever their gender. As more and more jobs require brain power, instead of physical strength, this trend will accelerate. If the economy depends on the equal deployment of male and female workers, then families who send their members into the work force must operate on the same basis.

Another image that emerges is of a society in which children are considered a public treasure—the cornerstone of the nation's survival. In such a society, the fate of children would not be affected by the socioeconomic backgrounds of their parents. In such a society, private and public interests would converge to form a partnership to ensure that children would grow to their fullest potential; it would also be the key to preventing teenage girls from bearing children out of wedlock.

In more technical terms, this two-dimensional, horizontal redistribution of income would accomplish two objectives at the same time: the prevention of absolute poverty for mothers and their children and the prevention of relative poverty of women in comparison to men.

If horizontal redistribution is implemented along these two dimensions, the rate of poverty would decline drastically. The problem of those who remained poor could then be dealt with by the traditional, antipoverty approach: the vertical redistribution of income from the rich to the poor through public assistance. But the scope of vertical redistribution that would be required to deal with the residual poor would be narrower than what is required today. Such a change in redistributional strategy would result in more adequate provision with less social controversy.

The future I envisage poses a great challenge and opportunities for policymakers in the United States. Policymakers must deal with the immediate challenge of meeting the income maintenance needs of women at different junctures of the life cycle. But they should also realize that to enhance the future viability of the United States, they need to develop social policies regarding the role of women in a broader context of economic and social development. Only by so doing can policymakers ensure that this nation develops into one in which children are born, in which the family is the preferred form of living, and in which all individuals are allowed to contribute to the nation's social and economic progress.

NOTES

1. The same can be said about the pregnancy and childbearing of nonmarried women.

2. U.S. Bureau of the Census, *Household and Family Characteristics: March*

1985, Series P-20, No. 411 (Washington, D.C.: U.S. Government Printing Office, 1986), Table D, p. 5.

3. K. A. Moore and M. R. Burt, *Private Crisis, Public Cost: Policy Perspectives on Teenage Childbearing* (Washington, D.C.: The Urban Institute, 1982).

4. National Center for Health Statistics, *Monthly Vital Statistics Report* 33,6 (1984): Table 18, pp. 31–32.

5. U.S. Department of Health and Human Services, Social Security Administration, *Social Security Programs Throughout the World 1983* (Washington, D.C.: Social Security Administration, 1984); A. J. Kahn and S. B. Kamerman, *Income Transfers for Families with Children: An Eight-Country Study* (Philadelphia: Temple University Press, 1983).

6. Kousei Tokei Kyoukai, *Kokumin no Fukushi no Doukou* (Tokyo: Kousei Tokei Kyoukai, 1987); Kouseishou Nenkin Kyoku, *Shin Nenkin Seido no Kaisetsu* (Tokyo: Shakai Hoken Kenkyuu Jyo, 1985); Kouseishou Shakaikyoku, *Shakai Hoshou no Tebiki* (Tokyo: Shakai Fukushi Chousakai, 1984).

7. Kouseishou, Shakaikyoku, Hogoka, *Seikatsu Hogo Techou* (Tokyo: Zenkoku Shakai Fukushi Kyoukai, 1984).

8. Kouseishou, Shakaikyoku, Hogoka, *Seikatsu Hogo Sokuhou*, November 1986; and Social Security Administration, *Social Security Bulletin* 51 (August 1988): Tables M18 and M27, pp. 45 and 51.

9. For detailed discussion, see M. Nakajima, "Jyosei no Roudou to Chingin," in *Jyosei no Life Cycle: Shotoku Hoshoo no Nichibei Hikaku*, ed. M. N. Ozawa, S. Kimura, and H. Ibe (Tokyo: University of Tokyo Press, 1989).

10. S. Hijikata, "Jyosei to Kyoiku," in *Jyosei no Life Cycle: Shotoku Hoshoo no Nichibei Hikaku*, ed. M. N. Ozawa, S. Kimura, and H. Ibe (Tokyo: University of Tokyo Press, 1989).

11. A. S. Earl, "Marital Property: Reform in the Wisconsin Tradition," *Marquette Law Review* 68 (Spring 1985): 381–82.

12. W. P. Cantwell, "The Uniform Marital Property Act: Origin and Intent," *Marquette Law Review* 68 (Spring 1985): 383–89; L. Adelman, D. Hanaway, and M. L. Munts, "Departures from the Uniform Marital Property Act Contained in the Wisconsin Marital Property Act," *Marquette Law Review* 68 (Spring 1985): 390–403.

13. D. S. Hamermesh and A. Rees, *The Economics of Work and Pay*, 3d ed. (New York: Harper & Row, 1984), 310–18.

14. M. N. Ozawa, "Work and Social Policy," in *Work, Workers, and Work Organizations: A View from Social Work*, ed. S. H. Akabas and P. A. Kurzman (Englewood Cliffs, N.J.: Prentice-Hall, 1982), 41.

15. V. Zelizer, "The Price and the Value of Children: The Cost of Children's Insurance," *American Journal of Sociology* 86 (March 1981): 1038.

16. V. R. Fuchs, "Why Are Children Poor?" Working Paper Series, No. 1984 (New York: National Bureau of Economic Research, 1986).

17. U.S. House of Representatives, Committee on Ways and Means, *Background Material and Data on Programs within the Jurisdiction of the Committee on Ways and Means*, 1988 ed., 100th Cong., 2d sess. (Washington, D.C.: U.S. Government Printing Office, 1988), Table 16, p. 742.

18. A. C. Carlson, "What Happened to the Family Wage?" *The Public Interest* 83 (Spring 1986): 7.

19. U.S. Department of Commerce, Bureau of the Census, "Population Pro-file of the United States, 1983–84," *Current Population Reports: Special Studies,* Series P-23, No. 145 (Washington, D.C.: U.S. Government Printing Office, 1985), 18; U.S. Department of Commerce, Bureau of the Census, "Projections of the Population of the United States, by Age, Sex, and Race: 1983 to 2080," *Current Population Reports,* Series P-25, No. 952 (Washington, D.C.: U.S. Government Printing Office, 1984), Tables A-4, A-5, and A-6, pp. 130–32.

20. R. T. Michael, "Education and the Derived Demand for Children," *Journal of Political Economy* 81 (March-April 1973), Part 2: S128–S164.

21. D. E. Bloom and N. G. Bennett, "Marriage Patterns in the United States," Working Paper No. 1701 (Washington, D.C.: National Bureau of Economics, 1985). Also see D. E. Bloom and J. Trussell, "What Are the Determinants of Delayed Childbearing and Permanent Childlessness in the United States?" *Demography* 21 (November 1984): 591–612; D. E. Bloom, "What's Happening to the Age at First Birth in the United States? A Study of Recent Cohorts," *Demography* 19 (August 1982): 351–70.

22. "Imported Youth," *The Economist* 309 (December 3, 1988): 75.

23. M. Teitelbaum and J. M. Winter, *The Fear of Population Decline* (New York: Academic Press, 1985).

SELECTED BIBLIOGRAPHY

Abrams, M. "Title IX—A Modest Success." *Graduate Woman* 76 (January/February 1982): 23–25.

Adelman, L., D. Hanaway, and M. L. Munts. "Departures from the Uniform Marital Property Act Contained in the Wisconsin Marital Property Act." *Marquette Law Review* 68 (Spring 1985): 390–403.

American Association of Retired Persons. *Income Security and Long-Term Care for Women in Midlife and Beyond: U.S. and Canadian Perspectives.* W13976 (887), D12890. Washington, D.C.: American Association of Retired Persons, 1987.

Andrews, E. *The Changing Profile of Pensions in America.* Washington, D.C.: Employee Benefit Research Institute, 1985.

Apple, M. "Teaching and 'Women's Work': A Comparative Historical and Ideological Analysis." *Teachers College Record* 86 (Spring 1985): 455–73.

Atkinson, A. B. *Social Justice and Public Policy.* Cambridge: M.I.T. Press, 1983.

Auerbach, A. J., and L. J. Kotlikoff. "Life Insurance and the Elderly: Its Adequacy and Determinant." In *Work, Health, and Income among the Elderly*, edited by G. Burtless. Washington, D.C.: The Brookings Institution, 1987.

Bancroft, G. *The American Labor Force.* New York: John Wiley and Sons, 1958.

Bane, M. J., and P. A. Jargowsky. "The Links between Government Policy and Family Structure: What Matters and What Doesn't." In *The Changing American Family and Public Policy*, edited by A. J. Cherlin. Washington, D.C.: Urban Institute Press, 1988.

Becker, G. *A Treatise on the Family.* Cambridge: Harvard University Press, 1981.

Behrman, J., R. Pollak, and P. Taubman. "Parental Preferences and Provision for Progeny." *Journal of Political Economy* 90 (1982): 52–73.

Bem, S. L. "Gender Schema Theory and Its Implications for Child Development: Raising Gender-Aschematic Children in a Gender-Schematic Society." *Signs* 8 (Summer 1983): 598–616.

Bernheim, B. D., A. Shleifer, and L. Summers. "The Strategic Bequest Motive." *Journal of Political Economy* 93 (1985): 1045–76.

Blackman, S. "The Masculinity-Femininity of Women Who Study College Mathematics." *Sex Roles* 15 (1986): 33–41.

Blinder, A. "A Model of Inherited Wealth." *Quarterly Journal of Economics* 87 (1973): 608–26.

Bloom, D. E. "What's Happening to the Age at First Birth in the United States? A Study of Recent Cohorts." *Demography* 19 (August 1982): 351–70.

Bloom, D. E., and N. G. Bennett. "Marriage Patterns in the United States." Working Paper No. 1701. Washington, D.C.: National Bureau of Economics, 1985.

Bloom, D. E., and J. Trussel. "What Are the Determinants of Delayed Childbearing and Permanent Childlessness in the United States?" *Demography* 21 (November 1984): 591–612.

Blumenthal, D., M. Schlesinger, P. B. Drumheller, and the Harvard Medical Project. "Special Report: The Future of Medicare." *New England Journal of Medicine* 314 (March 13, 1986): 722–28.

Bowen, H. R., and J. H. Schuster. *American Professors: A National Resource Imperiled*. New York: Oxford University Press, 1986.

Bowman, M. J., and M. Osawa. "Developmental Perspectives in the Education and Economic Activities of Japanese and American Women." Unpublished paper, 1985.

Brittain, J. *Inheritance and the Inequality of Material Wealth*. Washington, D.C.: Brookings Institution, 1978.

Brooks-Gunn, J., and F. F. Furstenberg, Jr. "Adolescent Sexuality." *American Psychologist* (in press).

Brooks-Gunn, J., and F. F. Furstenberg, Jr. "The Children of Adolescent Mothers: Physical, Academic, and Psychological Outcomes." *Developmental Review* 6 (1986): 224–51.

Brooks-Gunn, J., and F. F. Furstenberg, Jr. "Continuity and Change in the Context of Poverty." In *The Malleability of Children*, edited by J. J. Gallagher and C. T. Ramey. Baltimore: Brooks Publishing Co., 1987.

Browder, O. L., Jr. "Recent Patterns of Testate Succession in the United States and England." *Michigan Law Review* 67 (1968–1969): 1303–60.

Bumpass, L. "Children and Marital Disruption: A Replication and Update." *Demography* 21 (February 1984): 71–82.

Bureau of National Affairs. *Highlights of the New Pension Reform Law*. Washington, D.C.: Bureau of National Affairs, 1974.

Burkhauser, R. V., and K. C. Holden, eds. *A Challenge to Social Security: The Changing Roles of Women and Men in American Society*. New York: Academic Press, 1982.

Burkhauser, R. V., K. C. Holden, and D. Feaster. "Incidence, Timing, and Events Associated with Poverty: A Dynamic View of Poverty in Retirement." *Journal of Gerontology* 43 (March 1988): 46–52.

Burkhauser, R. V., K. C. Holden, and D. A. Myers. "Widowhood and Poverty: The Role of Survey Procedures in Artificially Creating Poverty." *Demography* 23 (November 1986): 621–31.

Burkhauser, R. V., and J. F. Quinn. "Work and Retirement: The American Experience." In *Redefining the Process of Retirement*, edited by W. Schmahl. New York: Springer, 1989.

Butz, W., and M. Ward. "The Emergence of Counter Cyclical Fertility." *American Economic Review* 69 (June 1979): 318–28.

Cain, G. G., and D. A. Wissoker. "Do Income Maintenance Programs Break

Up Marriages? A Reevaluation of SIME-DIME." Institute for Research on Poverty Discussion Paper no. 850–87, University of Wisconsin, Madison, 1987.

Campbell, R., and E. M. Brody. "Women's Changing Roles and Help to the Elderly: Attitudes of Women in the United States and Japan." *The Gerontologist* 25,6 (1985): 584–92.

Cantwell, W. P. "The Uniform Marital Property Act: Origin and Intent." *Marquette Law Review* 68 (Spring 1985): 383–89.

Card, J. J., and L. L. Wise. "Teenage Mothers and Teenage Fathers: The Impact of Early Childbearing on the Parents' Personal and Professional Lives." In *Teenage Sexuality, Pregnancy, and Childbearing*, edited by F. F. Furstenberg, Jr., R. Lincoln, and J. Menken. Philadelphia: University of Pennsylvania Press, 1981.

Carlson, A. C. "What Happened to the Family Wage?" *The Public Interest* 83 (Spring 1986): 3–17.

Cates, J. N., and M. B. Sussman. "Family Systems and Inheritance." *Marriage and Family Review* 5 (1982): 1–24.

Chambers, D. *Making Fathers Pay: The Enforcement of Child Support.* Chicago: University of Chicago Press, 1979.

Chang, T. M. *Support for National Caregiving.* Report #3, Bureau of Human Resources, Division of Community Services, Wisconsin Department of Health and Social Services, 1984.

Cherlin, A. J. *Marriage, Divorce, Remarriage.* Cambridge: Harvard University Press, 1981.

Chilman, C. S. *Adolescent Sexuality in a Changing American Society: Social and Psychological Perspectives for the Human Services Professions,* 2d ed. New York: John Wiley & Sons, 1983.

Clark, B. R., ed. *The School and the University.* Berkeley: University of California Press, 1985.

Clark, R. L., and D. A. Sumner. "Inflation and the Real Income of the Elderly: Recent Evidence and Expectations for the Future." *The Gerontologist* 25 (April 1985): 146–52.

Clark, S. M., and M. Corcoran. "Perspectives on the Professional Socialization of Women Faculty: A Case of Accumulative Disadvantage?" *Journal of Higher Education* 57 (January/February 1986): 20–43.

Clewell, B. C., J. Brooks-Gunn, and A. A. Benasich. "Child-Focused Programs for Teenage Parents: Anticipated and Unanticipated Benefits." *Family Relations* (in press).

Cogan, J. F., and F. Berger. *Family Formation, Labor Market Experience, and the Wages of Married Women.* Santa Monica, Calif.: The RAND Corporation, R-2310-NICHD, May 1978.

Commonwealth Fund Commission on Elderly People Living Alone. *Old, Alone, and Poor,* Baltimore, April 16, 1987.

Danziger, S. "Poverty and Inequality under Reaganomics." *Journal of Contemporary Studies* 5 (1982): 17–30.

Danziger, S. "Economic Growth, Poverty, and Inequality in an Advanced Economy." Institute for Research on Poverty Discussion Paper no. 862–88, University of Wisconsin, Madison, 1988.

Danziger, S., R. H. Haveman, and R. D. Plotnick. "Antipoverty Policy: Effects on the Poor and the Nonpoor." In *Fighting Poverty: What Works and What Doesn't*, edited by S. H. Danziger and D. H. Weinberg. Cambridge: Harvard University Press, 1986.

Danziger, S., G. Jakubson, S. Schwartz, and E. Smolensky. "Work and Welfare As Determinants of Female Poverty and Household Headship." *Quarterly Journal of Economics* 97 (August 1982): 519–34.

David, M., and P. Menchik. "Distribution of Estate Wealth and Its Relationship to Intergenerational Transfers." In *Statistics of Income and Related Administrative Record Research*. United States Department of Treasury. Washington, D.C.: U.S. Government Printing Office, 1982.

Davies, J. "The Relative Impact of Inheritance and Other Factors on Economic Inequality." *Quarterly Journal of Economics* 97 (1982): 471–98.

Donovan, E. T. "The Retirement Equity Act of 1984: A Review." *Social Security Bulletin* 48 (May 1985): 38–44.

Doty, P., K. Liu, and J. Weiner. "An Overview of Long-Term Care." *Health Care Financing Review* 6, 3 (Spring 1985): 69–78.

Dryfoos, J. "The Epidemiology of Adolescent Pregnancy: Incidence, Outcomes, and Interventions." In *Pregnancy in Adolescence: Needs, Problems, and Management*, edited by I. R. Stuart and C. F. Wells. New York: Van Nostrand Reinhold, 1982.

Duncan, G. J., and S. D. Hoffman. "A Reconsideration of the Economic Consequences of Marital Dissolution." *Demography* 22 (November 1985): 485–97.

Durand, J. D. *The Labor Force in the United States, 1890–1960*. New York: Social Science Research Council, 1948.

Earl, A. S. "Marital Property: Reform in the Wisconsin Tradition." *Marquette Law Review* 68 (Spring 1985): 381–82.

Elder, G. *Adolescent Socialization and Personality Development*. Chicago: Rand McNally, 1968.

Ellwood, D. T. "Targeting the Would-Be Long-Term Recipients of AFDC: Who Should Be Served?" Unpublished preliminary report, Harvard University, 1985.

Ellwood, D. T. *Poor Support: Poverty in the American Family*. New York: Basic Books, 1988.

Employee Benefit Research Institute. *Fundamentals of Employee Benefit Programs*, 3d ed. Washington, D.C.: Employee Benefit Research Institute, 1987.

Estes, C. L., R. J. Newcomer, and Associates. *Fiscal Austerity and Aging*. Beverly Hills: Sage Publications, 1983.

Feistritzer, E. *Profile of Teachers in the United States*. Washington, D.C.: National Center for Educational Information, 1987.

Fox, M. F., and S. Hesse-Biber. *Women at Work*. Palo Alto, Calif.: Mayfield Publishing Co., 1984.

Fries, J. F. "Aging, Natural Death, and the Compression of Morbidity." *New England Journal of Medicine* 303 (July 17, 1980): 130–35.

Fuchs, V. R. "Sex Differences in Economic Well-Being." *Science* 232 (April 1986): 459–64.

Fuchs, V. R. "Why Are Children Poor?" Working Paper Series, No. 1984, National Bureau of Economic Research, New York, 1986.

Furstenberg, F. F., Jr., J. Brooks-Gunn, and L. Chase-Lansdale. "Teenaged Pregnancy and Childbearing." *American Psychologist* (in press).

Furstenberg, F. F., Jr., J. Brooks-Gunn, and S. P. Morgan. *Adolescent Mothers in Later Life.* New York: Cambridge University Press, 1987.

Furstenberg, F. F., Jr., and G. Condran. "Family Change and Adolescent Well-Being: A Reexamination of U.S. Trends." In *The Changing American Family and Public Policy,* edited by A. J. Cherlin. Washington, D.C.: The Urban Institute Press, 1988.

Garfinkel, I., and S. McLanahan. *Single Mothers and Their Children: A New American Dilemma.* Washington, D.C.: Urban Institute, 1986.

Garfinkel, I., and M. Melli. *Child Support: Weaknesses of the Old and Features of a Proposed New System.* Vol. 1. Institute for Research on Poverty Special Report 32A, University of Wisconsin, Madison, 1982.

Goldin, C., and K. Sokoloff. "The Relative Productivity Hypothesis of Industrialization: The American Case, 1820–1850." *Quarterly Journal of Economics* 99 (August 1984): 461–87.

Graham, P. A. "Expansion and Inclusion: A History of Women in American Higher Education." *Signs* 3 (Summer 1978): 759–73.

Hamermesh, D. S., and A. Rees. *The Economics of Work and Pay.* 3d ed. New York: Harper & Row, 1984.

Hanna, C. "The Organizational Context for Affirmative Action for Women Faculty." *Journal of Higher Education* 59 (July/August 1988): 390–411.

Harbury, C. D., and D.M.W.N. Hitchens. *Inheritance and Wealth Inequality in Britain.* London: Allen and Unwin, 1979.

Harrington, C., R. J. Newcomer, C. L. Estes, and Associates. *Long-Term Care of the Elderly.* Beverly Hills: Sage Publications, 1985.

Hawkins, J. "Computers and Girls: Rethinking the Issues." *Sex Roles* 13 (1985): 165–80.

Hayes, C. D., ed. *Risking the Future: Adolescent Sexuality, Pregnancy, and Childbearing,* Vol. I. Washington, D.C.: National Academy Press, 1987.

Hearn, J. C., and S. Olzak. "The Role of College Major Departments in the Reproduction of Sexual Inequality." *Sociology of Education* 54 (July 1981): 195–205.

Hess, R. D., and I. T. Miura. "Gender Differences in Enrollment in Computer Camps and Classes." *Sex Roles* 13 (1985): 193–203.

Hijikata, S. "Jyosei to Kyoiku." In *Jyosei no Life Cycle: Shotoku Hoshoo no Nichibei Hikaku,* edited by M. N. Ozawa, S. Kimura, and H. Ibe. Tokyo: University of Tokyo Press, 1989.

Hing, E. "Use of Nursing Homes by the Elderly: Preliminary Data from the 1985 National Nursing Home Survey." *NCHS Advance Data from Vital and Health Statistics of the National Center for Health Statistics,* No. 135. Hyattsville, Md.: National Center for Health Statistics, May 14, 1987.

Hofferth, S. L. "Updating Children's Life Course." *Journal of Marriage and the Family* 47 (1985): 92–116.

Hofferth, S. L., and C. D. Hayes, eds. *Risking the Future: Adolescent Sexuality, Pregnancy, and Childbearing.* Vol. II. Washington, D.C.: National Academy Press, 1987.

Hofferth, S. L., J. R. Kahn, and W. Baldwin. "Premarital Sexual Activity among

U.S. Teenage Women over the Past Three Decades." *Family Planning Perspectives* 19,2 (1987): 46–53.

Holden, K. C. "Poverty and Living Arrangements among Older Women: Are Changes in Economic Well-Being Underestimated?" *Journal of Gerontology* 43 (January 1988): S22–S27.

Holden, K. C. "The Income Shock of Widowhood: Findings from the Survey of Income and Program Participation." Final Report to the American Association of Retired Persons, December 1988.

Holden, K. C. "The Transition from Wife to Widow: Data Issues in Measuring First-Period Income Effects in SIPP and the RHS." In *Individuals and Families in Transition: Understanding Change through Longitudinal Data.* Washington, D.C.: U.S. Bureau of the Census, forthcoming.

Holden, K. C., R. V. Burkhauser and D. J. Feaster. "The Timing of Falls into Poverty after Retirement and Widowhood." *Demography* 25 (August 1988): 405–14.

Holden, K. C., R. V. Burkhauser, and D. A. Myers. "Income Transitions at Older Stages of Life: The Dynamics of Poverty." *The Gerontologist* 26 (June 1986): 292–97.

Hutchens, R. M. "Welfare, Remarriage, and Marital Search." *American Economic Review* 69 (1973): 303–22.

Japan Institute of Labor. *Problems of Working Women.* Japanese Industrial Relation Series, no. 8 (1986).

Jones, E. F., J. D. Forrest, S. K. Henshaw, J. Silverman, and A. Torres. "Unintended Pregnancy, Contraceptive Practice, and Family Planning Services in Developed Countries." *Family Planning Perspectives* 20,2 (1988): 53–67.

Kahn, A. J., and S. B. Kamerman. *Income Transfers for Families with Children: An Eight-Country Study.* Philadelphia: Temple University Press, 1983.

Kahn, A. J., and S. B. Kamerman. *Child Care: Facing the Hard Choices.* Dover, Mass.: Auburn Publishing Co., 1987.

Kane, R. L., and R. A. Kane. "Long-Term Care: Can Our Society Meet the Needs of Its Elderly?" *Annual Review of Public Health* 1 (1980): 227–53.

Kelly, P. "The Influence of Reading Content on Students' Perceptions of the Masculinity or Femininity of Reading." *Journal of Reading Behavior* 15 (1986): 243–56.

Kitagawa, E. M., and P. M. Hauser. *Differential Mortality in the United States.* Cambridge: Harvard University Press, 1973.

Kotlikoff, L. J., and D. E. Smith. *Pensions in the American Economy.* Chicago: University of Chicago Press, 1983.

Kousei Tokei Kyoukai. *Kokumin no Fukushi no Doukou.* Tokyo: Kousei Tokei Kyoukai, 1987.

Kouseishou Nenkin Kyoku. *Shin Nenkin Seido no Kaisetsu.* Tokyo: Shakai Hoken Kenkyuu Jyo, 1985.

Kouseishou Shakaikyoku. *Shakai Hoshou no Tebiki.* Tokyo: Shakai Fukushi Chousakai, 1984.

Kouseishou, Shakaikyoku, Hogoka. *Seikatsu Hogo Techou.* Tokyo: Zenkoku Shakai Fukushi Kyoukai, 1984.

Kouseishou, Shakaikyoku, Hogoka. *Seikatsu Hogo Sokuhou.* Tokyo: Kouseishou, November 1986.

Krause, H. O. *Child Support in America: The Legal Perspective*. Charlottesville, Va.: Michie, 1981.

Laitner, J. "Household Bequests, Perfect Expectations, and the National Distribution of Wealth." *Econometrica* 47 (1979): 1175–93.

Laws, J. L. *The Second X: Sex Role and Social Role*. New York: Elsevier North Holland, Inc., 1979.

Lazear, E. P., and R. T. Michael. "Family Size and the Distribution of Real Per Capita Income." *American Economic Review* 70 (March 1980): 91–107.

Lebergott, S. *Income, Wealth, and Want*. Princeton: Princeton University Press, 1976.

Lee, V. E., and R. B. Ekstrom. "Student Access to Guidance Counseling in High School." *American Educational Research Journal* 24 (Summer 1987): 287–310.

Liebow, E. *Talley's Corner*. Boston: Little, Brown and Co., 1967.

Liu, K., K. G. Manton, and B. M. Liu. "Home Care Expenses for the Disabled Elderly." *Health Care Financing Review* 2 (1985): 51–58.

Long, C. *The Labor Force under Changing Income and Employment*. Princeton: Princeton University Press, 1958.

Lucas, G. I. "Caregiving: A Growing Workforce Issue." *The Aging Connection* 8, 6 (December 1987/January 1988): 7.

McAnarney, E. R., and C. Schreider. *Identifying Social and Psychological Antecedents of Adolescent Pregnancy: The Contribution of Research to Concepts of Prevention*. New York: William T. Grant Foundation, 1984.

Maccoby, E. E., and C. N. Jacklin. *The Psychology of Sex Differences*. Stanford: Stanford University Press, 1974.

McLanahan, S. "Family Structure and Stress: A Longitudinal Comparison of Two-Parent and Female-Headed Families." *Journal of Marriage and the Family* (May 1983): 347–57.

McLanahan, S. "Family Structure and the Reproduction of Poverty." *American Journal of Sociology* 90 (January 1985): 873–901.

McLanahan, S. "Family Structure and Dependency: Early Transition to Female Household Headship." *Demography* 25 (February 1988): 1–16.

McLanahan, S., and L. Bumpass. "Intergenerational Consequences of Family Disruption." *American Journal of Sociology* 94 (July 1988): 130–52.

Manton, K. G. "Changing Concepts of Morbidity and Mortality in the Elderly Population." *Milbank Memorial Fund Quarterly* 60 (1982): 183–244.

Manton, K. G., and K. Liu. "The 1982 and 1984 National Long Term Care Surveys: Their Structure and Analytic Uses." Unpublished paper prepared for the National Conference on Long-Term Care Data Bases, Washington, D.C., May 21–22, 1987.

Marsiglio, W. "Teenaged Fatherhood: High School Completion and Educational Attainment." In *Adolescent Fatherhood*, edited by A. B. Elster and M. E. Lamb. Hillsdale, N.J.: Lawrence Erlbaum Associates, 1986.

Marsiglio, W., and F. L. Mott. "The Impact of Sex Education on Sexual Activity, Contraceptive Use and Premarital Pregnancy among American Teenagers." *Family Planning Perspectives* 18,4 (1986): 151–62.

Mauldin, C. "Life-Cycle Labor Force Participation of Married Women: Historical Evidence and Implications." Unpublished paper, 1986.

Menchik, P. L. "A Study of Inheritance and Death Taxation: A Microeconometric Approach." Ph.D. dissertation, University of Pennsylvania, 1976.

Menchik, P. L. "Intergenerational Transmission of Inequality: An Empirical Study of Wealth Mobility." *Economica* 46 (1979): 346–62.

Menchik, P. L. "The Importance of Material Inheritance." In *Modelling the Distribution and Intergenerational Transmission of Wealth*, edited by J. D. Smith. Chicago: University of Chicago Press, 1980.

Menchik, P. L. "Primogeniture, Equal Sharing, and the U.S. Distribution of Wealth." *Quarterly Journal of Economics* 94 (1980): 299–316.

Menchik, P. L. "Is the Family Wealth Squandered? A Test of the Merry-Widow Model." *Journal of Economic History* 44 (1984): 835–38.

Menchik, P. L. "Unequal Estate Division: Is It Altruism, Reverse Bequests, or Simply Noise?" In *Modelling the Accumulation and Distribution of Wealth*, edited by D. Kessler and A. Masson. Oxford, Great Britain: Oxford University Press, 1987.

Menchik, P. L. and M. David. "The Incidence of a Lifetime Consumption Tax." *National Tax Journal* 35 (1982): 189–204.

Menchik, P. L. and M. David. "Income Distribution, Lifetime Savings, and Bequests." *American Economic Review* 73 (1983): 672–90.

Michael, R. T. "Education and the Derived Demand for Children." *Journal of Political Economy* 81 (March-April 1973), Part 2: S128–S164.

Mincer, J. "Labor Force of Married Women." In *Aspects of Labor Economics*, edited by H. G. Lewis. Princeton: Princeton University Press, 1962.

Moore, K. A., and M. R. Burt. *Private Crisis, Public Cost: Policy Perspectives on Teenage Childbearing*. Washington, D.C.: The Urban Institute Press, 1982.

Moore, K. A., and L. J. Waite. "Marital Dissolution, Early Motherhood, and Early Marriage." *Social Forces* 60 (September 1976): 20–40.

Moore, K. A., J. L. Peterson, and F. F. Furstenberg, Jr. "Starting Early: The Antecedents of Early Premarital Intercourse." Presented at Population Association of America Meetings, Minneapolis, 1984.

Moore, K. A., M. C. Simms, and C. L. Betsey. *Choice and Circumstance: Racial Differences in Adolescent Sexuality and Fertility*. New Brunswick, N.J.: Transaction Books, 1986.

Morgan, L. A. "The Financial Experience of Widowed Women: Evidence from the LRHS." *Gerontologist* 26 (December 1986): 663–68.

Mortimer, J. T., and R. Simmons. "Adult Socialization." *Annual Review of Sociology* 4 (1978): 421–54.

Moynihan, D. P. *The Negro Family: The Case for National Action*. Washington, D.C.: Department of Labor, Office of Policy Planning and Research, 1965.

Murray, C. *Losing Ground: American Social Policy 1950–1980*. New York: Basic Books, 1984.

Myers, D. A., R. V. Burkhauser, and K. C. Holden. "The Transition from Wife to Widow." *Journal of Risk and Insurance* 54 (December 1987): 752–59.

Nakajima, M. "Jyosei no Roudou to Chingin." In *Jyosei no Life Cycle: Shotoku Hoshoo no Nichibei Hikaku*, edited by M. N. Ozawa, S. Kimura, and H. Ibe. Tokyo: University of Tokyo Press, 1989.

National Center for Health Statistics, *Americans Needing Help to Function at Home*. Advance Data from Vital and Health Statistics, No. 92, DHHS Publication No. (PHS) 83–1250. Hyattsville, Md.: U.S. Public Health Service, September 1983.

National Council of Organizations for Children and Youth. *America's Children 1976: A Bicentennial Assessment*. Washington, D.C.: National Council, 1976.

Natriello, G., ed. *School Dropouts: Patterns and Policies*. New York: Teachers College Press, 1987.

Nichols-Casebolt, A., I. Garfinkel, and P. Wong. "Reforming Wisconsin's Child Support System." Institute for Research on Poverty Discussion Paper no. 793–85, University of Wisconsin, Madison, 1985.

Nuckols, R. C. "Widowhood, Income Maintenance, and Economic Well-Being." *Marriage and Family Review* 5 (1982): 39–60.

Osawa, M. "The Wage Gap in Japan: Changing Patterns of Labor Force Participation, Schooling and Tenure." Unpublished paper, 1986.

Ozawa, M. N. "Work and Social Policy." In *Work, Workers, and Work Organizations: A View from Social Work*, edited by S. H. Akabas and P. A. Kurzman. Englewood Cliffs, N.J.: Prentice-Hall, 1982.

Ozawa, M. N. "Women and Social Security." *Public Law Forum* 4 (1984): 307–24.

Ozawa, M. N. "A Critical Look at the Present-Day Welfare Responses." In *The Proceedings of the 23rd International Conference on Social Welfare*, edited by Y. Yaguchi, L. Thompson, and C. Thompson. Tokyo: The International Conference on Social Welfare, 1987.

Ozawa, M. N. "American Nursing Homes and Elderly Residents: An Overview from the 1985 National Nursing Home Survey." *Nenkin to Koyo* 23 (1988): 4–25.

Parelius, A. P. and R. J. Parelius. *The Sociology of Education*. Englewood Cliffs, N.J.: Prentice-Hall, Inc., 1978.

Parke, R. D., and B. Neville. "Teenage Fatherhood." In *Risking the Future: Adolescent Sexuality, Pregnancy, and Childbearing*, edited by S. L. Hofferth and C. D. Hayes. Washington, D.C.: National Academy Press, 1987.

Parke, R. D., and B. R. Tinsley. "Fatherhood: Historical and Contemporary Perspectives." In *Life Span Developmental Psychology: Historical and Generational Effects*, edited by K. A. McCluskey and H. W. Reese. New York: Academic Press, 1984.

Preston, S. H., and A. T. Richards. "The Influence of Women's Work Opportunities on Marriage Rates." *Demography* 12 (May 1975): 209–22.

Price, J. R. "The Transmission of Wealth at Death in a Community Property Jurisdiction." *Washington Law Review* 50 (1975): 277–340.

Reno, V., and S. Grad. "Special Anniversary Feature: Economic Security, 1935–85." *Social Security Bulletin* 48 (December 1985): 5–20.

Rice, D. P. "Long-Term Care of the Elderly and Disabled." *International Social Security Review* 3 (1983): 299–326.

Rice, D. P. "Demographic Realities and Projections of An Aging Population." In *Health Care for an Aging Society*, edited by S. Andreopoulos and J. R. Hogness. New York: Churchill Livingstone, 1989.

Rice, D. P., and C. E. Estes. "Health of the Elderly: Policy Issues and Challenges." *Health Affairs* 3 (Winter 1984): 25–49.

Rice, D. P., and J. J. Feldman. "Living Longer in the United States: Demographic Changes and Health Needs of the Elderly." *Milbank Memorial Fund Quarterly* 61 (1983): 362–96.

Rice, T., and J. Gabel. "Protecting the Elderly against High Health Care Costs." *Health Affairs* 5,3 (1986): 6–21.

Ross, C. M., S. Danziger, and E. Smolensky. "Interpreting Changes in the Economic Status of the Elderly, 1949–1979." *Contemporary Policy Issues* 5 (April 1987): 98–112.

Ross, C. M., S. Danziger, and E. Smolensky. "Level and Trend of Poverty in the United States." *Demography* 25 (November 1987): 587–600.

Ross, H., and I. Sawhill. *Time of Transition: The Growth of Families Headed by Women*. Washington, D.C.: Urban Institute, 1975.

Safilios-Rothschild, C. "Sex Differences in Early Socialization and Upbringing and Their Consequences for Educational Choices and Outcomes." In *Girls and Women in Education*. Paris: OECD, 1986.

Sandler, B. *The Campus Climate Revisited: Chilly for Women Faculty, Administrators, and Graduate Students*. Washington, D.C.: Association of American Colleges, 1986.

Sawhill, I. V. "Discrimination and Poverty among Women Who Head Families." *Signs* 2 (1976): 201–11.

Sawhill, I. V. "Poverty in the U.S.: Why Is It So Persistent?" *Journal of Economic Literature* 26 (September 1988): 1073–1119.

Schneider, E. L., and J. A. Brody. "Aging, Natural Death, and the Compression of Morbidity: Another View." *New England Journal of Medicine* 309 (October 6, 1983): 854–56.

Schoen, R. "United States Marital Status Life Tables for Periods 1910–1975 and Cohorts Born 1888–1945." Unpublished manuscript. Department of Sociology, University of Illinois, Urbana, 1983.

Seltzer, J. A., and I. Garfinkel. "Property Settlements and Child Support Awards: Inequality in Divorce Settlements." Institute for Research on Poverty Discussion Paper no. 867–88, University of Wisconsin, Madison, 1988.

Sherman, S. R. "Assets of New Retired-Worker Beneficiaries: Findings from the New Beneficiary Survey." *Social Security Bulletin* 48 (July 1985): 27–43.

Shimada, H., and Y. Higuchi. "An Analysis of Trends in Female Labor Force Participation in Japan." *Journal of Labor Economics* 3 (January 1985): S355–S374.

Shorrocks, A. "On the Structure of Intergenerational Transfers between Families." *Economica* 46 (1979): 415–25.

Siegel, J. S., and C. M. Taeuber. "Demographic Dimensions of an Aging Population." In *Our Aging Society: Paradox and Promise*, edited by A. Pifer and L. Bronte. New York: W. W. Norton and Company, 1986.

Simeone, A. *Academic Women Working Towards Equality*. South Hadley, Mass.: Bergin and Garvey, 1987.

Smeeding, T. M. "Nonmoney Income and the Elderly: The Case of the

Tweeners," *Journal of Policy Analysis and Management* 5 (1986): 707–24.

Smith, J. P. "Family Labor Supply over the Life Cycle." *Exploration in Economic Research* 4 (Spring 1977): 205–76.

Smith, J. P. *Female Labor Supply: Theory and Estimation.* Princeton: Princeton University Press, 1980.

Smith, J. P. "Poverty and the Family." In *Divided Opportunities,* edited by G. Sandefur and M. Tienda. New York: Plenum, 1988.

Smith, J. P., and M. P. Ward. *Women's Wages and Work in the Twentieth Century.* Santa Monica, Calif.: The RAND Corporation, R–3119–NICHD, 1984.

Smith, J. P., and M. P. Ward. "Time Series Growth in the Female Labor Force." *Journal of Labor Economics* 3 (January 1985): 59–90.

Smith, J. P., and M. P. Ward. "Women in the Labor Market and the Family." *Journal of Economic Perspectives,* forthcoming (Winter 1989).

Smith, J. P., and F. Welch. "Affirmative Action and Labor Markets." *Journal of Labor Economics* 2 (April 1984): 269–98.

Snyder, D. C. "Pension Status of Recently Retired Workers on Their Longest Job: Findings from the New Beneficiary Survey." *Social Security Bulletin* 49 (August 1986): 5–21.

Solomon, B. M. *In the Company of Educated Women.* New Haven: Yale University Press, 1985.

Somers, A. R. "Insurance for Long-Term Care." *New England Journal of Medicine* 317 (July 2, 1987): 23–29.

Steinmetz, S. K., and D. J. Amsden. "Dependent Elders, Family Stress, and Abuse." In *Family Relationships in Later Life.* Beverly Hills: Sage Publications, 1983.

Stockard, J., and M. M. Johnson. *Sex Roles: Sex Inequality and Sex Role Development.* Englewood Cliffs, N.J.: Prentice-Hall, 1980.

Stone, R., G. L. Cafferata, and J. Sangl. "Caregivers of the Frail Elderly: A National Profile." *The Gerontologist* 27,5 (1987): 616–26.

Sweet, J., and L. Bumpass. *American Families and Households.* New York: Russell Sage, forthcoming.

Taubman, P. *Income Distribution and Redistribution.* Reading, Mass.: Addison-Wesley, 1978.

Taylor, R. "Equity in Mathematics: A Case Study." *Mathematics Teacher* 76 (1983): 12–17.

Teitelbaum, M., and J. M. Winter. *The Fear of Population Decline.* New York: Academic Press, 1985.

Thornton, A., and D. Freedman. "The Changing American Family." *Population Bulletin* 38,4 (1983): 3–43.

Tobias, S. *Overcoming Math Anxiety.* New York: Norton, 1978.

Tomes, N. "The Family, Inheritance and the Intergenerational Transmission of Inequality." *Journal of Political Economy* 89 (1981): 928–58.

Uhlenberg, P., and M.A.P. Salmon. "Change in Relative Income of Older Women, 1960–1980." *The Gerontologist* 26 (April 1986): 164–70.

U.S. Bureau of the Census. "Household and Family Characteristics, March 1985." *Current Population Reports,* Series P-10, no. 411. Washington, D.C.: U.S. Government Printing Office, 1986.

U.S. Bureau of the Census. "Money Income and Poverty Status of Families and Persons in the United States: 1985 (Advance Data from the March 1986 Current Population Survey)." *Current Population Reports*, Series P-60, no. 154. Washington, D.C.: U.S. Government Printing Office, 1986.

U.S. Bureau of the Census. "Child Support and Alimony: 1985." *Current Population Reports*, Special Studies Series P-23, no. 152. Washington, D.C.: U.S. Government Printing Office, 1987.

U.S. Congressional Budget Office. *Trends in Educational Achievement.* Washington, D.C.: Congressional Budget Office, April 1986.

U.S. Department of Health and Human Services. *Life Tables for the United States: 1900–2050*, Actuarial Study No. 87. Washington, D.C.: U.S. Government Printing Office, 1982.

U.S. Department of Health and Human Services, Social Security Administration. *Social Security Programs Throughout the World 1983*. Washington, D.C.: Social Security Administration, 1984.

U.S. House of Representatives, Committee on Ways and Means. *Background Material and Data on Programs within the Jurisdiction of the Committee on Ways and Means.* 1988 ed. 100th Cong., 2d sess. (Washington, D.C.: U.S. Government Printing Office, 1988).

U.S. House of Representatives, Select Committee on Children, Youth, and Families. *Children, Youth, and Families: 1983.* 98th Cong., 2d sess. (Washington, D.C.: U.S. Government Printing Office, 1984).

U.S. Senate, Special Committee on Aging. *Aging America: Trends and Projections.* 1987–1988 ed. Washington, D.C.: U.S. Senate Committee on Aging, 1984.

Vinovskis, M. A. *An "Epidemic" of Adolescent Pregnancy? Some Historical and Policy Considerations.* New York: Oxford University Press, 1988.

Waite, L. J., G. H. Haggstrom, and D. E. Kanouse. "Changes in the Employment Activities of New Parents." *American Sociological Review* 50 (April 1985): 263–72.

Wedgewood, J. "The Influence of Inheritance on the Distribution of Wealth." *Economic Journal* 38 (1928): 38–55.

Weitzman, L. J. *The Divorce Revolution: The Unexpected Social and Economic Consequences for Women and Children in America.* New York: Free Press, 1985.

Widnall, S. E. "AAAS Presidential Lecture: Voices from the Pipeline." *Science* 241 (September 1988): 1740–45.

Wilson, W. J. *The Truly Disadvantaged.* Chicago: University of Chicago Press, 1987.

Wilson, W. J., and K. M. Neckerman. "Poverty and Family Structure: The Widening Gap between Evidence and Public Policy Issues." In *Fighting Poverty: What Works and What Doesn't*, edited by S. H. Danziger and D. H. Weinberg. Cambridge: Harvard University Press, 1986.

Zabin, L. S., J. F. Kantner, and M. Zelnik. "The Risk of Adolescent Pregnancy in the First Months of Intercourse." *Family Planning Perspectives* 11,4 (1979): 215–22.

Zelizer, V. "The Price and the Value of Children: The Cost of Children's Insurance." *American Journal of Sociology* 86 (March 1981): 1038–56.

Zelnik, M., and J. F. Kantner. "Sexual Activity, Contraceptive Use and Pregnancy among Metropolitan Area Teenagers: 1971–1979." *Family Planning Perspectives* 12,5 (1980): 230.

Zick, C. D., and K. R. Smith. "Immediate and Delayed Effects of Widowhood on Poverty: Patterns from the 1970's." *The Gerontologist* 26 (October 1986): 669–75.

Zigler, E. F., and E. W. Gordon, eds. *Day Care: Scientific and Social Policy Studies*. Boston: Auburn House Publishing Co., 1982.

INDEX

ABOUT THE EDITOR AND CONTRIBUTORS

J. Brooks-Gunn, Senior Scientist, Educational Testing Services, Princeton, NJ, and Visiting Scholar, Russell Sage Foundation, New York, NY

Shirley M. Clark, Chairperson, Department of Education Policy and Administration, The University of Minnesota, Minneapolis, MN

Frank F. Furstenberg, Jr., Professor, Department of Sociology, The University of Pennsylvania, Philadelphia, PA

Irwin Garfinkel, Professor, School of Social Work, The University of Wisconsin, Madison, WI

Karen C. Holden, Senior Scientist, Institute for Research on Poverty, The University of Wisconsin, Madison, WI

Sara McLanahan, Associate Professor, Department of Sociology, The University of Wisconsin, Madison, WI

Paul L. Menchik, Professor, Department of Economics, The Michigan State University, East Lansing, MI

Martha N. Ozawa, Bettie Bofinger Brown Professor of Social Policy, The George Warren Brown School of Social Work, Washington University, St. Louis, MO

Dorothy P. Rice, Professor, Department of Social and Behavioral Sciences, University of California, San Francisco, San Francisco, CA

James P. Smith, Director of Labor and Population Program, The RAND Corporation, Santa Monica, CA

Dorothy Watson, Project Assistant, Institute for Aging and Adult Life, The University of Wisconsin, Madison, WI